Before and After Waterloo

LE COURIER DU RHIN

Before and After Waterloo

Observations on the Napoleonic Era in
Continental Europe Before & After
its Principal Conflicts

By Edward Stanley

LEONAUR

Before and After Waterloo
Observations on the Napoleonic Era in
Continental Europe Before & After
its Principal Conflicts
by Edward Stanley

First published under the title
Before and After Waterloo

Leonaur is an imprint
of Oakpast Ltd

Copyright in this form © 2010 Oakpast Ltd

ISBN: 978-0-85706-282-6(hardcover)
ISBN: 978-0-85706-281-9 (softcover)

http://www.leonaur.com

Contents

ECHOES OF

PAST DAYS AT

ALDERLEY RECTORY

The originals of most of the letters now published are, with the drawings that illustrate them, at Llanfawr, Holyhead.

Some extracts from these letters have already appeared in the *Early Married Life of Maria Josepha, Lady Stanley*, but are here inserted again by kind permission of Messrs. Longman, and complete Bishop Stanley's correspondence.

Portions of letters quoted in Dean Stanley's volume, *Edward and Catherine Stanley*, have also been used with Messrs. Murray's consent.

In addition to the MSS. at Llanfawr, Lord Stanley of Alderley has kindly contributed some original letters in his possession.

J.H.A.

(One of the original editors Jane H. Adeane)

EDWARD STANLEY, BISHOP OF NORWICH

Biographical Sketch of
Edward Stanley

The letters which are collected in this volume were written from abroad during the opening years of the nineteenth century, at three different periods: after the Peace of Amiens in 1802 and 1803, after the Peace of Paris in 1814, and in the year following Waterloo, June, 1816.

The writer, Edward Stanley, was for thirty-three years an active country clergyman, and for twelve years more a no less active bishop, at a time when such activity was uncommon, though not so rare as is sometimes now supposed.

Although a member of one of the oldest Cheshire families, he did not share the opinions of his county neighbours on public questions, and his voice was fearlessly raised on behalf of causes which are now triumphant, and against abuses which are now forgotten, but which acutely needed champions and reformers a hundred years ago.

His foreign journeys, and more especially the first of them, had a large share in determining the opinions which he afterwards maintained against great opposition from many of his own class and profession. The sight of France still smarting under the effects of the Reign of Terror, and of other countries still sunk in medievalism, helped to make him a Liberal with "a passion for reform and improvement, but without a passion for destruction."

He was born in 1779, the second son and youngest child of Sir John Stanley, the squire of Alderley in Cheshire, and of his wife Margaret Owen (the Welsh heiress of Penrhos in Holyhead Island), who was one of the "seven lovely Peggies," well known in Anglesey society in the middle of the eighteenth century.

The pictures of Edward Stanley and his mother, which still hang

Margaret Owen, Lady Stanley

on the walls of her Anglesey home, show that he inherited the brilliant Welsh colouring, marked eyebrows and flashing dark eyes that gave force as well as beauty to her face. From her, too, came the romantic Celtic imagination and fiery energy which enabled him to find interests everywhere, and to make his mark in a career which was not the one he would have chosen.

"In early years" (so his son the Dean of Westminster records) "he had acquired a passion for the sea, which he cherished down to the time of his entrance at college, and which never left him through life. It first originated, as he believed, in the delight which he experienced, when between three and four years of age, on a visit to the seaport of Weymouth; and long afterwards he retained a vivid recollection of the point where he caught the first sight of a ship, and shed tears because he was not allowed to go on board. So strongly was he possessed by the feeling thus acquired, that as a child he used to leave his bed and sleep on the shelf of a wardrobe, for the pleasure of imagining himself in a berth on board a man-of-war. . . . The passion was overruled by circumstances beyond his control, but it gave a colour to his whole after-life. He never ceased to retain a keen interest in everything relating to the navy. . . . He seemed instinctively to know the history, character, and state of every ship and every officer in the service. Old naval captains were often astonished at finding in him a more accurate knowledge than their own of when, where, how, and under whom, such and such vessels had been employed. The stories of begging impostors professing to be shipwrecked seamen were detected at once by his cross-examinations. The sight of a ship, the society of sailors, the embarkation on a voyage, were always sufficient to inspirit and delight him wherever he might be."

His life, when at his mother's home on the Welsh coast, only increased this liking, and till he went to Cambridge in 1798 his education had not been calculated to prepare him for a clerical life. He never received any instruction in classics; of Greek and Latin and mathematics he knew nothing, and owing to his schools and tutors being constantly changed, his general knowledge was of a desultory sort.

His force of character, great perseverance and ambition to excel are shown in the strenuous manner in which he overcame all these obstacles, and at the close of his college career at St. John's, Cambridge, became a wrangler in the Mathematical Tripos of 1802.

After a year passed in foreign travel Edward Stanley returned home at his brother's request, and took command of the Alderley Volunteers—a corps of defence raised by him on the family estate in expectation of a French invasion.

In 1803 he was ordained and became curate of Windlesham, in Surrey. There he remained until he was presented by his father in 1805 to the living of Alderley, where he threw himself enthusiastically into his work.

Alderley parish had long been neglected, and there was plenty of scope for the young rector.

Before he came, the clerk used to go to the churchyard stile to see whether there were any more coming to church, for there were seldom enough to make a congregation, but before Edward Stanley left, his parish was one of the best organised of the day. He set on foot schemes of education throughout the county as well as at Alderley, and was foremost in all reforms.

The chancellor of the diocese wrote of him:

He inherited from his family strong Whig principles, which he always retained, and he never shrank from advocating those maxims of toleration which at that time formed the chief watchwords of the Whig party.

He was the first who distinctly saw and boldly advocated the advantages of general education for the people, and set the example of the extent to which general knowledge might be communicated in a parochial school.

To analyse the actual effects of his ministrations on the people would be difficult, . . . but the general result was what might have been expected. Dissent was all but extinguished. The church was filled, the communicants many.

He helped to found a Clerical Society, which promoted friendly intercourse with clergy holding various views, and was never afraid of avowing his opinions on subjects he thought vital, lest he should in consequence become unpopular.

He grudged no trouble about anything he undertook, and the people rejoiced when they heard "the short, quick tramp of his horse's feet as he went galloping up their lanes." The sick were visited and cheered, and the children kindly cared for in and out of school.

It was said of him that "whenever there was a drunken fight in the village and he knew of it, he would always come out to stop it—there was such a spirit in him."

Tidings were once brought to him of a riotous crowd, which had assembled to witness a desperate prize fight, adjourned to the outskirts of his parish, and which the respectable inhabitants were unable to disperse.

"The whole field" (so one of the humbler neighbours represented it) "was filled and all the trees round about, when in about a quarter of an hour I saw the rector coming up the road on his little black horse as quick as lightning, and I trembled for fear they should harm him. He rode into the field and just looked round as if he thought the same, to see who there was that would be on his side. But it was not needed; he rode into the midst of the crowd and in one moment it was all over. There was a great calm; the blows stopped; it was as if they would all have wished to cover themselves up in the earth. All from the trees they dropped down directly. No one said a word and all went away humbled."

The next day the rector sent for the two men, not to scold them, but to speak to them, and sent them each away with a Bible. The effect on the neighbourhood was very great, and put a stop to the practice which had been for some time prevalent in the adjacent districts.

His influence was increased by his early knowledge of the people, and by the long connection of his family with the place.

Two years after Edward had accepted the incumbency, his father died in London, but he had long before given up living in Cheshire, and Alderley Park had been occupied at his desire by his eldest son, afterwards Sir John, who had made his home there since his marriage in 1796.

Both the Stanley brothers married remarkable women. Lady Maria Josepha Holroyd, Sir John's wife, was the elder daughter of the first Lord Sheffield, the friend and biographer of Gibbon, and her strong personality impressed everyone who met her.

Catherine, wife of the rector, was the daughter of the Rev. Oswald Leycester, of Stoke Rectory, in Shropshire. Her father was one of the Leycesters of Toft House, only a few miles from Alderley, and at Toft most of Catherine's early years were spent. She was engaged to Edward Stanley before she was seventeen, but did not marry him till nearly two years later, in 1810.

During the interval she spent some time in London with Sir John and Lady Maria Stanley, and in the literary society of the opening years of the nineteenth century she was much sought after for her charm and appreciativeness, and for what Sydney Smith called her "porcelain understanding." The wits and lions of the Miss Berrys' parties vied with each other in making much of her; Rogers and Scott delighted in her conversation—in short, everyone agreed, as her sister-in-law Maria wrote, that "in Kitty Leycester Edward will indeed have a treasure."

After her marriage she kept up with her friends by active correspondence and by annual visits to London. Still, "to the outside world she was comparatively unknown; but there was a quiet wisdom, a rare unselfishness, a calm discrimination, a firm decision which made her judgment and her influence felt through the whole circle in which she lived." Her power and charm, coupled with her husband's, made Alderley Rectory an inspiring home to their children, several of whom inherited talent to a remarkable degree.

Her sister Maria [1] writes from Hodnet, the home of the poet Heber:

I want to know all you have been doing since the day that bore me away from happy Alderley. Oh! the charm of a rectory inhabited by a Reginald Heber or an Edward Stanley!

That rectory and its surroundings have been perfectly described in the words of the author of *Memorials of a Quiet Life*[2]:

A low house, with a verandah forming a wide balcony for the upper storey, where bird-cages hung among the roses; its rooms and passages filled with pictures, books, and old carved oak furniture. In a country where the flat pasture lands of Cheshire rise suddenly to the rocky ridge of Alderley Edge, with the Holy Well under an overhanging cliff; its gnarled pine-trees, its storm-beaten beacon tower ready to give notice of an invasion, and looking far over the green plain to the smoke which indicates in the horizon the presence of the great manufacturing towns.

There was constant intercourse between the park and the rectory, and the two families with a large circle of friends led most interest-

---

1. Maria Leycester, m. 1829 Rev. Augustus Hare.
2. *Memorials of a Quiet Life*, by Augustus Hare, adopted son of Mrs. Augustus Hare (Maria Leycester).

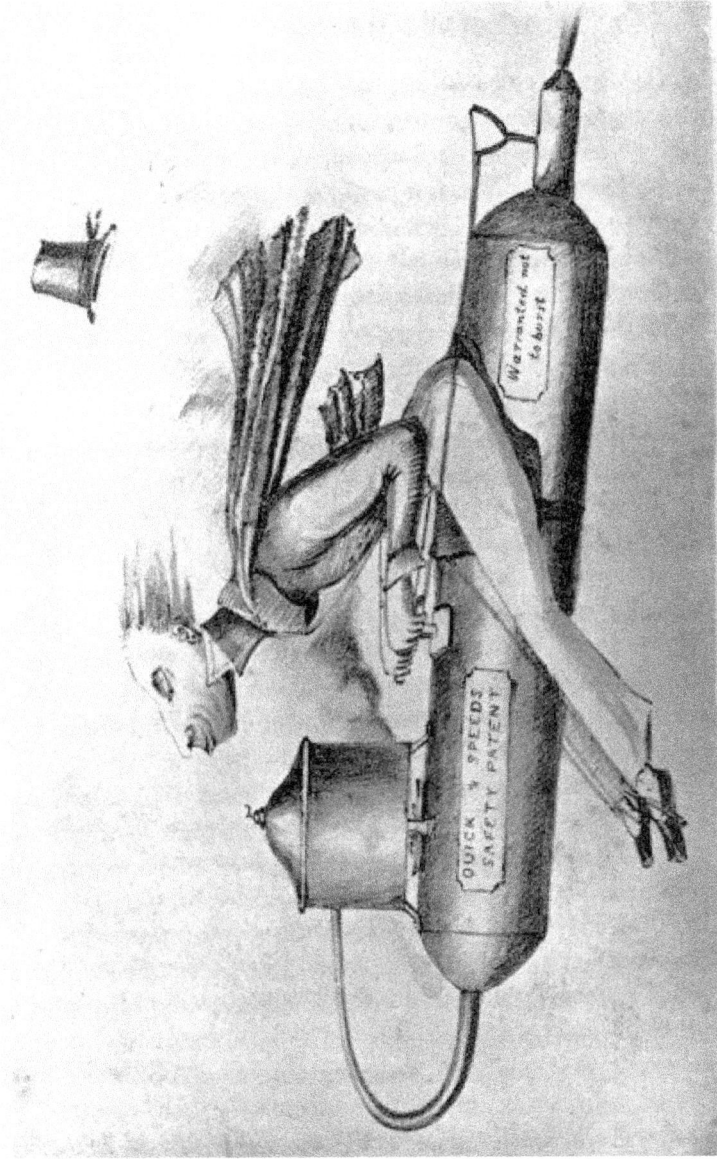

The Flight of Intellect

ing and busy lives. The rector took delight in helping his seven nieces with their Italian and Spanish studies, in fostering their love of poetry and natural history, and in developing the minds of his own young children. He wrote plays for them to act and birthday odes for them to recite.

Legends of the countryside, domestic tragedies and comedies were turned into verse, whether it were the Cheshire legend of the Iron Gates or the fall of Sir John Stanley and his spectacles into the Alderley mere, the discovery of a butterfly or the loss of "a superfine piece of Bala flannel."

His caricatures illustrated his droll ideas, as in his sketches of the six *Ologies from Entomology to Apology*. His witty and graceful *Bustle's Banquet* or the *Dinner of the Dogs* made a trio with the popular poems then recently published of the *Butterfly's Ball* and *The Peacock at Home*.

And since Insects give Balls and Birds are so gay
'Tis high time to prove that we Dogs have our day.

He wrote a *Familiar History of Birds,* illustrated by many personal observations, for throughout his life he never lost a chance of watching wild bird life. In his early days he had had special opportunities of doing so among the rocks and caverns of Holyhead Island. He tells of the myriads of sea-birds who used to haunt the South Stack Rock there, in the days when it was almost inaccessible; and of their dispersal by the building of the first lighthouse there in 1808, when for a time they deserted it and never returned in such numbers.

His own family at Alderley Rectory consisted of three sons and two daughters.

The eldest son, Owen, had his father's passion for the sea, and was allowed to follow his bent. His scientific tastes led him to adopt the surveying branch of his profession, and in 1836, when appointed to the *Terror* on her expedition to the North Seas, he had charge of the astronomical and magnetic operations.

When in command of the *Britomart*, in 1840, he secured the North Island of New Zealand to the English by landing and hoisting the British flag, having heard that a party of French emigrants intended to land that day. They did so, but under the protection of the Union Jack.

In 1846 Owen Stanley commanded the *Rattlesnake* in an important and responsible expedition to survey the unknown coast of New Guinea; this lasted four years and was very successful, but the great strain and the shock of his brother Charles' death at Hobart Town, at this time, were too much for him. He died suddenly on board his ship at Sydney in 1850, "after thirty-three years' arduous service in every clime."

Professor Huxley, in whose arms he breathed his last, was surgeon to this expedition, and his first published composition was an article describing it. He speaks of Owen Stanley thus:

Of all those who were actively engaged upon the survey, the young commander alone was destined to be robbed of his just rewards; he has raised an enduring monument in his works, and his epitaph shall be the grateful thanks of many a mariner threading his way among the mazes of the Coral Seas.

The second and most distinguished of the three sons was Arthur Penrhyn Stanley, of whom it was said "that in the wideness of his sympathies, the broadness of his toleration, and the generosity of his temperament the brilliant Dean of Westminster was a true son of his father, the Bishop of Norwich."

The third son, Charles Edward, a young officer in the Royal Engineers, who had done good work in the Ordnance Survey of Wales, and was already high in his profession, was suddenly cut off by fever at his official post in Tasmania in 1849.

The eldest daughter, Mary, had great powers of organisation, was a keen philanthropist and her father's right hand at Norwich. In 1854 she took charge of a detachment of nurses who followed Miss Nightingale's pioneer band to the East, and worked devotedly for the Crimean sick and wounded at the hospital at Koulalee.

Katherine, the youngest daughter, a most original character, married Dr. Vaughan, headmaster of Harrow, Master of the Temple, and Dean of Llandaff. She survived her whole family and lived till 1899.

The home at Alderley lasted for thirty-three years, during which Edward Stanley had changed the whole face of the parish and successfully organised many schemes of improvement in the conditions of the working classes in his neighbourhood. He could now leave his work to other hands, and felt that his energies required a wider field, so that when in 1838 Lord Melbourne offered him the See of Norwich he was induced to accept the offer, though only "after much hesitation and after a severe struggle, which for a time almost broke down his usual health and sanguine spirit."

"It would be vain and useless," he said, "to speak to others of what it cost me to leave Alderley"; but to his new sphere he carried the same zeal and indomitable energy which had ever characterised him, and gained the affection of many who had shuddered at the appointment of a "Liberal Bishop."

At Norwich his work was very arduous and often discouraging. He came in the dawn of the Victorian age to attack a wall of customs and abuses which had arisen far back in the early Georgian era, with no hereditary connection or influence in the diocese to counteract the odium that he incurred as a newcomer by the institution of changes which he deemed necessary.

It was no wonder that for three or four years he had to stem a steady torrent of prejudice and more or less opposition; but though his broadminded views were often the subject of criticism, his bitterest opponents could not withstand the genial, kindly spirit in which he met their objections.

At the time of his entrance upon his office party feeling was much more intense than it has been in later years, and of this the county of Norfolk presented, perhaps, as strong examples as could be found in any part of the kingdom.

The bishop was "a Whig in politics and a staunch supporter of a Whig ministry," but in all the various questions where politics and theology cross one another he took the free and comprehensive instead of the precise and exclusive views, and to impress them on others was one chief interest of his new position.

The indifference to party which he displayed, both in social matters and in his dealings with his clergy, tended to alienate extreme partisans of whatever section, and at one time caused him even to be unpopular with the lower classes of Norwich in spite of his sympathies.

The courage with which the rector had quelled the prize fight at Alderley shone out again in the bishop.

"I remember," says an eyewitness, "seeing Bishop Stanley, on a memorable occasion, come out of the Great Hall of St. Andrew's, Norwich. The Chartist mob, who lined the street, saluted the active, spare little Bishop with hooting and groans. He came out alone and unattended till he was followed by me and my brother, determined, as the saying is, '*to see him safe home*,' for the mob was highly excited and brutal. Bishop Stanley marched along ten yards, then turned sharp round and fixed his eagle eyes on the mob, and then marched ten yards more and turned round again rapidly and gave the same hawk-like look."

His words and actions must often have been startling to his contemporaries; when temperance was a new cause he publicly spoke in support of the Roman Catholic Father Mathew, who had promoted it in Ireland; when the idea of any education for the masses was not universally accepted he advocated admitting the children of dissenters to the national schools; and when the stage had not the position it now holds, he dared to offer hospitality to one of the most distinguished of its representatives, Jenny Lind, to mark his respect for her life and influence.

For all this he was bitterly censured, but his kindly spirit and friendly intercourse with his clergy smoothed the way through apparently insurmountable difficulties, and his powerful aid was ever at hand in any benevolent movement to advise and organise means of help.

In his home at Norwich the bishop and Mrs. Stanley delighted to welcome guests of every shade of opinion, and one of them, a member of a well-known Quaker family, has recorded her impression of her host's conversation. "The Bishop talks, darting from one subject to another, like one impatient of delay, amusing and pleasant," and he is described on coming to Norwich as having "a step as quick, a voice as firm, a power of enduring fatigue almost as unbroken as when he traversed his parish in earlier days or climbed the precipices of the Alps."

In his public life the liveliness of his own interest in scientific pursuits, the ardour with which he would hail any new discovery, the vividness of his own observation of Nature would illustrate with an unexpected brilliancy the worn-out topics of a formal speech. Few who were present at the meeting when the Borneo Mission was first proposed to the London public in 1847 can forget the strain of naval ardour with which the bishop offered his heartfelt tribute of moral respect and admiration to the heroic exertions of Sir James Brooke.

It was his highest pleasure to bear witness to the merits or to contribute to the welfare of British seamen. He seized every opportunity of addressing them on their moral and religious duties, and many were the rough sailors whose eyes were dimmed with tears among the congregations of the crews of the *Queen* and the *Rattlesnake*, when he preached on board those vessels at Plymouth, whither he had accompanied his eldest son, Captain Owen Stanley, to witness his embarkation on his last voyage.

"The sermon," so the Admiral told Dean Stanley twenty years afterwards, "was never forgotten. The men were so crowded that they almost sat on one another's shoulders, with such attention and admiration that they could scarcely restrain a cheer."

For twelve years his presence was felt as a power for good through the length and breadth of his diocese; and after his death, in September, 1849, his memory was long loved and revered.

"I felt as if a sunbeam had passed through my parish," wrote a clergyman from a remote corner of his diocese, after a visit from him, "and had left me to rejoice in its genial and cheerful warmth. From that day I would have died to serve him; and I believe that not a few of my humble flock were animated by the same kind of feeling."

His yearly visits to his former parish of Alderley were looked forward to by those he had known and loved during his long parochial ministrations as the greatest pleasure of their lives.

"I have been," he writes (in the last year of his life), "in various directions over the parish, visiting many welcome faces, laughing with the living, weeping over the dying. It is gratifying to see the cordial familiarity with which they receive me, and Norwich clergy would scarcely know me by cottage fires, talking over old times with their hands clasped in mine as an old and dear friend."

Under the light which streams through the stained glass of his own cathedral the remains of Bishop Stanley rest in the thoroughfare of the great congregation.

"When we were children," said a grey-haired Norfolk rector this very year, "our mother never allowed us to walk upon the stone covering Bishop Stanley's grave. I have never forgotten it, and would not walk upon it even now."

We pass; the path that each man trod
Is dim, or will be dim, with weeds:
What fame is left for human deeds
In endless age? It rests with God.

Edward Stanley circa 1800.

CHAPTER 1

New France and Old Europe

In June, 1802, Edward Stanley started on the first of those foreign journeys which, throughout his life, continued to be his favourite form of holiday.

He had just left Cambridge, having obtained a brilliant degree, and before taking Orders he set out with his college friend, Edward Hussey,[1] on the Grand Tour which was then considered necessary to complete a liberal education.

They were fortunate in the moment of their journey, for the Treaty of Amiens, which had been concluded only a few months before, had enabled Englishmen to tour safely in France for the first time for many years; and every scene in France was full of thrilling interest. The marks of the Reign of Terror were still plainly to be seen, and the new order of things which the First Consul had inaugurated was only just beginning.

It was an epoch-making journey to a young man fresh from college, and Edward Stanley was deeply impressed by what he saw.

He could compare his own experiences with those of his brother and father, who had been in France before the Revolution, and of his sister-in-law, Maria Josepha, who had travelled there just before the Reign of Terror; and in view of the destruction which had taken place since then, he was evidently convinced that Napoleon's iron hand was the greatest boon to the country.

He and his companion had the good fortune to leave France before the short interval of peace ended abruptly, and they were there-

---

1. E. Hussey, of Scotney Castle, Kent. He died in 1817 and left his only son Edward (married, 1853, Henrietta Clive, daughter of Baroness Windsor) to the guardianship of Edward Stanley.

fore saved from the fate of hundreds of their friends and fellow-travellers who had thronged across the Channel in 1802, and who were detained by Napoleon for years against their will.

Edward Stanley and Edward Hussey left France at the end of June, and went on to Switzerland, Italy, and finally to Spain, where the difficulties and dangers which they met, reveal the extraordinary dearth of personal comfort and civilised habits among that nation at the time.

The dangers and discomforts did not, however, interfere with the interest and pleasure of the writer who describes them. Then and ever after, travelling was Edward Stanley's delight, and he took any adventure in the spirit of the French song—

Je suis touriste
Quel gai metier.

His letters to his father and brother show that he lost no opportunity of getting information and of recording what he saw; and he began on this journey the first of a long series of sketchbooks, by which he illustrated his later journeys so profusely.

EDWARD STANLEY TO HIS FATHER, SIR JOHN T. STANLEY, BART.

Rouen, June 11, 1802.

My Dear Father,—You have already heard that I arrived here, and have been fortunate in everything since I left England. Our passage from Brighton to Dieppe was short and pleasant, and so was our stay at Dieppe, which we left the morning after we arrived in it. I never saw France before the Revolution, and therefore cannot judge of the contrasted appearance of its towns, but this I can safely say, that I never before saw such strong marks of poverty both in the houses and Inhabitants. I have as yet seen nothing like a gentleman; probably many may affect the dress and manners of the lower orders, in order to screen themselves and may consider that an outward show of poverty is the only way of securing what riches they have. I can conceive nothing so melancholy.

When I saw fine seats without windows or with shattered roofs, and everywhere falling to decay, I could not help thinking of their unfortunate owners, who, even if they were lucky enough to be reinstated in their possessions, might fear to repair their places, lest an appearance of comfort might tempt the Government to seize their effects. The only buildings at all tolerable are the barracks, which in general are large and well taken care of, and plenty of them there are in every town and village. Every person is here a soldier, ready to turn out at a moment's warning. This town is in a flourishing state at present, though during the war not a single ship made its appearance in its ports; now there are a great number of vessels, chiefly Dutch. The trade is cotton, for the manufactory of stuffs and handkerchiefs. It is said to be one of the dearest towns in France; certainly I have not found things very cheap.

We were at the play last night. An opera called *La Dot*, and an after piece called *Blaise and Bullet* were performed. The actors were capital, at Drury Lane they could not have acted better. The house is very large for a country theatre and very pretty, but so shockingly filthy and offensive, that I wondered any person could go often, but habit, I suppose, reconciles everything. There were a great many officers in the boxes, a haughty set of beings, who treat their *compatriotes* in a very scurvy way. They are the kings of the place and do what they please. Indeed, we had a fine specimen of liberty during the performances. An actress had been sent to Rouen from Paris, a wretched performer she was, but from Paris she came, and the managers were obliged to accept her and make her act.

The consequence was, she soon got hissed, and a note was thrown on the stage; whatever it was they were not permitted to read or make it public till they had shewn it to the officer of police, who in the present case would not let them read it. The hissing was, however, continued from corners of the house, and one man who sate near us talked in a high style about the people being imposed on, when in the middle of his speech I saw this man of liberty jump out of the box and disappear in an instant. I opened the box door to see what was the cause, when lo! the lobby was filled with soldiers, with their bayonets fixed, and the officer was looking about for any person who might dare to whistle or hiss, and silent and contented were the audience the rest of the performance. I cannot help mentioning a speech I heard this very evening at the play.

A man was sitting near a lady and very angry he was, and attempted often to hiss, but was for some time kept quiet by the lady. At last he lost all patience and exclaimed, "*Ma Foi, Madame, Je ferai ici comme si jétais en Angleterre où on fait tout ce qu'on plait.*" And away he went to hiss; with what effect his determination a *l'Angloise* was attended, I have mentioned. I afterwards entered into conversation with the lady, and when she told me about the police officer not giving permission to read the note, she added, looking at us, "to you, gentlemen, this must be a second comedy." Last night (Sunday) I went to a *fête* about a mile from the town; we paid 1s. 3d. each. It concluded with a grand firework. It was a sort of Vauxhall. In one part of the gardens they were dancing *cotillons*, in another swinging. In another part bands of music. I was never so much entertained as with the dancers; most of them were children. One little set in a *cotillon* danced in a style I could not have fancied possible; you will think I am telling a *traveller's* story when I tell you I thought they performed nearly as well as I could have seen at the opera.

Here, as at the theatre, soldiers kept everybody in awe; a strong party of dragoons were posted round the gardens with their horses saddled close at hand ready to act. I dined yesterday at a *table d'hôte*, with five French officers. In my life I never saw such ill bred blackguards, dirty in their way of eating, overbearing in their conversation, though they never condescended to address themselves to us, and more proud and aristocratical than any of the *ci-devant noblesse* could ever have been. From this moment I believe all the accounts I have heard from our officers of the French officers who were prisoners during the war. They were always insolent, and excepting in some few cases, ungrateful in the extreme for any kindness shewn to them.

Paris, June 17th.

The day before yesterday I arrived in this Metropolis. We left Rouen in a diligence and had a pleasant journey; the country we passed over was throughout extremely fertile; whatever scarcity exists at present in France, it must be of short duration, as the harvest promises to be abundant, and as every field is corn land, the quantity of grain will be immense. Government has indeed now taken every precaution. The ports of Rouen and Dieppe were filled with ships from Embden and Dantzig with corn. Our diligence was accompanied all the night by a guard of dragoons, and we passed every now and then parties of foot soldiers on the watch. The reason was, that the road had lately been infested with robbers, who attacked the public carriages in great numbers, sometimes to the amount of forty together. They in general behaved well to the passengers, requiring only any money belonging to Government which might happen to be in the carriage.

At present as the leader is taken and the band dispersed, there is no danger, but it is a good excuse to keep a number of troops in that part of the country. We entered Paris by St. Denis, but the fine church and Royal Palace are not now as they were in your time. The former is in part unroofed and considerably damaged—the latter is a barrack

THE PRISON OF THE TEMPLE,
PARIS, JUNE, 1802

and from its outward appearance seems to have suffered much in the Revolution. The city of Paris on entering it by no means strikes a stranger. In your time it must have been but tolerable, now it is worse, as every other house seems to be falling down or to be deserted. We have taken our abode in the Rue de Vivienne at the Hôtel de Boston, a central situation and the house tolerably dear. The poor Hussey suffered so much from a nest of bugs the first night, that he after enduring them to forage on his body for an hour, left his bed and passed the night on a sofa.

À propos, I must beg to inform Mr. Hugh Leycester that I paid attention to the conveyances on the road and think that he will have no reason to complain of them; the vehicles are not quite so good as in England nor are the horses, but both are still very tolerable. The inns I slept at were very good, and the roads by no means bad. I have been to a play every night since my arrival in Paris and shall continue so to do till I have seen all the theatres. The first evening I went to the "*Théâtre de la République*"; I am told it is the best. At least the first actors performed there. It is not to be compared with any of ours in style of fitting up. The want of light which first strikes a stranger's eye on entering a foreign play-house has its advantage. It shews off the performers and induces the audience to pay more attention to ye stage, but the brilliant effect we are used to find on entering our theatres is wanting.

This house is not fitted up with any taste. I thought the theatre at Rouen preferable. The famous Talma, the Kemble, acted in a tragedy, and Mme. Petit, the Mrs. Siddons of Paris, performed. The former, I think, must have seen Kemble, as he resembles him both in person and style of acting, but I did not admire him so much. In his silent Acting, however, he was very great. Mme. Petit acted better than any tragic actress I have ever seen, excepting Mrs. Siddons. After the play last night I went to the Frascati, a sort of Vauxhall where you pay nothing on entering, but are expected to take some refreshments. This, Mr. Palmer told me, was the lounge of the *beau monde*, who were all to be found here after the opera and plays. We have nothing of the sort in England, therefore I shall not attempt to describe it.

We staid here about an hour. The company was numerous, and I suppose the best, at least it was better than any I had seen at the theatres or in the walks, but it appeared to me to be very bad. The men I shall say nothing more of, they are all the same. They come to all places in dirty neckcloths or pocket handkerchiefs tied round their necks and most of them have filthy great coats and boots, in short, dress amongst the bucks (and I am told that within this month or two they are very much improved) seems to be quite out of the Question. As for the Ladies, O *mon Dieu!* Madame Récamier's [2] dress at Boodles was by no means extraordinary. My sister can describe that and then you may form some idea of them.

By what I can judge from outward appearance, the morals of Paris must be at a very low ebb. I may perhaps see more of them, when I go to the opera and parties. I have a thousand things more to say, but have no room. This letter has been written at such out of the way times and by little bits at a time, that I know not how you will connect it, but I have not a moment to spare in the regular course of the day. It is now between 6 and 7 o'clock in the morning, and as I cannot find my cloaths am sitting in a dress *à la Mode d'une Dame Française* till Charles comes up with them. Paris is full of English, amongst others I saw Montague Matthews at the Frascati.

I shall stay here till 5th July, as my chance of seeing Buonaparte depends on my staying till 4th, when he reviews the Consular Guard. He is a fine fellow by all accounts; a Military Government when such a head as his manages everything cannot be called a grievance. Indeed, it is productive of so much order and regularity, that I begin not to dislike it so much. At the theatres you have no disturbance. In the streets carriages are kept in order—in short, it is supreme and seems to suit this country vastly well, but God forbid I should ever witness it in England. You may write to me and tell others so to do till the 25th of June. *Adieu;* I cannot tell when I shall write again. This you know is a family epistle, therefore farewell to you all.

Ed. Stanley.

I have just paid a visit to Madame de D. She received me very graciously, and strongly pressed me to stay till 14th of July to be present at the Grand Day. She says Paris is not now worth seeing, but then every person will be in town. If there is no other way of seeing Buonaparte I believe I shall stay—but I do not wish it—I shall prefer Geneva.

EDWARD STANLEY TO HIS BROTHER, J. T. STANLEY.

Hotel de Boston, Rue Vivienne,
June 21, 1802.

My Dear Brother,— I sailed from Brighton on the evening of 8th and was wafted by a fine breeze towards this coast, which we made

2. Madame Récamier, famous French beauty, 1777-1849.

early on the morning of 9th, but owing to the tide, which had drifted us too much to leeward of Dieppe, we were unable to land before noon. We were carried before the officer of the municipality, who after taking down our names, ages, and destination, left us to ramble about at pleasure. Whatever Dieppe might have been before the Revolution, it is now a melancholy-looking place, large houses falling to ruin, inhabitants poor, streets full of soldiers, and churches turned into stables, barracks, or magazines. We staid there but one night and then proceeded in one of their diligences to Rouen.

These conveyances you of course have often seen; they are not as speedy in their motion as an English mail coach, or as easy as a curricle, but we have found them very convenient, and shall not complain of our travelling accommodation if we are always fortunate enough to meet with these vehicles. At Rouen we staid four days, as the town is large and well worth seeing; I then made an attempt to procure you some painted glass; as almost all the churches and all the convents are destroyed, their fine windows are neglected, and the panes broken or carried off by almost every person.

The *stable* from whence our diligence started had some beautiful windows, and had I thought of it in time I think I might have sent you some. As it was I went to the owner of the churches and asked him if he would sell any of the windows. Now though ever since he has had possession of them everybody has been permitted to demolish at pleasure, he no sooner found that a stranger was anxious to procure what to him was of no value, and what he had hitherto thought worth nothing, than he began to think he might take advantage and therefore told me that he would give me an answer in a few days if I would wait till he could see what they were worth. As I was going the next morning I could not hear the result, but I think you could for one guinea purchase nearly a whole church window, at least it may be worth your while to send to Liverpool to know if any ship is at any time going there. The proprietor of these churches is a banker, by name Tezart; he lives in la Rue aux Ours.

I arrived in Paris on the 15th, and intend staying even till the 14th of July if I cannot before then see the chief consul. Hitherto I have been unfortunate; I have in vain attended at the Thuilleries when the consular guard is relieved, and seated myself opposite his box at the opera. On the 4th of July, however, there is a review of his Guard, when he always appears, then I shall do my utmost to get a view of him. I cannot be introduced as I have not been at our court, and no king was ever more fond of court etiquette than Buonaparte. He resides in the Thuilleries; opposite to his windows is the place de Carousel, which he has separated from the great area by a long iron railing with three gates. On each side of the two side gates are placed the famous brazen horses from Venice, the middle gate has two lodges, where are stationed Horse Guards. Above this gate are four gilt spears on which are perched the cock and a civic wreath which I at first took for the Roman eagle, borne before their consuls, resembling it in every other respect. These gates are shut every night and also on every review day. Paris, like all the country, swarms with soldiers; in every street there is a barrack. In Paris alone there are upwards of fifteen thousand men. I must say nothing of the Government.

It is highly necessary in France for every person, particularly strangers, to be careful in delivering their opinions; I can only say that the *slavery* of it is infinitely more to my taste than the *freedom* of France. The public exhibitions (and indeed almost everything is public) are on a scale of liberality which should put England to the blush. Everything is open without money. The finest library I ever saw is open daily to every person. You have but to ask for any book, and you are furnished with it, and accommodated with table, pens, ink, and paper. The Louvre, the finest collection of pictures and statues in the world, is likewise open, and not merely open to view. It is filled, excepting on the public days, with artists who are at liberty to copy anything they please. Where in England can we boast of anything like this?

Our British museum is only to be seen by interest, and then shewn in a very cursory manner. Our public libraries at the universities are equally difficult of access. It is the most politic thing the Government could have done. The arts are here encouraged in a most liberal manner. Authors, painters, sculptors, and, in short, all persons in France, have opportunities of improving themselves which cannot be found in any other country in the world, not even in Britain. You may easily conceive that I who am fond of painting was most highly entertained in viewing the Great Gallery of the Louvre, and yet you will, I am sure, think my taste very deficient when I tell you that I do not admire the finest pictures of Raphael, Titian, Guido, and Paul Veronese, so much as I do those of Rubens, Vandyck, and le Brun, nor the landscapes of Claude and Poussin so much as Vernet's.

Rembrandt, Gerard Dow and his pupils Mieris and Metsu please me more than any other artists. In the whole collection they have but one of Salvator's, but that one, I think, is preferable to all Raphael's.

I have not yet seen statues enough to be judge of their beauties. The Apollo of Belvidere and the celebrated Laocoon lose, therefore, much of their excellence when seen by me. There is still a fine collection in the palace of Versailles, but the view of that once Royal Palace excites the most melancholy ideas. The furniture was all sold by auction, and nothing is left but the walls and their pictures. The gardens are much neglected, and will soon, unless the consul again makes it a royal residence, be quite ruined. You have, I daresay, often heard that the morals and society of Paris were very bad; indeed, you have heard nothing but the truth. As for the men, they are the dirtiest set of fellows I ever saw, and most of them, especially the officers, very unlike gentlemen.

The dress of the women, with few exceptions, is highly indecent; in London, even in Drury Lane, I have seen few near so bad. Before I left England, I had heard, but never believed, that some ladies paraded the streets in men's clothes. It is singular that in the first genteel-looking person I spoke to in Paris to ask my way, I was answered by what I then perceived a lady in Breeches and boots, since when I have seen several at the Theatres, at the Frascati and fashionable lounges of the evening, and in the streets and public walks!

I have not heard from you since I left England. Excepting the letter which was forwarded from Grosvenor Place. I hope to hear at Geneva, where I shall go as soon as the great consul will permit me by shewing himself. The country is in the finest state possible, and their weather most favourable. They have had a scarcity of corn lately, but the approaching harvest will most assuredly remove that. *Adieu*; I hope Mrs. Stanley has already received a very trifling present from me; I only sent it because it was classic wood. I mean the necklace made of Milton's mulberry-tree. I brought the wood from Christ's College garden, in Cambridge, where Milton himself planted it.

> Believe me,
> Yours sincerely,
> Edwd. Stanley.

FROM EDWARD STANLEY TO HIS FATHER AND MOTHER.

Lyons, July 20, 1802.

I shall not write you a very long letter as I intend to send you a more particular account of myself from Geneva, for which place we propose setting out tomorrow, not by the diligence, but by the *vetturino*, a mode of travelling which, of course, you are well acquainted with, being the usual and almost only method practised throughout

Italy unless a person has his own carriage. I am to pay £3 10s. for ourselves and suite, but not including bed and provisions. South of the Alps these are agreed for.

After every endeavour to see Buonaparte had proved vain, on the 6th of July we quitted Paris in a cabriolet. All this night, and especially the next day, we thought we should be broiled to death; the thermometer was at 95 the noon of July 7th; as you relish that, you may have some idea of the luxury you would have enjoyed with us.

We arrived at Troyes on the evening of the 7th, an old town in Champagne. People civil and excellent living, as the landlord was a *ci-devant* head cook to a convent of Benedictines, but Hussey and Charles were almost devoured in the night by our old enemies the bugs. Hussey was obliged to change his room and sleep all next day. I escaped without the least visit, and I am persuaded that if a famine wasted the bugs of the whole earth, they would sooner perish than touch me.

We left Troyes early on the morning of the 9th, arrived at Chatillon at four, and stayed there all night, for the diligences do not travel so fast as in England. We left it at four the next morning, Hussey, as usual smarting, and I very little refreshed by sleep, as owing to a compound of ducks and chickens who kept up a constant chorus within five yards of my bed, a sad noise in the kitchen from which I was barely separated, dogs barking, waggon bells ringing, &c., I could scarcely close my eyes.

At Dijon, beautiful Dijon, we arrived on the evening of the 10th. Had I known it had been so sweet a town I should have stayed longer, but we had taken our places to Châlons and were obliged to pass on. You, I believe, staid some time there, but, alas! how different now! The Army of rescue was encamped for some time in its neighbourhood, and the many respectable families who lived in or near it rendered it a sad prey to the hand of Robespierre. Its churches and convents are in a deplorable state, even as those of this still more unfortunate town. The best houses are shut up, and its finest buildings are occupied by the military. We left on the morning of the 11th, travelled safely (except a slight breakdown at our journey's end) to Châlons sur Saône, and on the 11th went by the water-diligence to Macon, where we stopped to sleep. We arrived at dusk, and as we were in a dark staircase exploring our way and speaking English, we heard a voice say, "This way, Sir; here is the supper." We were quite rejoiced to hear an English voice, particularly in such a place.

We soon met the speaker, and passed a most pleasant hour with

THE GUILLOTINE AT CHALON-SUR-SAÔNE.

him. He proved to be a passenger like ourselves in the diligence from Lyons which met ours here at the common resting-place. He was a surgeon of the staff, returning from Egypt, by name Shute. We all three talked together, and as loud as we could; the company, i believe, thought us strange beings. We told him what we could of England in a short time, he of the South, and we exchanged every species of information, and were sorry when it was necessary to part.

We arrived at Lyons on the 14th, the day of the Grand Fête. We saw the town hall illuminated, and a review on the melancholy plains of Buttereaux, the common tomb of so many Lyonnese. Here we have remained since, but shall probably be at Geneva on the 23rd. I lodge at the Hotel de Parc looking into the Place de Ferreant.

The landlady, to my great surprise, spoke to me in English very fluently. She is also a very excellent Spaniard. She has seen better days, her husband having been a merchant, but the Revolution destroyed him. She was prisoner for some time at Liverpool, taken by a privateer belonging to Tarleton and Rigge, who, I am sorry to say, did not behave quite so handsomely as they should, the private property not having been restored.

Of all the towns I have seen this has suffered most. All the *châteaux* and villas in its most beautiful environs are shut up. The fine square of St. Louis le Grand, then Belle Cour, now Place Buonaparte, is knocked to pieces; the fine statue is broken and removed, and nothing left that could remind you of what it was.

I have been witness to a scene which, of course, my curiosity as a traveller would not let me pass over, but which I hope not to see again—an execution on the guillotine. Charles saw a man suffer at Châlons; we did not know till it was over, but the machine was still standing, and the marks of the execution very recent. On looking out of my window the morning after our arrival here, I saw the dreadful instrument in the Place de Ferreant, and on inquiry found that five men were to be beheaded in the morning and two in the evening. They deserved their fate; they had robbed some farmhouses and committed some cruelties.

In England, however, they would probably have escaped, as the evidence was chiefly presumptive. They were brought to the scaffold from the prison, tied each with his arms behind him and again to each other; they were attended by a priest, not, however, in black, and a party of soldiers. The time of execution of the whole five did not exceed five minutes. Of all situations in the world, I can conceive of none half so terrible as that of the last prisoner. He saw his companions ascend one after another, heard each fatal blow, and saw each body thrown aside to make room for him. I shall never forget his countenance when he stretched out his neck on the fatal board. He shut his eyes on looking down where the heads of his companions had fallen, and instantly his face turned from ghastly paleness to a deep red, and the wire was touched and he was no more. Of all deaths it is far the most easy; not a convulsive struggle could be perceived after the blow. The sight is horrid in the extreme, though not awful, as no ceremony is used to make it so. Those who have daily seen 200 suffer without the least ceremony or trial get hardened to the sight.

The mode of execution in England is not so speedy certainly nor so horrid, but it is conducted with a degree of solemnity that must impress the mind most forcibly. I did not see the two who suffered in the evening, the morning's business was quite enough to satisfy my curiosity.

The next morning I saw a punishment a degree less shocking, though I think the prisoner's fate was little better than those of the day before. He was seated on a scaffold in the same place for public view, there to remain for six hours and then to be imprisoned in irons for eighteen years, a term (as he is 41) I think he will not survive.

What with the immediate effects of the siege and events that followed, the town has suffered so much in its buildings and inhabitants, that I think it will never recover. The manufactories of silk are just beginning to shoot up by slow degrees. Formerly they afforded employment to 40,000 men, now not above half that number can be found, and they cannot earn so much. Were I a Lyonese I should wish to plant the plains of Buttereaux with cypress-trees and close them in with rails. The place had been a scene of too much horror to remain open for public amusement.

The fine Hôpital de la Charité, against which the besiegers directed their heaviest cannon in spite of the Black ensign, which it is customary to hoist over buildings of that nature during a siege, is much damaged, though scarcely so much as I should have expected. The romantic castle of the Pierre Suisse is no longer to be found, it was destroyed early in the troubles together with most of the Roman antiquities round Lyons. I yesterday dined with two more Englishmen at the *table d'hôte*; they were from the South; one, from his conversation a Navy officer, had been absent seven years, and had been in the garrison of Porte Ferrajo in the Isle of Elba, the other an Egyptian

35

hero. There is also a colonel from the same place whose name I know not.

I heard it was an easy thing to be introduced to the Pope,[3] if letters are to be had for our Minister, whose name is Fagan, or something like it. Now, as I may if I can get an opportunity when at Geneva to pay a visit to Rome and Florence previous to passing the Pyrenees, I should like a letter to this Mr. Fagan, if one can be got. As Buonaparte's Pope is not, I believe, so particular as the Hero himself with regard to introductions, I may perhaps be presented to him. I look forward with inexpressible pleasure to my arrival at Geneva, to find myself amongst old friends and to meet with, I hope, an immense collection of letters.

The vineyards promise to be very abundant; of course we tasted some of the best when in Burgundy and Champagne. What a country that is! The corn to the East of Paris is not so promising as that in Normandy. The frosts which we felt in May have extended even more to the south than to this town. The apple-trees of Normandy have suffered most, and the vines in the northern parts of France have also been damaged. . . . I shall go from Geneva to Genoa, and there hold a council of war.

Geneva.

. . .Between Lyons and Geneva we supped with the Passengers of a *vetturino*. Two of these were officers in the French Service, one of them a Swiss, the other a Frenchman. The conversation soon fell upon Politics, in which I did not choose to join, but was sufficiently entertained in hearing the discourse. Both agreed in abominating the present state of affairs. The Swiss hated the consul, because he destroyed his country, the other because he was too like a king. Both were philosophers, and each declared himself to be a moralist. The Frenchman was by far the most vehement of the two, and the Swiss seemed to take much pleasure in leading him on. His philosophy seemed to be drawn from a source equally pure with his morality; assuming for his motto his first and favourite maxim, "*que tous les hommes sont égaux par les lois de la Nature,*" &c., he thought himself justified in wishing Buonaparte (I was going to say) at the Devil (but I soon found out that the existence of that gentleman was a matter of great doubt with the philosopher) for daring to call himself the head of the French Republic. His hatred of power was only equalled by his aversion to the English, whom he

---

3. Pius VII., made Pope in 1800.

seemed to abhor from the bottom of his heart, so much so, that when I attempted to defend the First Consul, he dashed out with a torrent of abuse, and ended by saying, "*Et enfin c'est lui qui a fait la paix avec l'Angleterre.*"

I was for some time in doubt what part of the Revolution he preferred, but by defending Robespierre, he soon gave me an idea of his love of liberty, morality, equality, and so forth. I was sorry he retired so soon after supper, as I never was more entertained in my life in so short a time as with this little fellow, as singular in his figure and dress as in his manner, and he contrived to be always eating as well as talking.

EDWARD STANLEY TO HIS BROTHER J, T. STANLEY.

Argonauta, off Hyères,
Sept. 29, 1802.

My Dear Brother,—Before I left Geneva I firmly intended writing to you, but as I left it unexpectedly and sooner than I intended I had not time, but this, and all my adventures till I left it, I hope you have already heard, as I wrote two letters, one to my Father, the other to my Mother before I quitted Geneva. You will no doubt be Surprised, and perhaps envy my present situation. Where do you think I am? Why, truly, writing on a cot between two 24-pounders in a Spanish 84. You will wonder, I am sure, at seeing the date of this letter, and perhaps wish to know by what good fortune I found a berth in a Spanish man-of-war, an Event which I little expected when I wrote last. I shall begin my story from Geneva, and you shall hear my adventures to the present moment.

We left Geneva in a *vetturino* for Turin, a journey which took up eightdays longer than it naturally should have done, but our coachman was taken ill, and we were on his account obliged to travel slowly. But I was not impatient, as you will know the scenery is beautiful; we crossed Mount Cenis, which, after St. Bernard's, cannot be called a difficult pass. At Turin we stayed three days. It is now a melancholy town, without commerce, and decreasing daily in population. The celebrated Jourdan [4] is the ruler of the place, and with his wife lives in the King's palace. From Turin we went to Genoa, passing through country not equal in scenery, but infinitely more interesting than that between

---

4. General Jourdan, 1762-1833, Marshal. He fought in the Peninsular War, and rallied to Napoleon during the Hundred Days, but later on served the Bourbons and was made Governor of the Hôtel des Invalides under Louis Philippe.

Geneva and Turin, every step almost having been the scene of battle, and every town the object of a siege.

But the most interesting spot of all was the plain of Marengo, near Alessandria. As we travelled in the diligence I had not so good an opportunity of viewing it as I should have had in a *vetturino*, but we stopped a short time to see the monument which is raised to commemorate the victory; it is erected near two remarkable spots, one where Desaix[5] fell, the other the House from which Buonaparte wrote an account of the event to the Directory.

We passed also through Novi, every house in which is marked by shot; that unfortunate town has been three times pillaged during the war. We arrived at Genoa on the 10th of September, in my opinion the most magnificent town for its size I ever saw. The palaces are beyond conception beautiful, or rather were, for the French troops are not at this moment admitted within the gates; they are quartered in the suburb in great numbers. As for the new Government, it is easily seen who is at the head of it. There is a *doge*, to be sure, but his orders come all from Paris. While we were waiting there expecting a ship to sail to Barcelona, the *Medusa*, English Frigate, came in, and amongst its passengers who came with her we found a Cambridge acquaintance, who advised us to go without delay to Leghorn as the Spanish squadron was waiting there for the King of Etruria [6] in order to carry him to Barcelona.

Fortunately the next day an English brig was going, and in her we took our passages; we were fortunate enough to receive a large packet of letters from England a few hours before she sailed, which had she sailed at the time the captain intended we should have missed. Will you let my sisters know that they arrived safe? I am not without hopes of making some use of the interesting letters to Italy, though I am now steering to the westward. After a good passage of two days we arrived at Leghorn and found the Spaniards still there.

As soon as I landed I delivered a letter to a Mr. Callyer, a Liverpool gentleman who is settled there, and by his means was introduced to the Admiral's first lieutenant, who promised to secure me a berth in some of the ships. In short, here I am in a very fine ship, though a horrid sailer. I have now given you a short sketch of my tour till arriving at Leghorn; I have only to say something of Leghorn and the

5. General Desaix; killed at Marengo, 1800.
6. Louis, King of Etruria, son of Ferdinand, Duke of Parma married Mary, *Infanta* of Spain; died 1803.

Argonauta. The town has suffered very much by the war, supported nearly as it was by its commerce with England. The inhabitants saw with little pleasure a French army take possession of the place and drive away the English. They still have a strong force in the town— upwards of 2,000—and its fortifications have been dismantled. It is singular enough to see the French and Tuscan colours flying together on the same staff.

When we entered the port the Tuscan ensign was becalmed and the French flag was flying *by itself.* I was much grieved not to be able to visit Florence when so near it, but as the squadron was in daily expectation of sailing I did not venture to be absent for four days, which the Journey would have required. I was therefore obliged to content myself with a view of Pisa, which I would not have missed on any account. The leaning tower is a curiosity in itself sufficient to induce a stranger to make a long journey to visit it. Here the King of Etruria lived and was hourly expected to set out for Leghorn. But his health, as it was believed, was in so precarious a state that it was sometimes reported that he would not go at all. The Queen, indeed, was in a very critical state, and were it not that her children, she being an *Infanta* of Spain, are entitled to a certain sum of money by no means small, provided they were born in Spain, it would have been madness in her to have undertaken the voyage; indeed, I think it highly probable that a young prince will make his appearance ere we arrive at Barcelona.

After having spent a longer time than I liked at Leghorn, which has nothing curious to recommend it, at length it was given out that on the 26th the King would certainly arrive from Pisa and embark as soon as possible. Accordingly at 6 o'clock on that day all the houses were ornamented in the Italian style by a display of different coloured streamers, etc., from the windows, and His Majesty entered the town. Had I been a king I should have been not altogether pleased with my reception. He appeared in the balcony of the Grand Duke's palace, no one cried, "*Viva Ludovico I!*"

He went to the theatre the same evening, which was illuminated on the occasion, and, of course, much crowded. I do not think our opera could have boasted a finer display of diamonds than I saw that evening in the ladies' heads, but, be it remembered, that there are 7,000 Jews in Leghorn, not one of whom is poor; some are reported to be worth a million. Many of the Italians are also very rich. Next day we were informed that it was necessary to repair on board our ship, as the King was to go early on the 20th. The naval scene received an addition on 26th by the arrival of two French frigates from Porto Ferrajo. They had carried a fresh garrison there and landed 500 men of the former one at Leghorn; they marched immediately, as it was said, to garrison Florence.

On the 27th the Spaniards and French, the only ships of war in the roads, saluted, were manned and dressed. At eleven o'clock of the 27th (after having again seen the King at the opera) in the launch of the *Argonauta* we left Leghorn and went on board, for the first time in my life, to spend I hope many days in so large a ship. She was one of that unfortunate squadron which came forth from Cadiz to convey home Admiral Linois[7] and his prize the *Hannibal*, after our unsuccessful attack in Algeciras bay. This ship suffered little; she was then a better sailer than she is now, or most probably she would not be at present in the service of Spain. Early on the morning of the 28th the marines were on the deck. It blew fresh from the shore, and it was doubted whether the King would venture; at 8 o'clock, however, the Royal barge was seen coming out of the Mole.

The Admiral's ship, *La Reyna Louisa*, gave the signal and at the instant Every ship fired three royal salutes. The effect was very beautiful; we were the nearest to the Admiral, nearer the land were the two other Spanish frigates, and abreast of us the two French ships. They were all dressed, and as the King passed near them they were manned and three cheers were given. The King's boat came first, then the Queen's. After them followed the consuls of the different nations who were at Leghorn, and after them a boat from each of the ships. There were besides a great number of other boats and ships sailing about.

Soon after the King had arrived on board the *Reyna Louisa*, of 120 guns, the signal was made for preparing to sail, and soon after the signal for sailing. We all got under weigh, but as our ship was a bad sailer we had the mortification of seeing ourselves left far behind in a short time. We have had nothing but light winds ever since, and for the last two days contrary, but I am not in the smallest degree impatient to get to Barcelona. The novelty of scene, more especially as it is a naval

---

7. Comte de Linois, 1761-1848. On June 13, 1801, he, with three ships, defeated six British ships in Algeciras Bay, and being protected by the Spanish batteries, he forced the British admiral to retreat, leaving the *Hannibal* in possession of the enemy. In recognition of this triumph Linois received a sword of honour from Napoleon. The English fleet avenged this disaster on July 12, 1801, when the Spanish and French squadrons set out from Cadiz with the captured *Hannibal* and Admiral Saumarez forced the combined fleets to retire shattered into harbour again.

one, pleases me more than anything I have met with hitherto. We are, however, now (Oct. 3rd) looking out for land. Cape Sebastian will be the point we shall first see in Spain, and I much fear that tomorrow night I shall sleep in Barcelona.

Of the discipline of the Spanish navy I cannot say much, nor can I praise their cleanliness. I wish much to see a storm. How they manage then I do not know, for when it blows hard the sailors will not go aloft; as for the officers or midshipmen, they never think of it. Indeed, the latter live exactly as well as the officers; they mess with them, have as good berths, and are as familiar with them as they are with each other; very different in every respect from the discipline in English men of war. I shall write another letter to my sisters by this post; as they are at Highlake you may exchange letters.

Soon I shall write to you again. I have to thank you for a very long letter which I received at Geneva, chiefly relating to the proper judgement of paintings. I am not yet quite a convert, but experience may improve me. In Spain I understand I shall see some very good ones by the first masters. I fear much that my desire of visiting Spain will not be so keen as it was when I have seen a very little of it. By all accounts, even from Spaniards themselves, travelling is very inconvenient, and what is infinitely worse, very expensive; added to which the intolerable Suspicion and care of the Government renders any stay there very unpleasant.

In case I find myself not at my ease there I shall, when at Gibraltar, take a passage back to Italy, for Rome and Naples must be seen. Now I think of it I must mention one ship well known to you which I saw at Leghorn, namely, the *John of Leith*. I accidentally saw her boat with the name written; you may be sure I looked at her with no small pleasure.[8] When I sought for her next day she was gone. I little thought when I last saw you to see a ship in which you had spent so much time, up the Mediterranean.

I am learning Spanish at present, and the progress I have made in it is not the least pleasure I have received during my stay in the *Argonauta*. It is a language extremely difficult to understand when spoken, but easy to read, and very fine. I can already understand an easy book. If I can add Spanish and Italian, or some knowledge of those languages, to my stock, I shall consider my time and money as well spent, independent of the countries I shall have seen.

---

8. The vessel in which Edward Stanley's elder brother John had made his Icelandic Expedition, 1788.

Before I close this letter, which you will receive long after its original date, I must tell you I have been making a most interesting visit to the celebrated Lady of Mont Serrat,[9] and was even permitted to kiss her hand, an honour which few, unless well recommended, enjoy. I have not time to say so much of it as I could, I can only assure you that it fully answered the expectations I had raised. The singular scenery and the more singular customs of its solitary inhabitants, excepting the monks of the convent, who lead a most merry, sociable life, are well worth the trouble of going some distance to visit. The formation of the mountain is also very extraordinary. Entirely pudding stone, chiefly calcarious, some small parts of quartz, red granite, and flint only to be found. I have preserved some pieces for your museum, which I hope will arrive safe in England, as also the small collection of stones which I sent from the Alps.

Yours sincerely,

Edwd. Stanley.

Malaga, Jan., 1803.

My Dear Father,—To this place am I once more returned, after having made an excursion to the far-famed city of Granada and still more renowned palace of the Alhambra. My last letter was dated from Gibraltar on the 17th of December. We left the Rock in a vile *tartan*, [10] rendered still less agreeable by belonging to Spaniards, who, at no time remarkable for cleanliness, were not likely to exert themselves in that point in a small trading vessel. We were crowded with passengers and empty casks—both equally in the way; though the latter were not then noisy nor sick, I considered them as the least nuisance. Fortunately a strong W. breeze soon carried us from the Rock, and in one night we found ourselves close to the Mole of Malaga.

We introduced ourselves on landing to the English consul laird, to whose attentions we have been since much indebted. On the 2nd day after our arrival we heard of a muleteer who was on his return to Granada, and with whom we agreed for three mules. The distance is eighteen leagues over the mountains, a journey of three days; this is a country wild as the Highlands of Scotland, and in parts, if possible, more barren. The first night we slept at Vetey Malaga and the 2nd at Alhama, a town famous for its hot baths, which, thanks to the

9. A famous image of the Virgin, said to have been found A.D. 880 on a mountain of Catalonia, and in honour of which a magnificent church was built by Philip II. and Philip III. of Spain.
10. *Tartana*—a vessel peculiar to the Mediterranean.

Moors—who built walls about them—the Spaniards still enjoy.

The accommodations in the country are rather inferior to those of England, though perhaps you may consider me so prejudiced in favour of my own, and therefore unjust in my accounts of other countries. This may be the case, and I dare say a muleteer would find infinite fault with an English inn, where accommodation may be found for the rider as well as the mule. On entering one of these *ventas*, or inns, you find yourself in the midst of jack asses and mules, the necks of which, being usually adorned with bells, produce a music highly entertaining to a traveller after a long day's journey over these delightful roads. If you can force your way through this crowd of musical quadrupeds it is necessary that you should attempt to find out the landlord and petition for a room, which in general may be had, and if you are fortunate, mattrasses are laid on the floor.

Eating, however, is always out of the question. It is absolutely necessary to carry your own stock and look for yourself if a frying-pan can be found. If you are very much tired and the bugs, mosquitos, fleas, and other insects (sent into the world, I believe, to torment mankind) are also tired or satiated with sucking the blood from the travellers the preceding night, you may chance to sleep till 3 o'clock in the morning, when the carriers begin to load their beasts and prepare for the day's journey. The pleasure of travelling is also considerably diminished by the numbers of crosses by the road side, which, being all stuck up wherever a murder has been committed, are very unpleasant hints, and you are constantly put in mind of your latter end by these confounded monuments of mortality.

Fortunately, we met with no *tromboners* on the road, and hitherto we have saved the country the expense of erecting three crosses on our account. At last we arrived at Granada, the 3rd town in Spain in extent, being surpassed only by Seville and Toledo. You will, I suppose, expect a long account of the Alhambra and romantic gardens of the Generalife, a minute account of the curiosities in the City and a long string of *etceteras* relative to the place. You must, however, remain in ignorance of all these things till we meet, as at present I have neither time or inclination or paper sufficient to repeat my adventures and observations: suffice it to say that on the whole I was much disappointed both with the Alhambra and Granada, which are I cannot say lasting monuments, for they are falling fast to ruin.

Of the indolence and negligence of the people, you will scarcely believe that so large a town so near the sea, and situated in one of the finest vales in Spain, is almost without trade of any sort—neither troubling itself with importations or exerting its powers to provide materials for exportation. The captain general, however, is doing all he can to restore it to its former dignity, and were he well seconded, Granada might again hope to become one of the brightest ornaments of Spain. We returned by way of Loja and Antiquiera on the 27th of December, and have been wind bound ever since, and likely to be for another month—sure never was a wind so obstinate as the present.

We have here, I believe, quite formed a party to visit another quarter of the globe—a short trip to Africa is at present in agitation. A Captain Riddel from Gibraltar is one of the promoters, and if we can get to Gibraltar in any decent time you may possibly in my next letter hear some account of the good Mahometans at Tangiers. We are but to make a short stay and carry our guns and dogs, as we are told the country is overrun with game of every sort. I have been most agreeably surprised in finding Malaga a very pleasant place: we have met with more attention and seen more company here than we ever did in Barcelona.

I am this evening going to a ball; unfortunately *fandangos* are not fashionable dances, but they have another called the *bolero*, which in grace and elegance stands unrivalled, but would scarcely be admitted in the less licentious circles of our northern climate. I shall take lessons at Cadiz, and hope to become an adept in all those dances before I see you. If you write within a fortnight—and of course you will after receiving this—you may still direct to Cadiz.

There has been a disturbance at Gibraltar, which was hatching when we were there, and during our absence has broken out. The many strange reports and particulars which have reached Malaga—as I cannot vouch for their truth, I shall not mention; the grand point, however, was to put His Royal Highness on board of a ship and send him back to England. There has been also a desperate gale of wind in the straights—three Portuguese frigates, one with the loss of her rudder, were blown in here.

Some vessels, I understand, were also lost at the Rock. I hope our little brig, *ye Corporation*, with the young pointers has arrived in the Thames in spite of the constant gales and contrary winds which we met with. I was sorry when the wind became fair and the Rock appeared ahead. My taste for salt water is not at all diminished by experience. It is no doubt a strange one, but there is no accounting for these things, you know. Malaga is warm enough—we have green peas and asparagus every day. But we experienced very severe weather at Granada—frost and snow. The baths of the Alhambra were even covered with ice an inch thick. *Adieu!* this is post day.

Loves to all,

Yours Sincerely,

E. S.

Gibraltar, Jan. 22, 1803.

My Dear Brother,—I promised in my last, which I wrote when I was on the point of setting out on a tour to Granada, to write again and give some account of myself immediately on my return, which was delayed on account of sundry unfortunate circumstances till the day before yesterday. From Malaga I wrote to my father, and you probably have heard that a fair wind carried us in a vile vessel from this place to Malaga in one night, from whence, staying as short a time as possible, I set out on mules to Granada, distant a journey of three days. Till this time I had never, excepting from hearsay, formed a true idea of the perfection to which travelling in Spain could be carried, and yet, bad as it was, my return to land from Gibraltar has shown that things might be a degree worse.

Of the roads I can only say that most probably the Spaniards are indebted to the Moors for first marking them out, and that the present race follow the steps of their ancestors, without troubling themselves with repairs or alterations of any description. You may well then imagine the delicate State in which they now are. The *ventas* or inns are in a state admirably corresponding to that of the high-roads. Provisions of every sort must necessarily be carried unless the traveller wishes to fast; beds are occasionally, and indeed I may say pretty generally, to be met with, such as they are; of course, bugs, fleas, mosquitos, and so forth must not be considered: they are plentifully diffused over the country, and are by no means confined to the inferior houses.

With a substitution for "*Pallida Mors*" the quotation from Horace may with truth be applied, "*aequo pulsant pede pauperum tabernae, Regum turres.*" We passed through Alhama, near which are some very fine hot baths; the exact heat I could not ascertain (as my thermometer was actually jolted to pieces though in its case in my pocket, travelling from Turin to Genoa), but it is so great that I could scarcely keep my hand immersed for a minute. In another country they would be much frequented; as it is there are only some miserable rooms for those who repair to them from necessity.

On the evening of the 21st of December we arrived at our journey's end, and found, what we did not expect, a very tolerable inn, though as Granada is considered the third town in Spain, those who are unacquainted with the country might expect a better. I have so much to say that I cannot enter into a minute account of the famous palace of the Alhambra and other curiosities in the town, which is most beautifully situated at the foot of a range of snow-covered mountains at the extremity of what is said to be the most luxuriant and delightful valley in Spain. I hope for the credit of the inhabitants that it is not so, as certainly it is in a disgraceful state of cultivation, and were it not for the acqueducts erected by the Moors for the convenience of watering the land would, I fear, in a few years be burnt up by the intense heat of summer. Its chief produce is corn and oil; silk and wine are also cultivated, but the cold of winter sometimes injures the two latter.

The place is badly peopled and has no trade; it is chiefly supported by being the chief criminal port of Spain, and the richest people are consequently the lawyers. We saw the baths of Alhambra in a state very different from what they usually are—actually frozen over and the ice nearly an inch thick. I must say I was greatly disappointed with these famed remains of Moorish magnificence, though certainly when everything was kept in order, the fountains all playing, it must have been very different; at present it is falling fast to ruin. The Governor is a man appointed by the Prince of Peace,[11] and I believe would be unwilling to bestow any attention on anything in the world but his own person, of which by all accounts he takes special care. We returned to Malaga through Loja and Antequerra, both Moorish towns.

At Malaga we were detained by contrary winds for three weeks; we might, indeed, have passed our time less advantageously at other places, as we experienced much unexpected civility and saw a great deal of Spanish society. Wearied at length with waiting for winds, we determined to set out on our return to the Rock by land, and accordingly hired four horses, and, under the most favourable auspices, left Malaga. We soon found that even a Spanish sky could not be trusted; it began before we had completed half our first day's journey to pour with rain. To return was impossible, as we had forded the first river. In short, for three days we suffered every inconvenience which can be conceived, but were still to meet with another disappointment, for on the morning of the day in which we had certainly calculated to arrive

---

11. Emanuel Godoy, favourite Minister of Charles IV. of Spain.

at Gibraltar we came to a river which was so much swelled that the boatman could not ferry us over.

Nearly a hundred muleteers and others were in the same predicament, and we had the satisfaction of passing two most miserable days in a horrid *cortigo*, a house of *accommodation* a degree lower than a *venta*. Our provisions were exhausted, and nothing but bread and water were to be met with. Beds, of course, or a room of any sort were unobtainable. Conceive to yourself a kitchen filled with smoke, without windows, in which were huddled together about forty of the lowest order of Spaniards. As it poured with rain we could not stir out, and as for staying within doors it was scarcely possible. If we tried to sleep we were instantly covered with fleas and other insects equally partial to a residence on the human body.

After two days' penance, as the waters began to abate, we determined to cross the river in a small boat and proceed on foot, which we did, and though we had to skip through two or three horrible streams and wade through mud and marshes we performed the journey lightly, as anything was bearable after the Cortigo del rio Zuariano. We passed through St. Roque and the Spanish lines and arrived at Gibraltar on 20th, out of patience with the Spaniards and everything belonging to Spain. Indeed, the country is a disgrace to Europe. I wish indolence was the only vice of the inhabitants, but added to laziness they are in general mean in their ideas, the women licentious in their manners, and both sexes sanguinary to a degree scarcely credible.

In Malaga particularly, few nights pass without some murders. Those who have any regard for their safety must after dark carry a sword and a lantern. You may form some idea of the people when there was one fellow at Granada who had with his own hand committed no less than twenty-two murders. Nothing could be more gratifying to an Englishman than finding wherever he goes the manufactures of his own country. This in Spain is particularly the case; there is scarcely a single article of any description which this people can make for themselves, consequently English goods are sure of meeting with a quick sale. Perhaps it may be from prejudice, but certainly the idea I had of England before I left it has been raised many degrees since I have had an opportunity of comparing it with other countries.

But now for some news respecting Gibraltar itself, which has during my absence been a scene of confusion, first by a dreadful gale of wind, and secondly from a much more serious cause, a spirit of mutiny in the garrison. By the former sixteen or eighteen vessels were either lost or driven on shore; by the latter some lives were sacrificed before tranquillity was restored, and three men have since suffered death by the verdict of a court martial. No doubt you will see something of it in the papers; I cannot now enter into a detail as it would take some time.

The two regiments principally, and I believe I may say only, concerned were the Royals, which is the Duke's[12] own regiment, and the 25th; fortunately they did not act in concert. The other regiments of the garrison, the 2nd, 8th, 23rd, and 54th, particularly the latter, behaved well. The design was to seize the Duke and put him on board a ship and send him to England. He is disliked on account of his great severity: whether he carries discipline to an unnecessary degree military men know better than myself. Despatches have been sent to England, and I believe some of the men concerned; the greatest anxiety prevails to know what answers or orders will be returned. Of war and the rumours of war, though we it seems are nearer the scene of action than those who dwell at home, little is known, and what little is seems to be more inclined to peace than the English papers allow. It is here said, on what grounds I know not, that the Spaniards have entirely ceded Minorca to their good neighbours the French.

We have but a small naval force in the bay; and a few frigates and ships of war, one of the latter the *Bittern*, I believe, arrived yesterday from England, but without any particular news. Many gun boats were fitting out at Malaga, but I was informed they were only meant for "*Guarda Costas*," which may or not be the truth. We sailed for Cadiz the moment an E. wind would give us leave; it has now blown almost constantly a W. wind for three months, and the season has been remarkably wet. I am impatient to get to Cadiz as I expect certainly to find letters, the receipt of which from home is, I think, the greatest pleasure a traveller can experience.

Of Louisa's[13] marriage I have as yet not heard, though no doubt, however, it has taken place. How are my nephews and nieces? I do

---

12. H.R.H. Edward, Duke of Kent; appointed Governor of Gibraltar, 1802. In order to establish strict discipline in the garrison, which he found in a very demoralised state, he issued a general order forbidding any private soldiers to enter the wine shops, half of which he closed at a personal sacrifice of £4,000 a year in licensing fees. In consequence, a mutiny broke out on Christmas Eve, 1802. Though the mutiny was quelled, the Home Government did not support the Duke, who was recalled in March, 1803.

13. Edward Stanley's sister, Louisa; m., November, 1802, to Sir Baldwin Leighton, Bart., of Loton, Shropshire.

indeed look forward with pleasure to my next visit to Alderley. Remember it is now nearly two years since I have seen you; how many things have happened in the time to yours most sincerely

Edwd. Stanley.

EDWARD STANLEY TO HIS BROTHER J. T. STANLEY.

Gibraltar, January 16, 1803.

My Dear Brother,— . . . I shall pass over the greater part of the rest of your long letter and proceed without further delay to talk of myself. The last time you heard from me I think was soon after I arrived in Barcelona; what occurred during my stay there you have most probably heard from my sisters, as I wrote to Highlake just before I left that place. I consider myself as extremely fortunate in being at Barcelona during a time when I had a better opportunity of seeing the court of Spain and the different amusements of the country than I could have witnessed by a much longer residence even in Madrid itself. I was, however, unfortunately only a spectator; as no regular English consul had arrived in Barcelona, I had no opportunity of being introduced either at court or in the first circles. Another difficulty also was in my way; unfortunately I was not in the army and consequently had no uniform, without which or a court dress no person is considered as a gentleman in this country. I have repeatedly regretted that before I left England I did not put my name down on some military list, and under cover of a red coat procure an undisputed right to the title of gentleman in Spain.

As for the people, both noble and vulgar, it requires but a very short residence amongst them to be highly disgusted; few receive any thing which deserves the name of a regular education, and I have been told from, I believe, undoubted authority, that a nobleman unable to write his name, or even read his own pedigree, is by no means a difficult thing to meet with. The Government is in such a state that ere long it must fall, I should think. The King is entirely under the power of the Prince of Peace,[14] a man who from being a common *corps de garde* has risen by degrees, and being naturally ambitious and extremely avaricious has gained a rank inferior only to that of the King, and a fortune which makes him not only the richest man in Spain but probably in Europe. He is disliked by every class of people, and it is not, I believe, without good ground that he is considered as little better than a tool

14. Godoy (Emanuel—b. 1767, d. 1851), Prince of Peace. Prime Minister to Charles IV. of Spain.

of Buonaparte's.

The conduct of France to Spain in many particulars, which are too numerous now to mention, shews in what a degraded state the latter is—how totally unable to act or even think for herself. One instance I need only mention, though I do not vouch for the truth of it, further than as being a report current in the garrison. The French have *kindly* offered to send 4,000 troops to Minorca in order to *take care* of it for your good friends the Spaniards, and a squadron is fitting out at Toulon to carry them there. After your alarming account of the naval preparations in the three kingdoms you will expect that I, who am here in the centre of everything, should be able to tell you a great deal; you will, therefore, be surprised when you are informed that yours is almost the only account of another war which I have heard of.

A strong squadron, indeed, of six line of battle ships some time ago sailed with sealed orders and went aloft, but where is unknown. From Barcelona, as it was utterly impossible to get to Madrid on account of the King having put an embargo on every conveyance, which is easily done as the conveyances are bad as the roads and difficult to meet with, as well as enormously dear, we determined to steer for Gibraltar by sea, and accordingly took passage on an English brig, which was to stop on the coast for fruit we took on board. The voyage was uncommonly long, and we met with every species of weather, during which I had the pleasure of witnessing a very interesting collection of storms, with all the concomitant circumstances such as splitting sails and shipping seas, one of which did us considerable mischief, staving in all the starboard quarter boards, filling and very nearly carrying away the long-boat, drowning our live stock, and, of course, ducking us all on deck most thoroughly.

We stayed a week at Denia, a small but beautiful town on the south part of the K. of Valencia. We were fortunately put on shore here in the night of December 6th. I say fortunately, as in consequence of a very strong *levanter* the captain was for some hours in doubt whether he should not be under the necessity of running through the straits and carrying us to England, which was very near happening. Italy I have quite given up for the present. Rome and Naples I lament not to have seen, but you know that from Leghorn I turned to the westward in compliance with Hussey's wish, who was anxious to be near Lisbon. We have some idea of going from this place through Malaga to Granada, and soon after we return proceed to Cadiz, and after making some excursions from thence go on to Lisbon. Your letter which you promised to send to Madrid will, I fear, never reach me, though I have still hopes of paying that capital a visit. At Lisbon I shall arrive, I should think, about March, and hope to be in England about May, or perhaps sooner. At Lisbon I hope to find a letter from you; the direction is Jos. Lyne and Co. I have been very unfortunate in not finding some friends in the garrison, the only officer to whom I had a letter whom I found here has been of little service to us. I have, however, made the best use of my time and have been over the greatest part of this extraordinary fortress, but shall leave the description of it, as well as of an infinity of other things, till we meet, which shall be very soon after my arrival in England. I must send this instantly or wait for the next post day, so I shall conclude rather hastily. My best love to Mrs. S. and Believe me,

Yours sincerely,

Edwd. Stanley.

LORD SHEFFIELD

CHAPTER 2

After Napoleon's Fall

1814.

The sudden rupture of the Peace of Amiens in May, 1803, closed France to Englishmen, except to the miserable eight or nine thousand who were in the country at the time, and were forcibly detained there by orders of the First Consul. It was not until eleven years later, in April, 1814, when Napoleon had abdicated, and when the allies had triumphantly entered Paris and restored Louis XVIII. to the throne of his fathers, that peaceful British travellers could cross the frontier once more.

The busy parish life which had occupied Edward Stanley during the years which had elapsed since his first visit to France had not made him less keen for travel than he had been in his college days, and all his ardour was aroused by the news that there was to be an end to Napoleon's rule.

The excitement caused by the rumour of the capture of Paris and the deposition of the Emperor may be guessed at by a letter received at Alderley from Lord Sheffield, father of Lady Maria Stanley, in the spring of 1814.

LETTER FROM LORD SHEFFIELD.

Portland Place, April 6, 1814.

. . . I am just come from the Secretary of State's office. We are all gasping for further intelligence from Paris, but none has arrived since Captain Harris, a very intelligent young man who was despatched in half an hour after the business was completed, but of course cannot answer half the questions put to him. He came by Flanders, escorted part of the way by *Cossacks*, but was stopped nearly a day on the road. Schwartzenberg completely out-generalled Buonaparte. An intercepted letter of the latter gave him notice of an intended operation. He instantly decided on the measures which brought on the capture of Paris. I suppose you know that King Joseph sent the Empress and King of Rome previously to Rambouillet. It is supposed that Buonaparte has fallen back to form a junction with some other troops. A friend of Marshal Beresford's[1] has just called here who lately had a letter from the Marshal which says that he is quite sure that Soult has not 15,000 men left, and that in sundry engagements and by desertion he has lost about 16,000 men. I have no letter from Sir Henry[2] or William Clinton[3] since I saw you, but I learn at the War Office that the latter was, on the 20th of last month, within ten days' march of the right wing of Lord Wellington's army.[4]

Further news soon followed, and the authentic accounts of the Emperor's abdication at Fontainebleau on April 11th, and of his banishment to Elba, made it certain that his power was broken.

The Rector of Alderley was eager to seize the chance of viewing the wreck of Napoleon's Empire while the country was still ringing with rumours of battles and sieges, and he began to make plans to do so almost as soon as the French ports were open.

His wife was as keen as himself, and it was at first suggested that Sir John and Lady Maria, as well as Mrs. Edward Stanley, should join the expedition; but the difficulties of finding accommodation, and the fears of the disturbed state of the country, made them abandon the idea, to their great disappointment.

The following extracts from the correspondence of Lady Maria Stanley explain the reasons for the journey being given up by herself and her sister-in-law.

They describe the feeling in England on the foreign situation, and also give a glimpse of the wayward authoress, Madame de Staël, who was just then on her way back to France after a banishment of ten years.

LADY MARIA STANLEY TO HER SISTER, LADY LOUISA CLINTON.

Alderley Park, April 30, 1814.

So the Parisian expedition is at an end for us, in convention, that

---

1. Marshal Viscount Beresford, b. 1770, d. 1854, General in the English Army. He reorganised the Portuguese army in the Peninsular War.
2. Sir Henry Clinton, General; d. 1829.
3. Sir William Clinton, General, 1769-1854; married Louisa, second daughter of Lord Sheffield.
4. On April 10th Lord Wellington fought the Battle of Toulouse against Soult.

is, for I think Edward will brave all difficulties, and with Ed. Leycester, taking Holland first on his way, make a fight for Paris if possible; but all who know anything on the subject represent the present difficulties as so great, and the probable future ones so much greater, that Kitty (Mrs. Ed. Stanley) has given up all thought of making the attempt this year.

Lodging at Paris is difficult to be had, and there are even serious apprehensions of a scarcity of provisions there. Moreover, the wise ones would not be surprised if things were in a very unsettled and, perhaps, turbulent state for some months. This is Miss Tunno's information, confirmed by other accounts she has had from Paris.

Madame Moreau's [5] brother means to return to prepare for her reception and the mode of travelling, and when all is arranged to come again to fetch her.

There seems every reason to think another year preferable for a trip, especially as I have been making the same melancholy reflections as Cat. Fanshawe, [6] and feared there would not be one clever or agreeable person left in London a twelve-month hence; my only comfort is the expectation that House rent will be very cheap, and that the said Cat. will be better disposed to take up with second best company for want of perfection, and that we may have more of her society.

...All you say of the French nobility and their feelings is very true; but if they return with the sentiment that all the Senate who wish for a good constitution are "*des coquins*," which I very much suspect, I shall consider the emigrants are the greatest "*coquins*" of the two sets.

Surely, all the very bad Republicans and terrorists are exterminated. I should like to see a list of the Constituent Assembly, with an account of what has become of each. I have been reading all the accounts we have of the Revolution from the beginning. When I begin I am as fierce a Republican as ever, and think no struggle too much for the purpose of amending such a government or such laws. By the time I come to /93, however, one begins to hesitate, but I rejoice most heartily the old times are not restored, and hope Louis means to be sincere and consistent with his good beginning.

I return the *Conte de Cely*, which is very entertaining and interest-

---

5. Madame Moreau, widow of General Moreau, daughter of General Hulot, and a friend of the Empress Joséphine. Since the death of the General, who was killed at the battle of Dresden, in 1813, the Emperor Alexander had given Mme. Moreau a pension of 100,000 *francs* a year in recognition of her husband's services; and in 1814 Louis XVIII. gave her the rank of "*Maréchale de France*."
6. Catherine Fanshawe, poetess, and friend of most of the literary people in London of her day.

ing, as no doubt speaking the sentiments of all the old nobility. I do not think France has seen the end of her troubles entirely. It is impossible the senate and the emigrants can sit down quietly together, but the former—the marshals and the generals—would be formidable if they had reason given them to doubt the security of Louis' acceptation of the constitution. If the Bourbons share the sentiments of their nobles, will you not give me leave to think they are too soon restored?

Miss Tunno is very intimate with Mdme. Moreau and a cousin of hers. All her accounts have been conformable with yours.

LADY LOUISA CLINTON TO HER SISTER, LADY MARIA STANLEY.

Today I sat an hour with Cat. Fanshawe, and was highly amused by the account she gave of Mme. de Staël bolting up to her while standing speaking to Lord Lansdowne and some others at Mrs. Marcet's,[7] and saying, "I want to be acquainted with you. They say you have written a minuet. I am not a judge of English poetry, but those who are told me it is very good. Is it printed?" This intolerable impertinence, which, however, she probably meant for condescension, so utterly overset Cat., that she could find not a word to say, and treated the overture so coldly that nothing more came of it.

I exhort Cat. to recollect that the woman was so notorious for excessive ill-breeding, that no particular affront was intended, and hoped she would not continue coy, as I long to hear something of this Lioness from one who can judge.

Hitherto I have had no such luck. I hear the most exaggerated statements of the Baroness's absurdities, or of the necessity of her being one of every literary party.

LETTER FROM MISS CATHERINE FANSHAWE, AFTER MEETING
LORD BYRON AND MME DE STAËL AT
SIR HUMPHRY AND LADY DAVY'S.

Early Spring, 1814.

I have just stayed in London long enough to get a sight of the last imported lion,[8] Mme de Staël; but it was worth twenty peeps through ordinary show-boxes, being the longest and most entertaining dinner at which I ever in my life was present. The party being very small, her

---

7. Mrs. Marcet, b. 1785, a native of Geneva (*née* Halduriand). Well known for her economic and scientific works.
8. Madame de Staël, daughter of Louis XVI.'s Minister Necker, b. 1766, d. 1817. Married 1786 to the Baron de Staël, Swedish Minister to France. She had been exiled from France by Napoleon on account of her books, *Corinne* and *L'Allemagne.*

conversation was for the benefit of all who had ears to hear, and even my imperfect organ lost little of the discourse—happy if memory had served me with as much fidelity; for, had the whole discourse been written without one syllable of correction, it would be difficult to name a dialogue so full of eloquence and wit. Eloquence is a great word, but not too big for her. She speaks as she writes; and upon this occasion she was inspired by indignation, finding herself between two opposite spirits, who gave full play to all her energies.

She was astonished to hear that this pure and perfect constitution was in need of radical reform; that the only safety for Ireland was to open wide the doors which had been locked and barred by the glorious revolution; and that Great Britain, the bulwark of the world, the Rock which alone had withstood the sweeping flood, the ebbs and flows of democracy and tyranny, was herself feeble, disjointed, and almost on the eve of ruin. So, at least, it was represented by her antagonist in argument, Childe Harold, whose sentiments, partly perhaps for the sake of argument, grew deeper and darker in proportion to her enthusiasm.

The wit was his. He is a mixture of gloom and sarcasm, chastened, however, by good breeding, and with a vein of original genius that makes some atonement for the unheroic and uncongenial cast of his whole mind. It is a mind that never conveys the idea of sunshine. It is a dark night upon which the lightning flashes. The conversation between these two and Sir Humphry Davy,[9] at whose house they met, was so animated that Lady Davy[10] proposed coffee being served in the eating-room; so we did not separate till eleven. Of course we had assembled rather late. I should not say "assembled," for the party included no guests except Lord Byron and myself in addition to the "Staël" quartette. . . .

As foreigners have no idea that any opposition to Government is compatible with general obedience and loyalty, their astonishment was unbounded. I, perhaps I only, completely relished all her reasonings, and I thought her perfectly justified in replying to the pathetic mournings over departed liberty, "*Et vous comptez pour rien la liberté de dire tout cela, et même devant les domestiques!*" She concluded by heartily wishing us a little taste of real adversity to cure us of our plethora of

---

9. Sir Humphry Davy, 1778-1829; began life as a Cornish miner. He became a distinguished chemist and scientist.
10. Daughter of C. Kerr, Esq., of Kelso, and widow of S. Apreece, Esq., married Sir Humphry Davy, 1812.

political health.

In consequence of the difficulties and dangers anticipated in the above letters Edward Stanley finally decided to take as his only travelling companion his young brother-in-law, Edward Leycester, who was just leaving Cambridge for the Long Vacation. Mrs. Stanley accompanied her husband and brother as far as London, in order to see the festivities held in honour of the State visit of the Allied sovereigns to England in June, on their way from the Restoration ceremonies in France. Her letters to her sister-in-law during this visit describe some of the actors in the great events of the last few months and the excitement which pervaded London during their stay.

MRS. EDWARD STANLEY TO LADY MARIA STANLEY.

London, Friday, June 13, 1814.

Edward went for his passport the other day, and was told he must go to the Alien office, being taken for a Frenchman. . . .I forgot yesterday to beg Sir John would write Edward an introduction to Lord Clancarty, [11] and anybody else he can think of at Paris or the Hague, and send them to him as soon as possible.

We have been Emperor [12] hunting all morning. No, first we went to Mass with Miss Cholmondeley, and heard such music! Then with her to the Panorama of Vittoria, and since then we have been parading St. James's Street and Piccadilly. Oh! London forever! Edward saw a whiskered man go into a shop, followed him, and accosted him, and it was a man just arrived with despatches for the Crown Prince, who was thankful to be shewn his way. There was a gentleman came up to talk to Miss Cholmondeley, and he had been living in the house with Lucien Bonaparte. [13]

Then Edward was standing in Hatchard's shop, and he saw a strange bonnet in an open landau, and there was the Duchess of Oldenburg[14]

---

11. Second Earl of Clancarty, 1767-1837. Ambassador to the Netherlands.

12. The Emperor Alexander I. of Russia, 1777-1825.

13. Lucien, second brother of the Emperor Napoleon, 1775-1840.

14. Catherine, Grand Duchess of Russia, sister of the Emperor Alexander I., won golden opinions in England. "She was very clever, graceful, and elegant, with most pleasing manners, and spoke English well." Creevey says that the Emperor was much indebted to his sister, the Duchess of Oldenburg, for "keeping him in the course by her judicious interposition and observations." In 1808 Napoleon had wished for her as his bride, but, as she says in a letter to her brother, the *Czar*, "her heart would break as the intended wife of Napoleon before she could reach the limits of his usurped dominions, and she cannot but consider (continued over page.)

KITTY LEYCESTER – MRS EDWARD STANLEY

and her bonnet, and her brother sitting by her in a plain black coat, and he gave himself the toothache running after the carriage.

He saw, or fancied he saw, a great deal of character in the Duchess's countenance. I just missed this, but afterwards joined Edward, and walked up and down St. James's Street, trusting to Edward's eyes, rather than all the assurances we met with, that the Emperor was gone to Carlton House, and were rewarded by a sight of him in a quarter of an hour, which had sufficed him to change his dress and his equipage, and a very fine head he has. Such a sense of bustle and animation as there is in that part of the town! You and Sir John may, and I daresay will, laugh at all the amazing anxiety and importance attached to a glimpse of what is but a man after all; but still the common principles of sympathy would force even Sir John's philosophy to yield to the animating throng of people and carriages down St. James's Street, and follow their example all the time he was abusing their folly.

June 13, 1814.

At half-past ten we started for the illuminations, and nearly made the tour of the whole town from Park Lane to St. Paul's in the open barouche.

I cannot conceive a more beautiful scene than the India House; they had hung a quantity of flags and colours of different sorts across the street; the flutings and capitals of the pillars, and all the outlines of the buildings, marked out with lamps, so that it was much more like a fairy palace and a fairy scene altogether than anything else.

The flags concealed the sky, and formed such a fine background to the brilliant light thrown on all the groups of figures.

We did not get home till daylight. There was nothing the least good or entertaining in the way of inscriptions and transparencies, except a "Hosanna to Jehovah, Britain, and Alexander."

MRS. E. STANLEY TO LADY MARIA STANLEY.

London, Wednesday, June, 1814.

Where did we go to be made fools of by the Emperor yesterday

as frightfully ominous this offer of marriage from an Imperial Assassin to the daughter and grand-daughter of two assassinated Emperors" (see *Letters of Two Brothers*, by Lady G. Ramsden). The marriage of the Grand Duchess Catherine to the Duke of Oldenburg was hastily arranged to enable her to escape the alliance. The Duke died in 1812, and she afterwards married her cousin, the Crown Prince of Wurtemberg, to whom she had been attached in early youth. The Duchess attracted great attention by wearing a large bonnet, which afterwards became the fashion and was called after her.

for four hours? We went with Miss Tunno, got introduced to a gentleman's tailor in Parliament Street, and looked out of his window; saw a shabby coach and six pass, full of queer heads, one of which was so like the prints of Alexander, and bowed so like an Emperor, that I must and will maintain it to have been him till I can receive positive proof that it was not. We saw, too, what they said was Blücher, but we could hear or see nothing but that something was wrapped up in furs. However, Edward was more fortunate, and came in for the real bows which the real Emperor made from the Pulteney Hotel window, and you and Sir John may laugh as you please at all the trouble we have taken to see—nothing.

Nevertheless, though I was well disposed to kiss the Emperor and Prince, and all who contributed to disappoint the public expectation, it is certainly entertaining and enlivening to be in expectation of meeting something strange every corner you turn and every different report you hear. The Emperor has gone out this morning to look about at half-past nine, long before the Prince Regent called.

They say he will sail in one of his own ships from Leith and may pass through Manchester. But after all, it is something like what Craufurd described being in Paris, to be hearing yourself in the midst of a great bustle with your eyes shut and unable to see what was going on round you.

We talk of Monday se'enight for our separation. There is so much to be seen if one could but see it here, that Edward is in no hurry to be off. . . .

At Lady Cork's the other night Blücher was expected. Loud huzzas in the street at length announced him, the crowd gathered round the door, and in walked Lady Caroline Lamb [15] in a foreign uniform! This I had from no less authentic and accurate a source than Dr. Holland, who was an eyewitness. She had been at the party in female attire, and seeing Lady Cork's anxiety to see the great man, returned home and equipped herself to take in Lady C. and Co.

Monday, 8 a.m., June 16th.

Yesterday, after church, we went to the park. It was a beautiful day, and the Emperor may well be astonished at the population, for such a crowd of people I could not have conceived, and such an animated crowd. As the white plumes of the Emperor's guard danced among

15. Lady Caroline, daughter of the Earl of Bessborough, wife of Hon. William Lamb, afterwards Lord Melbourne, authoress of *Glenarvon*, &c.

the trees, the people all ran first to one side and then to the other; it was impossible to resist the example, and we ran too, backwards and forwards over the same hundred yards, four times, and were rewarded by seeing the ranger of the forest, Lord Sydney, who preceded the Royal party, get a good tumble, horse and all. We saw Lord Castlereagh almost pulled off his horse by congratulations and huzzahs as loud as the Emperor's, and a most entertaining walk we had.

We dined at Mr. Egerton's. Mr. Morritt[16] rather usurped the conversation after dinner, but I was glad of him to save me from the history of each lady's adventures in search of the Emperor or the illuminations. The Opera must have been a grand sight; it seems undoubted that the Emperor and Prince Regent, and all in the Royal box, rose when the Princess of Wales came in and bowed to her—it is supposed by previous arrangement. Lord Liverpool[17] declared that he would resign unless something of the sort was done.

One man made forty guineas by opening his box door and allowing those in the lobbies to take a peep for a guinea apiece. We made an attempt on Saturday to get into the pit, but it was quite impossible. I would not for the world but have been here during the fever, although what many people complain of is very true, that it spoils all conversation and society, and in another day or two I shall be quite tired of the sound or sight of Emperors.

The merchants and bankers invited the Emperor to dinner; he said he had no objection if they would promise him it should not exceed three-quarters of an hour, on which Sir William Curtis lifted up his hands and exclaimed, "God bless me!"

He is tired to death with the long sittings he is obliged to undergo. The stories of him quite bring one back to the *Arabian Nights*, and they could not have chosen a more appropriate ballet for him than *Le Calife Voleur*.

If he stayed long enough, he might revolutionise the hours of London.

I was close to Blücher yesterday, but only saw his back, for I never thought of looking at a man's face who had only a black coat on.

You may safely rest in your belief that I do not enjoy anything I see or hear without telling it to you, and you are quite right in your conjecture as to what your feelings would be here.

I have thought and said a hundred times what a fever of impatience

16. Mr. Morritt, of Rokeby.
17. Lord Liverpool, 1770-1828. Prime Minister in 1815.

disappointment, and fatigue you would be in. . . . You are also right in supposing that you know as much or more of the Emperor than I do, for one has not the time nor the inclination to read what one has the chance of seeing all the day long, and it is so entertaining that I feel it quite impossible to sit quiet and content when you know what is going on.

One person meets another: "What are you here for?"

"I don't know. What are you expecting to see?"

One says the Emperor is gone this way, and another that way, and of all the talking couples or trios that pass you in the street, there are not two where the word "Emperor" or "King" or "Blücher" is not in one, if not both mouths; and all a foxhound's sagacity is necessary to scent him successfully, for he slips round by backways and in plain clothes.

MRS. E. STANLEY TO LADY MARIA STANLEY.

London, June 17, 1814.

We were in high luck on Sunday in getting a private interview with the *Cossacks*, through some General of M.'s acquaintance. We saw their horses and the white one, 20 years old, which has carried Platoff[18] through all his engagements. They are small horses with very thick legs. The *Cossacks* themselves would not open the door of their room till luckily a gentleman who could speak Russian came up, and then we were admitted.

There were four, one who had been thirty years in the service, with a long beard and answering exactly my idea of a *Cossack*; the others, younger men with fine countenances and something graceful and gentleman-like in their figure and manner. They were very happy to talk, and there was great intelligence and animation in their eyes. No wonder they defy the weather with their cloaks made of black sheepskin and lined with some very thick cloth which makes them quite impenetrable to cold or wet.

Their lances were 11 feet long, and they were dressed in blue jacket and trousers confined round the waist with a leather belt, in which was a rest for the lance. I envied their saddles, which have a sort of pommel behind and before, between which is placed a cushion, on which they must sit most comfortably. We must see them on horseback to *have seen* them, but we shall probably have an opportunity of seeing them again.

---

18. Platoff, 1716-1818, Russian General.

On returning from Miss Fanshawe's we saw a royal carriage in George Street at Madame Moreau's, and we waited to see the Emperor and the Duchess (of Oldenburg) get into the carriage. He was in a plain blue coat; she without her curious bonnet, so that I had a good view of her face, which I had the satisfaction of finding exactly what I wished to see. The extreme simplicity of her dress—she had nothing but a plain white gown and plain straw hat, with no ornament of any sort—and her very youthful appearance made me doubt whether it was really the Duchess; but it was.

She is very little, and there is a strong expression of intelligence, vivacity, and youthful, unsophisticated animation in her countenance. I fancied I could see so much of her character in the brisk step with which she jumped into the carriage, and the unassuming, lively smile with which she bowed to the people.

The Emperor looks like a gentleman—but a country gentleman, not like an Emperor. His head is very like R. Heber's. The Duchess allowed herself to be pleased and to express her pleasure at all the sights without the least restraint. She asks few questions, but those very pertinent. She is impatient at being detained long over anything, but anxious to silence those who would hence infer that she runs over everything superficially, without gaining or retaining real knowledge.

At Woolwich she was asked if she would see the steam-engines. "No, she had seen them already, and understood them perfectly." As they passed the open door she turned her head to look at the machinery, and instantly exclaimed, "Oh, that is one of Maudesley's engines," her eye immediately catching the peculiarity of the construction.

London, June 22, 1814.

In the middle of Edward's sermon at St. George's today somebody in our pew whispered it round that there was the King of Prussia[19] in the gallery. I looked as directed, and fixed my eyes on a melancholy, pensive, interesting face, exactly answering the descriptions of the King, and immediately fell into a train of very satisfactory reflection and conjecture on the expression of his physiognomy, for which twenty minutes afforded me ample time. The King was the only one I had not seen, therefore this opportunity of studying his face so completely was particularly valuable.

When the prayer after the sermon was concluded, my informer

---

19. Frederick William III.

said the King was gone, when, to my utter disappointment, I beheld my hero still standing in the gallery, and discovered I had pitched upon a wrong person, and wasted all my observations on a face that it did not really signify whether it looked merry or sad, and entirely missed the sight of the real King, who was in the next pew.

Nothing but his sending to offer Edward a Chaplaincy in Berlin for his excellent sermon can possibly console me, except, indeed, the *honour by itself* of having preached before a King of Prussia, which can never happen again in his life.

...The Duchess of Oldenburg took all the merchants by surprise the other day. They had no idea she was coming to their dinner; she was the only lady, and she was rather a nuisance to them, as they had provided a hundred musicians, who could not perform, as she cannot bear music. [20] She was highly amused at the scene and with their "Hip! Hip!"

Monday, June 23, 1814.

At our dinner Mr. Tennant came in late, with many apologies, but really he had been hunting the Emperor—waiting for him two hours at one place and two hours at another, and came away at last without seeing him at all.

He said, in his dry way, that "Have you seen the Emperor?" has entirely superseded the use of "How do you do?"

In the morning he had gone into a shop to buy some gloves, and whilst he was trying them on the shopman suddenly exclaimed, "Blücher! Blücher!" cleared the counter at a leap, followed by all the apprentices, and Mr. Tennant remained soberly amongst the gloves to make his own selection, for he saw nothing more of his dealers.

Rooms are letting today in the city at 60 guineas a room, or a guinea a seat for the procession. Tickets for places to see it from White's to be had at Hookham's for 80 guineas; 50 have been refused.

Your letter revived me after five hours' walking and standing, and running after reviews, &c.

I did see the King of Prussia, to be sure, and the Prince, and the people climbing up the trees like the grubs on the gooseberry bushes, and heard the *feu de joie*, whose *crescendo* and *diminuendo* was very fine indeed, but altogether it was not worth the trouble of being tired and squeezed for.

---

20. The Duchess had been very fond of music, but since the death of her husband it had affected her so deeply that she feared breaking down on any public occasion.

At the reception at Sir Joseph Banks's house last night the most interesting object of the evening was a sword come down from heaven on purpose for the Emperor! Let the Prince Regent and his garters and his orders, and the merchants and the aldermen and everybody hide their diminished heads! What are they and their gifts to the philosophers'?

This is literally a sword made by Sowerby from the iron from some meteoric stones lately fallen—of course in honour of the Emperor. There is an inscription on it something to this effect, but not so neat as the subject demanded, and it is to be presented to Alexander—who does not deserve it, by the by, for having entirely neglected Sir Joseph amongst all the great sights and great men, which has rather mortified the poor old man.

London, Monday night.

They are off, and in spite of all my friends' predictions to the contrary, I am here.

Edward went this morning to Portsmouth on his way to Havre, but the Havre packet is employed in pleasuring people up and down to see the ships. Not a bed is to be had in the place, so he has secured his berth in the packet, if he can find her, and get on board at night after her morning's excursions.

Standing room is to be had in the streets for three shillings; seats are putting up in and for two miles out of the town; all the laurels cut down to stick upon poles; in short, everybody is madder there than in London.

Can the English ever be called cool and phlegmatic again? It is really a pity some metaphysicianising philosopher is not here to observe, describe, and theorise on the extraordinary symptoms and effects of enthusiasm, curiosity, insanity—I am sure I do not know what to call it—*en masse*.

One should have supposed that the great objects would have swallowed up the little ones. No such thing! they have only made the appetite for them more ravenous.

The mob got hold of Lord Hill [21] in the park at the review, and did literally pull his coat and his belt to pieces. He snatched off his Order of the Bath, and gave it to Major Churchill, who put it in the holster of his saddle, where he preserved it from the mob only by drawing his sword and declaring he would cut any man's hand off who touched

21. Rowland Hill. General Lord Hill, 1772-1842; distinguished in the Peninsular War.

it. Some kissed his sword, his boots, his spurs, or anything they could touch; they pulled hair out of his horse's tail, and one butcher's boy who arrived at the happiness of shaking his hand, they chaired, exclaiming, "This is the man who has shaken hands with Lord Hill!" At last they tore his sword off by breaking the belt and then handed it round from one to another to be kissed.

My regret at not having been at White's is stronger than my desire to go was; it must have been the most splendid and interesting sight one could ever hope to see.

On Friday, June 27th, Edward Stanley and Edward Leycester finally set off and sailed from Portsmouth, all gay with festivities in honour of the Allied Sovereigns.

Mrs. Stanley was left to spend the time of their absence at her father's house in Cheshire, but the keen interest with which she would have shared the journey was not forgotten by her husband.

The events of the tour were minutely chronicled in his letters to her, and not only in letters, but in sketch books, filled to overflowing with every strange group and figure which met the travellers on their way, through countries which had been, although so near, prohibited for such a long time that they had almost the interest of unknown lands.

MRS. E. STANLEY TO LADY MARIA STANLEY.

Stoke, July 4, 1814.

...That my curiosity may not catch cold in the too sudden transition from exercise to inaction, the Shropshire and Cheshire Heroes have followed me down here, and I have had the pleasure of seeing and hearing of the crowds going to touch (for that is the present fashion of seeing, or, to speak philosophically, *mode* of *perception*) Lord Hill; and yesterday I met Lord Combermere and his bride at Alderley, and a worthy hero he is for Cheshire!

A folio from Havre just arrived. I am very noble, very virtuous, and very disinterested—pray assure me so, for nothing else can console me—it is too entertaining to send one extract.

CHAPTER 3

Under the Bourbon Flag

EDWARD STANLEY TO HIS WIFE.

Letter 1.

Havre, June 26, 1814.

We have passed the Rubicon—*nous voilà en France*, all new, interesting, and delightful. I know not where or how to begin—the observations of an hour were I to paint in miniature would fill my sheet; however, you must not expect arrangement but read a sort of higgledy-piggledy journal as things run through my head. I must pin them down like my butterflies as they pass, or they will be gone forever.

At half-past four on Friday we sailed from Portsmouth, and saw the fleet in the highest beauty—amongst them all while they were under sail tacking, &c.; the delay has not been lost time. I should observe before I quit the subject of Portsmouth events, that the Emperor could not find time to sail about for mere amusement two days, this he left to the P.R.[1] He (the Emperor) and the Duchess of Oldenburg occupied themselves in visiting the dockyards, machinery, Haslar hospital—in short, everything worthy the notice of enlightened beings. . . .

Our passengers were numerous, about twenty-five in a vessel of as many tons, with only six what they called regular sleeping-places. . . . But I had no reason to complain, our party was in many respects excellent—one, a jewel of no ordinary value, by name Mr. John Cross, of whom I must enquire more. I have seldom met with a man of more general and at the same time deep information; he seemed perfect in everything. Mineralogy, antiquities, chemistry, literature, human nature were at his fingers' ends, and most gentlemanly manners into the

---

1. The Prince Regent, afterwards George IV.

bargain. . . .

Amongst others we had three French officers, prisoners returning home. They had not met before that evening, but had you heard their incomparable voices when they sang their trios, you would have supposed they had practised together for years. Mr. John Cross alone surpassed them in their art. These gentlemen were certainly not *hostile* to Bonaparte, but to gratify their musical taste they stuck at nothing— "God save the King," "Rule Britannia," "The Downfall of Paris" were chaunted in swift succession, and the following commencement of one of their songs will show the popular opinion of Bonaparte's campaign in Russia:—

Quel est le Monarque qui peut
Etre si fou
Que d'aller à Moscou
Pour perdre sa grande armée?

A fair wind brought us in sight of the French coast early on Saturday. At 11 we were under the headland of Havre, and at 12 anchored in the bay, and were in an instant surrounded by chattering boatfuls who talked much but did nothing. On landing we were escorted to the passport office and most civilly received there; the difference, indeed, between public offices in England and France is quite glaring. Even the Custom House officers apologised for keeping us waiting for the form of searching; and though the underlings condescended to take a *franc* or two, the officer himself, when I offered money, turned away his head and hand and cried, "*Ba, Ba, Non, Non*," with such apparent sincerity that I felt as if I had insulted him by offering it . . .

The whole process of getting our passports signed, &c., being over, we went to an hotel. "*Ici, garçon, vite mettez Messieurs les Anglois à l'onzième*," cried a landlady—and such a landlady! and up we scampered to the 5th storey (there are more still above us) and to this said, "*No onzième*." . . .

We lost no time in the evening in looking about us; the town is situated about two miles up the Seine on a sort of peninsula surrounded with very regular and strong fortifications. Its docks are incomparable, and Bonaparte would have added still more to their magnificence, but now all is at a stand—the grass is quietly filling up spaces hitherto taken up by soldiers, Workmen, shot and guns; the numberless merchant vessels in a state of decay proved sufficiently the entire destruction of all trade; but what gave me particular satisfaction was the sight of a flotilla of *praams*, luggers, intended for the invasion of England, all reposing in a happy progress to speedy putrefaction and decay. About a mile from the town on the hill is a beautiful village called St. Michel, where the Havre citizens have country houses.

The town itself is as singular as heart can wish—indeed, I am firmly convinced that the difference between the towns of the earth and moon is not greater than that between those of England and France. I scarcely know how to describe it to you. Conceive to yourself a long street of immensely tall houses from five to eight storeys, *huddled*, for huddling is the only word which can convey my meaning, and in truth their extraordinary height and narrow breadth seem rather the effect of compression than design. . . . These houses are inhabited by various families of various occupations and tastes, so that each storey has its own peculiar character—here you see a smart balcony with windows to the ground, garnished above and below with the insignia of washing woman or tailor. They are built of all materials, though I think chiefly of wood (like our old Cheshire houses) and *stucco*; and, thanks to time and the filth and poverty of the people, their exterior assumes a general tint of pleasing dirty picturesque. This said dirt may have its advantages as far as the eye is concerned, but the nose is terribly assailed by the innumerable compounded effluvias which flow from every alley-hole and corner.

For the people and their dress! who shall venture to describe the things I have seen in the shape of caps, hats and bonnets, cloaks and petticoats, &c.? There I meet a group of Oldenburg bonnets broader and more loaded with flowers, bunches, bows, plumes than any we saw in London, and would you believe it I am already not merely getting reconciled but absolutely an admirer of them.

Having passed the groups of bonnets I meet at the next moment a set of beings ycleped *poissardes*, caparisoned with coverings of all sorts, shapes, and sizes—here flaps a head decorated with lappets like butterflies' wings—here nods a bower of cloth and pins tall and narrow as the houses themselves, but I must not be too prolix on any one particular subject.

Sunday.

We have been to the great church. It was full, very full, but the congregation nearly all female.

There is certainly something highly imposing and impressive in that general spirit of outward devotion at least which pervades all ranks. Nothing can be finer than their music: we had a sermon, too, and not a bad one. The order of things is somewhat reversed. In England we wear white bands and black gown, here the preacher had black bands and white gown, and I fear the eloquence of St. Paul would not prevent the smiles of my hearers in Alderley Church were I to pop on my head in the middle of the discourse a little black cap of which I enclose an accurate representation.

What shall I say of political feeling? I think they appear to think or care very little about it; the military are certainly dissatisfied and the innkeepers delighted, but further I know not what to tell you; I am told, however, that the new proclamation for the more decent observance of Sunday, by forcing the shopkeepers to shut up their shops during Mass, is considered a great grievance. . . . .

Letter 2

Rouen, June 28, 1814.

Foolish people are those who say it is not worthwhile to cross the water for a week. For a week! why, for an hour, for a minute, it would be worth the trouble—in a glance a torrent of news, ideas, feelings, and conceptions are poured in which are valuable through life. We staid at Havre till Monday morning, and though a Cantab friend of Edward's, on bundling into his cabriolet, expressed his astonishment we would think of staying a day, when he had seen more than enough of the filthy place in an hour, we amused ourselves very well till the moment of departure. . . .

At 4 on Monday we stepped into the cabriolet or front part of our diligence, on the panels of which was written *"Fugio ut Fulgor,"* and though appearances were certainly against anything like compliance with this notice, the result was much nearer than I could have conceived. Five horses were yoked to this unwieldy caravan—two to the pole, and three before, and on one of these pole horses mounted a driver without stockings in jack boots, crack went an enormous whip, and away galloped our five coursers. It is astonishing how they can be managed by such simple means, yet so it was; we steered to a nicety sometimes in a trot, sometimes in a canter, sometimes on a full gallop.

The time for changing horses by my watch was not more than one minute—before you knew one stage was passed another was commenced; they gave us five minutes to eat our breakfast—an operation something like that of ducks in a platter, the dish consisting of coffee and milk with rolls sopped in it. The roads are incomparable—better than ours and nearly if not quite as good as the Irish. The country from Havre to Rouen is rich in corn of every description—there is nothing particular in the face of it, and yet you would, if awakened from a dream, at once declare you were not in England; in the first place there are no hedges—the road was almost one continuous avenue of apple-trees; the timber trees are not planted in hedgerows but in little clumps or groves, sometimes but generally rather removed from the road, and it is amongst these that the villages and cottages are concealed, for it is surprising how few in comparison with England are seen.

The trees are of two descriptions—either trimmed up to the very top or cut off so as to form underwood. I did not observe one that could be called a branching tree; the finest beech we saw looked like a pole with a tuft upon it. The cottages are mostly of clay, generally speaking very clean, and coming nearer to what I should define a cottage to be than ours in England.

You see no cows in the fields, they are all tethered by the road-side or other places, by which a considerable quantity of grass must be saved, and each is attended by an old woman or child. We passed through two or three small towns and entered Rouen eight hours after quitting Havre, 57 miles. Rouen, beautiful Rouen, we entered through such an avenue of noble trees, its spires, hills and woods peeping forth, and the Seine winding up the country, wide as the Thames at Chelsea.

Such a gateway! I have made a sketch, but were I to work it up for a month it would still fall far short and be an insult to the subject it attempts to represent. If Havre can strike the eye of a stranger, what must not Rouen do? Every step teems with novelty and richness, Gothic gateways, halls, and houses. What are our churches and cathedrals in England compared to the noble specimens of Gothic architecture which here present themselves?. . . Rouen has scarcely yet recovered from the dread they were in of the Cossacks, who were fully expected, and all valuables secreted—not that they were absolutely without news from the capital: the diligence had been stopped only once during the three days after the Allies entered Paris. Till then they had proceeded *comme à l'ordinaire*, and the diligence in which we are to proceed tonight left it when Shots were actually passing over the road during the battle of Montmartre—how they could find passengers to quit it at such an interesting moment I cannot conceive; had I been sure of being eaten up by a horde of *Cossacks*, I could not have left the spot.

What an odd people the French are! they will not allow they were in ignorance of public affairs before the entrance of the Allies. "Oh no, we had the *Gazettes*," they say, and I cannot find that they considered these *Gazettes* as doubtful authorities. We have plenty of troops here—genuine veterans horse and foot; I saw them out in line yesterday. The men were soldier-like looking fellows enough, but one of our cavalry regiments would have trotted over their horses in a minute without much ceremony; the army is certainly dissatisfied. Marmont is held in great contempt; they will have it he betrayed Paris, and say it would be by no means prudent for him to appear at the head of a line when there was any firing.

The people may or may not like their emancipation from tyranny, but their vanity—they call it glory—has been tarnished by the surrender of Paris, and they declare on all hands that if Marmont had held out for a day Bonaparte would have arrived, and in an instant settled the business by defeating the Allies. In vain may you hint that he was inferior in point of numbers (to say anything of the skill and merit of the Russians perhaps would not have been very prudent), and that he could not have succeeded. A doubting shake of the head, significant shrug of the shoulders, and expressive "*Ba, Ba,*" explain well enough their opinions on the subject.

I cannot conceive a more grating badge to the officers than the white cockade—the *fleur de lys* is now generally adopted in place of the N and other insignia of Bonaparte, but, excepting from some begging boys, I have never heard the cry of "*Vive Louis XVIII.!*" and then it was done, I shrewdly suspect, as an acceptable cry for the *Anglois*, and followed immediately by "*un pauvre petit liard, s'il vous plait, Mons.*" We went to the play last night; the house was filthy beyond description, and the company execrable as far as dress went; few women, and those in their morning dress and Oldenburg bonnets—the men almost all officers, and a horrid-looking set they were. I would give them credit for military talents; they all looked like chiefs of *banditti*—swarthy visages, immense *moustachios*, vulgar, disgusting, dirty, and ill-bred in their appearance.

From all I hear the account of the duels between these and the Russian officers at Paris were perfectly correct. [2]

2. "After the Restoration of the Bourbons several duels took place for the most frivolous causes. Duels were fought even by night. The officers of the Swiss guards were constantly measuring swords with the officers of the old '*Garde Impériale*'" (Gronow's *Memoirs*, vol. 2. p. 22).

I am just come in from a stroll about the town. Among the most interesting circumstances that occurred was the inspection of detachments of several regiments quartered there. I happened to be close to the general when he addressed some grenadiers *de la Garde Impériale* on the subject of their dismissal, which it seems they wanted. They spoke to him without any respect, and on his explaining the terms on which their dismissal could alone be had, they appeared by no means satisfied, and when he went I heard one of them in talking to a party collected round him say, *"Eh bien, s'il ne veut pas nous congédier, nous passerons."* A man standing by told me a short time ago a regiment of Imperial Chasseurs when called upon to shout *"Vive Louis XVIII.!"* at Boulogne, to a man, officers included, cried *"Vive Napoleon!"* and I feel very certain that had the same thing been required today from the soldiers on the field, they would have acted in the same manner, and that the spectators would have cried "Amen."

I heard abundance of curious remarks on the subject of the war, the peace, and the changes; they will have it they were not conquered. "Oh no." *"Paris ne fut jamais vaincue—elle s'est soumise seulement!"* I leave it to your English heads to define the difference between submission and conquest.

Beef and mutton are 5d. per lb. here. Chickens 3s. the couple, though 24 per cent. was probably added to me as an Englishman. Bread a 100 *per cent.* cheaper than in England—at least so I was informed by an Englishman in the commercial line. Fish cheap as dirt at Havre, 3 John Dorys for 6d.

From Havre to Rouen, 57 miles, cost us £1 6s. for both; from thence to Paris, 107 miles, £2; our dinners, including wine, are about 4s. a head; breakfast 2s., beds 1s. 6d. each.

Letter 3

Paris, June 30th.

Here we arrived about an hour ago; for the last two miles the country was a perfect garden—cherries, gooseberries, apple-trees, corn, vineyards, all chequered together in profusion; in other respects nothing remarkable. . . .

The first sight of Paris, or rather its situation, is about ten miles off, when the heights of Montmartre, on one side, and the dome of the Hôpital des Invalides on the other reminded us of their trophies and disasters at the same time. . . .

Now you must enter our rooms in *l'Hôtel des Etrangers, rue du Haz-*

3

Paris July 4, 1814

PARIS, 1814, OLD BRIDGE AND CHÂTELET.

ard, as I know you wish to see minutely. First walk, if you please, into an antechamber paved with red hexagon tiles (dirty enough, to be sure), and the saloon also, into which you next enter through a pair of folding doors. This saloon is in the genuine tawdry French style—gold and silver carving work and dirt are the component features. It is about twenty feet square, plenty of chairs, sofas of velvet, and so forth, but only one wretched rickety table in the centre. Two folding doors open into our bedroom, which is in furniture pretty much like the rest; the beds are excellent—fitted up in a sort of tent fashion—and mine has a looking-glass occupying the whole of one side, in which I may at leisure contemplate myself in my nightcap, for I cannot discover for what other purpose it was placed there.

Now let us take a walk—put on thick shoes or you will find yourself rather troubled with the paving stones, for nothing like a flagged footpath exists; a slight inclination from each side terminates in a central gutter, from which are exploded showers of mud by the passing carriages and cabriolets. You must get on as you can; horse and foot, coaches and carts are jumbled together, and he who walks in Paris must have his eyes about him. The streets are in general narrow and irregular, and so much alike that it requires no small skill to find one's way home again. Ariadne in Paris would wish for her clue. First we ascended the bronze column[3] in the Place de Vendôme—figure to yourself a column perfect in proportions much resembling Nelson's in Dublin, ornamented after the plan of Trajan's pillar—all of bronze, on which the operations of the wars and victories in Germany are recorded.

Bonaparte's statue crowned it, but that was removed. The column itself, however, will remain an eternal statue commemorating his deeds, and though the eagles and letter N are rapidly effacing from every quarter, this must last till Paris shall be no more. From the top of this pillar you of course have a magnificent view, and it must have been a choice spot from whence to behold the fight of Montmartre. It will scarcely interest you much to say much about the other public buildings, suffice it to say that all the improvements are in the very best style—magnificent to the last degree; they may be the works of a Tyrant, but it was a Tyrant of taste, who had more sense than to spend 120,000 Louis in sky-rockets. His public buildings at least were for the

---

3. The Colonne Vendôme. This stood on the site of a statue to Louis XIV. which had been melted down at the Revolution. It was made of Austrian cannon taken during the years from 1806 to 1810.

public good, and were ornaments to his capital.

But let us turn from inanimate to living objects; since I penned the last line I have been sitting with Mme. de Staël. . . . By appointment we called at 12.[4] For a few moments we waited in a gaudy drawing-room; the door then opened and an elderly form dressed *à la jeunesse* appeared; she is not ugly; she is not vulgar (Edward begs to differ from this opinion, he thinks her ugly beyond measure); her countenance is pleasing, but very different from anything my fancy had formed; a pale complexion not far from that of a white Mulatto, if you will allow me to make the bull; her eyebrows dark and her hair quite sable, dry and crisp like a negro's, though not quite so curling. She scarcely gave me time to make my compliments in French before she spoke in fluent English. I was not sorry she fought under British colours, for though she was never at a loss, I knew I could express and defend myself better than had she spoken in French.

I hurried her as much as decency would permit from one subject to another, but I found politics were uppermost in her thoughts. . . . She was equally averse to both parties—to the royal because she said it was despotism; the Imperial because it was tyranny.

"Is there," said I, "no happy medium; are there none who can feel the advantages of liberty, and wish for a free constitution?"

"None," said she, "but myself and a few—some twelve or fifteen—we are nothing; not enough to make a dinner party."

I ventured to throw in a little flattery—I knew my ground—and remarked that an opinion like hers, which had in some measure influenced Europe, was in itself an host; the compliment was well received, and in truth I could offer it *conscientiously* to pay tribute to her abilities.

On leaving Mme. de S. we paid another visit. From the greatest woman we went to see our greatest man in Paris, Sir Charles Stuart,[5] to whom Lord Sheffield had given me a letter of introduction. This had been sent the day before, and of course I now went to see the ef-

---

4. Madame de Staël had only returned to France after her long exile a few weeks after Napoleon's abdication. Her rooms were in *the Hôtel de Tamerzan, 105, Rue de Grenelle St. Germain.*

5. Stuart, Sir Charles, 1779-1845. Eldest son of Sir C. Stuart, General, and Louisa, daughter and co-heiress of Lord Vere Bertie. Minister at the Hague and Ambassador at Paris, and later on at St. Petersburg. British Envoy at the Congress of Vienna. Created Baron Stuart de Rothesay 1841. Married, 1816, Lady Elizabeth Yorke, third daughter of third Earl of Hardwicke. Gronow gives a more favourable account of him, "One of the most popular Ambassadors Great Britain ever sent to Paris."

fect. After waiting in the anti-chamber of the great man for about half an hour, and seeing divers and sundry faces pass and repass in review, we were summoned to an audience. We found a little, vulgar-looking man, whom I should have mistaken for the great man's butler if he had not first given a hint that he was *bonâ fide* the great man himself. I think the conversation was nearly thus:

E. S.: "Pray, Sir, are the Marshalls in Paris, and if so is it easy to see them?"

Sir C. S.: "Upon my soul I don't know."

E. S.: "Pray, Sir, is there anything interesting to a stranger like myself likely to take place in the course of the next fortnight?"

Sir C. S.: "Upon my soul I don't know."

E. S.: "Pray, Sir, is the interior of the Thuilleries worth seeing, and could we easily see the apartments?"

Sir C. S.: "Upon my soul I don't know."

This, I do assure you, was the cream of the conversation. Now certainly a great man ought to look wise and say he does not know so and so, when in fact he knows all about it, but somehow or other I could not help thinking that Sir Charles spoke the truth, for if I may draw any inference from Physiognomy, I never saw a face upon which the character of "upon my soul I don't know" was more visibly stamped. I left my card, bowed, and retired. . . .

I next turned my eyes to the Louvre.[6] What are the exhibitions of London, modern or ancient? What are Lord Stafford's, Grosvenor's, Angerstein's, &c., in comparison with this unrivalled gallery? Words cannot describe the *coup d'œil*. Figure to yourself a magnificent room so long that you would be unable to recognise a person at the other extremity, so long that the perspective lines terminate in a point, covered with the finest works of art all classed and numbered so as to afford the utmost facility of inspection; no questions asked on entering, no money to be given to bowing porters or butlers, no cards of admission procured by interest—all open to the public view, unfettered and unshackled; the liberality of the exhibition is increased by the appearance of Easels and desks occupied by artists who copy at leisure.

It is noble and grand beyond imagination. In the Halls below are the Statues, arranged with equal taste, though, as they are in different rooms, the general effect is not so striking. I recognised all my

6. Under the Treaty of Paris France had been allowed to keep the Art Treasures taken by Napoleon.

old friends, the Venus de Medicis was alone new to me. She is sadly mutilated, but is still the admiration of all persons of sound judgment and orthodox taste, amongst whom, I regret to say, I deserve not to be classed, as I really cannot enter into the merits of statues, and the difference between a perfect and moderate specimen of sculpture appears to me infinitely less than between good and moderate paintings.

After dining at a Restaurateur's, who gave us a most excellent dinner, wine, &c., for about 3s. a head, we went to the *Théâtre Français*, or the Drury Lane of Paris. We expected to see Talma [7] in Mérope, but his part was taken by one who is equally famous, Dufour, and the female part by Mme. Roncour. She was intolerable, though apparently a great favourite; he tolerable, and that is all I can say. In truth, French tragedy is little to my taste. . . . The best part of the play was the opportunity it afforded "*les bonnes gens*" *de* Paris to show their loyalty, and much gratified I was in hearing some enthusiastic applause of certain passages as they applied to the return of their ancient sovereign. There is something very sombre and vulgar in the French playhouses with the men's boots and the women's bonnets. Could I in an instant waft you from the solitudes of Stoke to the clatter of Paris, how you would stare to see the boxes filled with persons almost extinguished in their enormous *casques* of straw and flowers. I have seen several bearing, in addition to other ornaments, a bunch of five or six lilies as large as life. . . .

Letter 4

Paris, July 8, 1814.

You will take for granted we have seen all the exhibitions, libraries, &c., of Paris; they will wait for more ample description—a glance on one or two will be sufficient.

L'Hôpital des Invalides was, you know, famous for its magnificent dome, which was decorated with flags, standards, and trophies of the victorious arms of France; impatient to shew them to Edward, I hastened thither, but alas, not a pennant remains. On the near approach of the Allies they were taken down, and some say burnt, others buried, others removed to a distance. I asked one of the *invalides* whether the Allies had not got possession of a few. With great indignation and animation he exclaimed, "*Je suis aussi sûr que je suis de mon existence qu'il n'out pas pris un seul même.*"

On Sunday last, after having hunted everywhere for a Protestant

7. Talma, the celebrated tragic actor, 1763-1826.

Pompe Notre Dame - Paris July 11 1814

18

PARIS, LA POMPE,. NOTRE DAME.

church, one of which we found at last by some blunder quite empty, we went with our landlord, a sergeant in the national guard, to inspect the heights of Chaumont, Belleville, and Mont Martre. . . . We ascended from the town for about three miles to a sort of large rambling village, in situation and circumstances somewhat like Highgate. This was Belleville, whose heights run on receding from Paris a considerable distance, but terminate rather abruptly in the direction of Mont Martre, from which they are separated by a low, swampy valley containing all the dead horses, filth, and exuvious putrefactions of Paris. . . . Immediately below, extending for many miles, including St. Denis and other villages, are fine plains; upon which plains about 3 in the morning the Russians deployed, and the spectacle must have been interesting beyond measure. . . .

On the heights and towards the base were assembled part of Marmont's[8] army with their field pieces and some few heavier guns; there, too, were stationed the greater part of the students of *l'Ecole Polytechnique*, corresponding to our Woolwich cadets. Nothing could surpass their conduct when their brethren in arms fled; they clung to their guns and were nearly all annihilated. I was assured that their bodies were found in masses on the spot where they were originally stationed; their number was about 300. . . . I met a few in the course of the day who were, like ourselves, contemplating the field of battle, and who spoke like the rest of their countrymen of the baseness of Marmont and treachery of the day.

The cannonade must have been pretty sharp while it lasted, as about 5,000 Russians perished before they got possession of the heights—though the actual operation of storming did not occupy half an hour—but their lines were quite open to a severe fire of grape from eminences commanding every inch of the plain. Whilst this work was going on at Belleville, another Russian column performed a similar service at Mt. Martre, which is nearer Paris—in fact, immediately above the Barriers. . . . Thither our guide next conducted us, and pointed out the particular spots where the assault and carnage were most desperate. A number of Parties were walking about and all talking of the battle or Bonaparte. . . .

Till this day I had never heard him openly and honestly avowed,

8. On March 30th the Allies marched on Paris. They attacked in three divisions— the Silesian army on the side of Montmartre, Prince Eugene of Wurtemberg and Barclay de Tolly by Pantin and Romainville, the Crown Prince of Wurtemberg by Vincennes and Charenton. Marmont surrendered the same day.

but here I had several opportunities of incorporating myself in groups in which his name was bandied about with every invective which French hatred and fluency could invent. Their tongues, like Baron Munchausen's horn, seemed to run with an accumulated rapidity from the long embargo laid upon them. "*Sacré gueux, bête, voleur,*" &c., were the current coin in which they repaid his despotism, and I was happy to find that his conduct in Spain was by all held in utter detestation and considered as the ground work of his ruin.

I saw one party in such a state of bodily and mental agitation that I ran up expecting to see a battle, but the multiplicity of hands, arms, and legs which were rising, falling, wheeling, and kicking, were merely energetic additions to the general subject. . . . The National guard were not (with few exceptions) actually engaged. To the amount of 36,000 they occupied the towns and barriers, by all accounts guessing, or, as one intelligent conductor assured us, very certain that they would not be called upon to fight much for the defence of Paris. . . . Indeed, from all I have been able to learn, and from all I have been able to see, it appears pretty clear that no serious defence was intended—a little opposition was necessary for the look of the thing. And although Marmont might have done more, I feel convinced that had he exerted himself to the utmost, Paris must have perished.

The heights were defended in a very inadequate and unsoldierlike manner; not a single work was thrown up before the guns, no entrenchments, no bastions, and yet with three days' notice all this might have easily been done. The barriers all round Paris were, and still are, hemmed round with palisades with loop holes, each of which might have been demolished by half a dozen rounds from a 6-pounder; the French, indeed, laugh at them and consider them as mere divertissements of Bonaparte's, and feeble attempts to excite a spirit of defence amongst the people—a spirit which, fortunately for Europe, was never excited. The lads of Paris had determined to take their chance and not to do one atom more than they were called upon or compelled to do. These wooden barriers are made of *le bois de tremble* (aspen), and the pun was that the fortifications "*tremblaient partout.*"

You will like to hear something of Edgeworth's friend, St. Jean d'Angély;[9] he came up to the barrier where our landlord (who had been formerly an imperial guardsman and fought in the battle of Marengo [*also published by Leonaur*]) was posted; here he called loudly

---

9. Régnaud St. Jean d'Angély, 1762-1819.

for some brandy, for which he got laughed at by the whole line of guard; he then sallied forth and proceeded a short distance, when his horse took fright, and as St. Jean was, as our landlord told us, "*entiére-ment du même avis avec son cheval*," they both set off as fast as they could, and were in a few minutes far beyond all danger, nor did they appear again amid the din of arms.

The fate of Paris was decided with a rapidity and *sang-froid* quite astonishing. By 5 o'clock in the evening all was entirely at an end, and the national guard and allies incorporated and doing the usual duty of the town. They were, indeed, under arms a little longer than usual, and a few more sentries were placed and the theatre not open that evening, but that single evening was the only exception, and the next day the Palais Royal was as brilliant and more cheerful than ever, with its motley groups of visitors.

The *Cossacks* were not quartered in the Palais Royal, they were in the Ch. Elysées, the trees of which bear visible marks of their horses' teeth, but a good many came in from curiosity and hung their horses in the open space of the Palais. . . The Russian discipline was most se-vere, and not an article was taken from any individual with impunity, immediate death was the punishment. The field of battle bore few marks of the event—a few skeletons of horses and rags of uniforms; the more surprising thing is that, notwithstanding all the trampling of horse and foot on the plains below so late as the end of March, the corn has not suffered in the slightest degree. I wish the Alderley crops were as good.

You have no idea of the severity of the conscription. That men can be attached to a being who dragged them, with such violence to every feeling, from their homes would be astonishing, but for the well-known force of the "selfish principle" which amalgamates their glory with his. A friend of our landlord's paid at various times 18,000 *francs*, about £900; he thought himself safe, but Bonaparte wanted a Volunteer guard of honour; he was told it would be prudent to enrol himself, which in consideration of the great sums he had paid would be merely a nominal business, and that he would never be called upon. He did put his name down; was called out in a trice and shot in the next campaign. Our waiter at Rouen assured me his friends had bought him off by giving in the first instance £25 for a substitute, with an annuity to the said substitute of an equal sum—pretty well this, for a poor lad of about sixteen.

Thanks to our landlord and not to Sir Charles Stuart, we might have been introduced into the Thuilleries, but came too late. We lost nothing, as after Mass the King marched through a beautiful sort of glass gallery facing the Thuilleries Gardens, and then came out into a balcony to shew himself to the crowd there assembled! he was received with universal and loud applause. "*Vive le Roi!*" was heard as loud as heart could wish, hats, sticks and handkerchiefs were flying in all directions. When he entered Paris, in one of the barriers a sort of archway was made and so contrived that as the carriage passed under a crown fell upon it, a band at the same time striking up "*Où peut on être mieux que dans le sein de sa famille*," which is, you know, one of their favourite airs.

Poor man, he has enough to do, and will, I fear, experience a turbulent reign. Bonaparte has left his troops three years in arrears, the treasury empty, two parties equally clamorous for places and pensions, both of which must be satisfied. Their taxes are heavier than I thought they were. Our landlord has an estate worth about 2,000 *francs*, his father paid 200 *francs* a year for it, and he is now under the necessity of paying 1,200, having only a clear surplus of 800, and the finances are at too low an ebb to allow of any immediate reduction in their taxes. . . .

To take things in their course, I must now proceed to my dinner at Sir Charles Stuart's. I was shewn into a room where I found three or four Englishmen gaping at one another. Before many more had assembled, in came Sir C., and I *believe*, or rather I am willing to flatter myself, he made a sort of half bow towards us, and then we stood and gaped again; a few more words between him and one or two who were to go to court the day after, but to me and some others not a syllable of any description was uttered, and when some more English were shewn in who were, I presume, as respectable as myself, his behaviour was quite boorish, he did not condescend to look towards the door. These things went on till a throng of Spaniards with Stars and orders came in; with these he appeared tolerably intimate, and also with three Englishmen who afterwards appeared. We were about twenty-four in number, and all I had to do in the half-hour preceding dinner was to look out for the most intelligent, gentleman-like-looking Englishman I could, to secure a place by him. . . .

You will ask who I met. I protest to you that I went and returned without being able to learn more than that the secretary's name was Bidwell, and that one other person in company was a Mr. Martin, who had been agent for prisoners; of the rest I knew nothing, not even of my neighbour; birth, parentage, and education were alike involved in the cloud of diplomatic mystery which seemed to impend heavily over this mansion, and when my neighbour asked me, or I asked him, the names of any person present the answer was mutual—"I don't know." Sir Charles sat in the centre with a gold-coated *don* on each side of him, with whom he might have whispered, for though I sat within two of His Excellency, I never heard the sound of his voice: however, my opinion may not coincide with all that pass from Calais to Dover, as I heard one man remark to another that his countenance was very pleasing, to which was added in reply, "and he is a very sensible man." These things may be, but I never met with one more perfect in the art of concealing his talents.

Now for the *Jardin des Plantes* and its lectures. This same *Jardin* is a large space appropriated to botanical pursuits, public walks, menageries, museums, &c. There you see bears and lions and, in fact, the finest collection of birds and beasts alive, some in little paddocks, others in clean and airy dens. But this is the least part of this delightful establishment; its museums and cabinets are like the Louvre, the finest collection in the world. Everything is arranged in such order that it is almost impossible to see it without feeling a love of science; here the mineralogist, geologist, naturalist, entomologist may each pursue his favourite studies unmolested. Here, as everywhere else, the utmost liberality is shewn to all, but to Englishmen particularly, your country is your passport.

Like the mysterious "Open *Sesame*" in the *Arabian Nights*, you have only to say, "*Je suis Anglais*" and you go in and out at pleasure. I have seen Frenchmen begging in vain with ladies and officers of the party and turned away because they had happened on the wrong day or hour, and then we, without solicitation, have been desired to walk in. But all these museums and living animals, curious and interesting as they are, are surpassed by the still greater liberality shewn in the daily lectures given by the members of the Institute or Professors of the several sciences. I have attended Haiiy, [10] Duméril, [11] l'Ettorel, du Mare, and others upon mineralogy, nat. hist., and entomology, and Haiiy, you know, is the first mineralogist in Europe, and I never looked upon a more interesting being.

When he entered the lecture room, every one rose out of respect, and well they might. He is 80 years of age apparently, with a most heavenly patriarchal countenance and silver hair; his teeth are gone,

---

10. Abai Reny Just Haiiy, 1743-1822.
11. Duméril, naturalist and professor.

so that I could not understand a word he said, though, indeed, had he been possessed of all the teeth in Christendom I apprehend I should not have been much wiser, as he lectured on the angular forms of the Amphiboles. He looked like a man picked out of a crystal, and when he dies he ought to be reincarnated and placed in his own museum.

Another scene to which I found my way was equally interesting: I went to a lecture on iconographic drawing, or science, as it was called, of representing natural subjects. In other words, when I got there I found it was a professorship of drawing, everything connected with natural history, such as flowers, animals, insects; and the professor lectures one day and practically instructs on another. I happened to be present at one of the latter. Conceive my surprise at finding myself in a large library filled with tables, drawing books, ladies and gentlemen all sketching either from nature or excellent copies here. As it was not a public day except to those who wished to attend for instruction, I ought not with propriety to have intruded, but "*J'étais Anglois*" and every attention was paid.

You would have given a little finger to have seen the room; it was a hot summer's day, but there all was cool and fragrant; the windows opened on the gardens, the tables were covered with *groupes* of flowers in vases; the company, about forty, were seated up and down where ever they chose, each with a nice desk and drawing board—in short, it was a scene which excited feelings of respect for a nation which thus patronised everything which could add to the rational improvement of its members. Were France the seat of religion and pure virtue it would be Utopia verified; but, alas! there are spots which stain the picture and cast a balance decidedly in favour of England: we are rough, we are narrow-minded, but he who travels is brought to confess and say "*England! with all thy faults I love thee still.*" . . .

Letter 5.

Paris, July 10th.

Madame de Staëls party formed a fine contrast to the gloom and ponderosity of Sir Charles Stuart's dinner the day before. We went a quarter before nine, thinking, as it was the nominal hour, it would be ill-bred to go too early, but the French are more punctual in these matters, for we found the good people all assembled and Marmont [12]

---

12. Marmont, 1774-1852, Duc de Raguse. The defence of Paris had been left in his hands by Napoleon, and his surrender to the Allies was the finishing stroke which forced Napoleon to abdicate.

walked out not five minutes before we walked in.

In his stead we had General Lafayette,[13] the cornerstone of the Revolution. He is a tall, clumsy-made man, not much unlike Dr. Nightingale, though rather thinner. His countenance discovers thought and sound judgment, but by no means quickness or brilliancy; his manners were quiet, unassuming, and gentleman-like. He spoke little, and then said nothing particularly worth notice.

The next lion announced was a lioness, the celebrated Madame Récamier, [14] and though she is not in her *première jeunesse*, I can easily conceive how she could once dazzle the world. It would be too much to give her credit for superior talents, but her manners were very agreeable though rather like all other belles of France who have fallen in my way, somewhat *à la languissante*. But I am all this while forgetting the star of the evening, the Baroness herself. She sat in a line with about six ladies, before whom were arranged as many gentlemen, all listening to the oracular tongue of their political Sybil.

She was in high spirits because she had been warmed up by the decision of the court and commons concerning the liberty of the press, which had received an effectual check by limiting all liberty of speech and opinion to works containing not less than 480 pages, thus excluding the papers and pamphlets. The moment we were announced, before she asked me how I did, she enquired whether I had heard this notable decision, and then demanded what I thought of it. Of course, I assured her how much I lamented the prospect of an inundation of dull, prolix books to which France was thus inevitably exposed. This, as we spoke in English, she immediately translated for the benefit of the company, adding "*Ce Monsieur Anglois dit cela, et c'est bien vrai il a raison*," and then she laughed and seemed to enjoy the catalogue of stupid books which might be anticipated.

I must confess the party was a little formidable; in England I should have said formal, but there is something in French manners wholly foreign to any application of the word formal, and really after exchanging a few remarks I was glad to be introduced to her son[15] and daughter,[16] with both of whom I was much pleased. They are clever

---

13. Lafayette, 1757-1834, Liberal general and politician.
14. Madame Récamier, 1777-1849, a famous beauty. She had held a *salon* at Paris in the early days of the Empire, but had been exiled in 1811 and had just returned (June, 1814)
15. Auguste de Staël, 1790-1827.
16. Mademoiselle de Staël, married the Duc de Broglie.

and agreeable. She is not above eighteen or twenty, and if her complexion was good would be very pretty. She was not shy, beginning conversation in a trice upon interesting subjects. She compared the English and French character, in which she (and I presume it was a maternal opinion) would not allow an atom of merit to the latter.

On finding that I was a clergyman she immediately began upon Religion, talked of Hodgson, [17] Andrews, Wilberforce, [18] and then in questioning me about the Methodists (about whom she seemed to have heard much and entertained confused notions) we slid into mysticism, which carried us, of course, into the third vol. of *Allemagne*; she spoke in raptures of the mystic school, said she was quite one in heart—"*Cela se peut*," thought I; but somehow or other "*Je ne le crois pas*," for I have heard some little anecdotes of her mother, in which, whatever may be her theoretical views of mysticism, her practical opinions are rather more lax than Fénelon's. Much against my will I took my leave, willing to hope that Mme. S. spoke the truth when she said how glad she should be to see me if I visited Paris during the winter; she is off to Switzerland in a few days. The French say we have spoilt her—in fact, she occupies little of the public attention in Paris.

The next event most interesting was our visit to the *Corps Législatif*, or House of Commons. We went to a certain door, to which we were refused admittance, and told it was too full or too late. But said I, "*Nous sommes Anglois*"; in an instant a man came up and placed us in an inner gallery in the body of the house. The House is something like the Royal Institution—of course larger and beautifully fitted up. Considering it as the Royal Institution for your better comprehension, the president sits on a tribunal throne in a recess corresponding to the fireplace; immediately below is a sort of rostrum from whence the members speak, in situation like the lecturer of the R.I. In point of decoration and external appearance both of house and members, it is far superior to our House of Commons, as all the members wear uniforms of blue and gold, but taking it all together I know not that anything can be more illustrative of the French character—externally all correct and delightful, but within "a sad rottenness of the state of Denmark."

The president began the proceedings by ringing a bell; a paper was then read detailing, I believe, the orders of the day. A member then

17. Hodgson, Dean of Carlisle and Rector of St. George's, Hanover Square; d. 1844.
18. William Wilberforce, 1759-1833; distinguished among the promoters of Negro Emancipation and the Abolition of the Slave Trade.

arose and went to the rostrum. In the middle of his speech he was called to order and told it was a very bad speech, so down he came and another mounted. He was equally disliked, for they told him he spoke too low and they could not hear him, so he disappeared; then half a dozen got up and were so impatient that they began speaking altogether before they reached the Tribune. In vain did the president ring his bell, and stand up and gesticulate. Silence, however, was at length obtained, and he addressed them, but with little better success than the rest. One man then stept forward and did obtain a hearing, for he had good lungs and a fair share of eloquence. His speech was short, but it was by far the best; his name was Dumolard. [19] Soon afterwards the sitting broke up; the whole took up little more than an hour. I know not whether the perfect want of order was more ridiculous or disgusting; the sittings of the senate (peers) are private. . . .

We will now take you to Malmaison, the interesting retreat of the interesting Joséphine. Her character was scarcely known in England. We hear little more of her than as a discarded Empress or Mistress of Buonaparte's, but she had much to recommend her to public as well as private notice. The French all speak highly of her, and it is impossible, on seeing Malmaison and hearing of her virtues, not to join in their opinion. To be sure, as a Frenchman told me in running through a list of virtues, "*Elle avait été un peu libertine, mais ce n'est rien cela,*" and, indeed, I could almost have added, "*C'est bien vrai,*" for every allowance should be made; consider the situation in which she was placed, her education, her temptations; many a saint might have fallen from the eminence on which she stood; I never dwelt with more satisfaction or felt more inclined to coincide in that benevolent verdict of the best of judges of human nature and human frailty, "*Neither do I condemn thee, go and sin no more,*" than in criticising the character of Joséphine.

I am not sure whether you know exactly the history of Malmaison. The house and land attached to it were purchased by Buonaparte when First Consul, and given to Joséphine, who made it what it is, and bought more land, so that it is now in fact a little Estate. On being divorced, she retired thither with Eugène Beauharnais, her son, and younger children. Her pursuits and occupations will be best understood by describing what we saw. I should say, before I proceed, that it required some interest to get in, and that we went with the Hibberts, who knew the secretary of the Swedish ambassador, in whose suite we

---

19. Dumolard, 1766-1820; a French politician, a prominent figure in the Chamber of Representatives under the first Restoration.

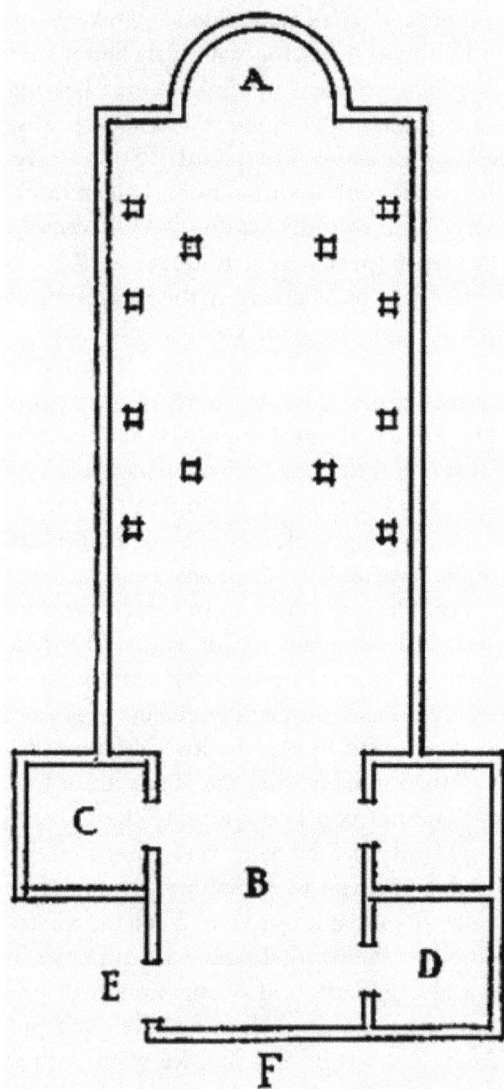

MALMAISON

were incorporated for admission.

The chief room in the house is what is called the gallery A, planned and finished according to her own designs; the floor is a mass of dark inlaid marble, the ceiling arched and light admitted from it, the whole not much unlike the gallery at Winnington on a much larger scale. It would be difficult to describe the fitting up of the interior. The walls are hung with the most exquisite selections from ancient masters, not stolen, but many given to her, and the rest purchased by herself; but I was more struck by the statues than with anything else. The dots represent them and their situations in the gallery; they are chiefly by two modern artists, Canova and Boher, though I fear the reputation of my taste and judgment will suffer by the confession. I still must confess that I felt far more pleasure than in looking either upon Apollo or the Venus de Medicis. There was a bust and statue of herself, the latter particularly beautiful, and if accurate, which I was assured it was, the original must have been elegant and interesting to the last degree. It reminded me much of Lady Charlemont, with a stronger expression of sense.

The rest of the room was furnished with tables inlaid with marble, upon which were a variety of bronzes, pieces of armour, &c., and her musical instruments were as she had left them, and everything wore an appearance of comfort which is seldom seen in the midst of such magnificence. Through folding doors you enter into a smaller room hung with pictures. C. was her chapel; before a little unostentatious altar, which had every appearance of having daily witnessed her devotions, was a beautiful Raphael; the walls were hung with seven small Scripture subjects by Poussin. I would have given a great deal to have been her invisible observer in this sacred retirement. She must have been alone, for it was scarcely large enough to admit priest or attendant.

D. was a room in which she breakfasted, during which time music was generally performed in B. From E. was a fine view of the aqueduct of Marly, and E. was the way to the garden, which she had fitted up in the English style. I have not time to enter into detail of these or her greenhouses. She was fond of society and patronised the arts. She allowed artists to sit at leisure in her gallery to copy pictures, and conversed with them a great deal. She did an infinity of good to all within her reach and was beloved by all. Her death was very sudden; she had complained of a sore throat, but not sufficiently to confine her to her room. On a certain Wednesday or Thursday she was in her park in high spirits, showing it to the Emperor Alexander and King of Prussia; being rather heated she drank some iced water; in the evening she was worse, on Sunday she was dead, sensible to the last; talked of death, seemed perfectly resigned—to use the words of a French lady, who told me many interesting particulars, "*sa mort était très chrétienne.*"

They were busied in packing pictures and making catalogues, but I believe there is no fear of dismantling the house, as Eugène Beauharnais[20] and the children are to have it in conformity to her will.[21] I have seen few things since my departure from England which have interested me more than Malmaison, and I could almost fancy that her statue, which is that of a pensive female, with the chin resting on the hand, was her ghost ruminating over the extraordinary events which had recently occurred, and which she had quitted forever. You will see Malmaison in my sketch-book, as well as the castle of Vincennes, which is as picturesque and imposing as it is interesting, from the circumstances attending the Duke d'Enghien's[22] death. It seems this event was known at Paris the next day and spoken of with as much freedom as the despotic government of Paris would admit. . . .

I went yesterday to see the house of peers in the Luxembourg. The hall of sittings is not unlike that of the *Corps Législatif,* but the decorations are more interesting, each niche being filled with Austrian standards and a few others. Under a gilt dome, supported by similar pillars, was the spot where Napoleon's throne was *not.* The remnants I saw lying in one of the ante-rooms, all of which were ornamented with immense pictures of the principal battles, but these, out of compliment to the Emperor, &c., had been covered over with green baize, even the very standards had been removed during the stay of the Emperor of Austria in Paris. There is a sitting on Tuesday, and if I stand at the door I may see the marshals alight, but my curiosity would not be satisfied, as no persons seem to know them; even the man who shewed us the hall, who actually keeps the door through which they enter and sees them all constantly, assured me he did not know one from the other. He did not even know whether Marmont [23] had one arm or two.

---

20. Eugène Beauharnais, 1780-1824, Viceroy of Italy, 1805-15. Son of Joséphine by her first marriage with the Vicomte de Beauharnais.

21. After the Second Restoration Prince Eugène Beauharnais sold Malmaison and removed its gallery of pictures to Munich.

22. Duc d'Enghien, 1772-1804, son of the Duc de Bourbon. Shot at Vincennes by order of Napoleon when First Consul, under the pretext that he had conspired against him.

23. Marmont lost his arm at the battle of Salamanca in 1812.

Letter 6

Thanks to our Landlord, and not to Sir Charles Stuart, we have just been elbowing the Marshals, as a sergeant of the National Guard offered to take us into the Thuilleries, and in we went with him in full uniform, on the very best day we could have selected since our arrival in Paris, as a corps of about 10,000 or 15,000 men were to be reviewed by the King *en masse* in the Place de Carousel, immediately in front of the Thuilleries.

We were stationed in a room of which I had heard much and wished above all things to see—"*la Salle des Maréchaux*," so called from the full-length portraits of eighteen of these gentlemen with which it is hung; the upper part of the room is surrounded by a gallery decorated with pictures of the chief battles—Lodi, Passage of the Po, and one sea piece descriptive of the capture of our frigate, the *Ambuscade*, by a smaller vessel. It is so good a picture that for the sake of the painting I never thought of lamenting the subject.

After standing in this hall for a few minutes in the midst of generals without number in full uniform, I had the satisfaction of being almost knocked over by Marshal Jourdan,[24] a sharp, queer-looking fellow not at all stamped with the features of a hero. I eyed him well, and had scarcely satiated my curiosity when half a dozen more came by, walking about without peculiar honours or attention, and only to be distinguished from the generals by a broad red ribbon, worn like those of our Knights of the Bath.

I looked at each and all, but as few could tell their names I was at a loss to distinguish one from another; my head and eyes were in a perfect fidget, flying from marshal to marshal and from picture to picture.

Of the Ducs de Treviso,[25] de Conegliano,[26] Serurier,[27] and Perignan[28] I had no doubt, as I saw them again several times, but I am not sure that I should know the others except from a recollection of their pictures.

---

24. Jourdan, General, 1762-1833.
25. Duc de Treviso, Marshal Mortier, 1768-1835.
26. Duc de Conegliano, Marshal Moncey, 1754-1842. He defended the walls of Paris as Major-General of the National Guard and laid down his arms only after the Capitulation was signed.
27. Serurier, General, 1742-1819.
28. Perignan, General, 1754-1819.

I will describe a few while their countenances are fresh upon my memory.

Ney [29] is a fine, handsome man, but remarkably fair with light curling hair, and struck us very like Mrs. Parker, of Astle.

Duc d'Istria [30] was reckoned by Robert Hibbert like me—that is to say, he had dark arched eyebrows, a fox-like sort of countenance, very dark, almost swarthy, and from his extreme bilious appearance, I should imagine might be troubled, like myself, with bad headaches.

Davoust! [31] I can scarcely recall his portrait without shuddering. If ever an evil spirit peeped through the visage of a human being, it was in Davoust. Every bad passion seemed to have set its mark on his face: nothing grand, warlike, or dignified. It was all dark, cruel, cunning, and malevolent. His body, too, seemed to partake of his character. I should fancy he was rather deformed. I never saw so good a Richard III. Let him pass and make way for one of a different description, Victor, [32] a fine, open, gentlemanly countenance, though not like a military hero. Marmont, a dark haired, sharp-looking man of military stature. Duc de Dantzig, [33] very ugly and squinting. Berthier, [34] remarkably quiet and intelligent. Murat, [35] an effeminate coxcomb with no characteristic but that of self-satisfaction. Moncey, a respectable veteran. Massèna, [36] the most military of all, dark hair and countenance, fine figure. Soult, [37] a stern soldier, vulgar but energetic; his mouth and lower part of his face like Edridge, [38] though not so large a man.

---

29. Ney, Prince de la Moskowa, Duc d'Elchingen, 1769-1815, "*Le Brave des Braves.*" He swore allegiance to Louis XVIII., but returned to Napoleon in 1815, fought under him at Waterloo, and was shot for treason under the Second Restoration.
30. Duc d'Istria, Bessières, Commander of the Old Guard.
31. Davoust, Prince d'Eckmuhl. In 1814 the unfortunate city of Hamburg was still suffering under the unrelenting severity of Davoust, who had appointed a commission having the power of condemning to death all persons who used inflammatory speeches to exasperate the soldiers or the inhabitants.
32. Victor, Duc de Belluno, 1764-1841.
33. Lefebre, Duc de Dantzig, 1755-1820.
34. Berthier, Prince de Wagram, 1753-1815, Chief of the Staff. A close friend of Napoleon from 1796 onwards. He escaped to Bamberg in 1815 in hopes of remaining neutral, but was killed there by the emissaries of a secret society.
35. Murat, 1778-1815, King of Naples and husband of Caroline Bonaparte. He had concluded a treaty with Austria against Napoleon in January, 1814. He was shot in Calabria in 1815.
36. Massèna, Duc de Rivoli, 1758-1817. "The favoured child of victory."
37. Soult, Duc de Dalmatie, 1769-1861. He decided the victory of Austerlitz.
38. Edridge, portrait painter, 1769-1821.

The King was to me a very secondary person; however, I was close to him as he tottered, like a good old well-meaning man, to Mass. On his return he appeared, as I described last Sunday, in the balcony facing the gardens for a few minutes and was loudly cheered, and then he came back to the *Salle des Maréchaux* and sat down in a fine chair of Bonaparte's, covered all over with his bees, in a balcony facing the Place de Carousel, from whence he looked down on the 10,000 troops who were there assembled. The shouts here were not what they ought to have been. Comparatively few cried "God bless him!" and I much fear the number who thought it was still less. The Duc de Berri,[39] on horseback with Marshal Moncey on one side and Du Pont[40] on the other, reviewed the troops, who passed in companies and troops before them. As each company passed the officer held up his sword and cried "*Vive le Roi!*" and some of the soldiers did the same, but not more than one out of ten.

I heard an anecdote of the Duc de Berri which is, I hope, true. A few days ago in reviewing some troops on the Champs Elysées an officer in passing chose to cry out, "*Vive Napoléon!*" upon which the *Duc* rode up to him, tore his epaulette from his shoulder and order from his breast, threw them on the ground, and instantly dismissed him the service; this spirit pleased the soldiers, and they all shouted "*Vive le Roi!*"

On Saturday we went to St. Cloud, Versailles, and the great and little Trianon. St. Cloud and the great Trianon were the especial residences of Buonaparte, and I looked at his bed and tables and chairs with some curiosity. I have not time to describe all these. I saw one public place yesterday which should be mentioned, a museum of models in every department of art and science, with all the machines, &c., connected with them. I would willingly conclude my observations on Paris with some remarks on its manners, principles, &c., and I would begin with religion first if I could, but the fact is there appears to be none. If any does exist it must approximate to mysticism and lie concealed in the recesses of the heart, for truly "*the right hand knoweth not what the left hand doeth.*"

But with all this non-appearance I should be cautious in passing

---

39. Duke de Berri, second son of the Comte d'Artois, afterwards Charles X., 1778-1820. He married Caroline of Naples, and was the father of the Comte de Chambord. He was assassinated by Louvel on the steps of the Opera House at Paris in 1820.
40. General Du Pont, 1759-1838.

too severe a censure. It must be remembered that the nation is military, that from the earliest years they "sing of arms," and Buonaparte carried this to such a degree that even children not much older than Owen [41] are to be seen in full uniforms. He wished to incorporate the two terms of man and soldier. We laughed, you remember, at the account of the little King of Rome appearing in uniform; in Paris this would not appear ridiculous. He had uniforms of all the favourite regiments horse and foot. . . .

But yet there appears to be less vice than in England, I should rather say less organised vice; I have not heard of a single robbery, public or private—I walk without fear of pickpockets; I should be inclined to say they seemed rather against themselves than against each other. Their principles may be more relaxed on some points than ours, but I doubt much whether a Frenchman would not be as much disgusted in England as an Englishman could possibly be in France; we call them a profligate race and condemn them in *toto*—something like Hudibras' John Bull—

Compounds for sin he is inclined to
By damning those he has no mind to.

Their public walks and theatres are less offensive to decency than ours. Drunkenness is scarcely known; at first sight I should pronounce them an idle, indolent people; the streets are almost always full; the gardens, public walks, &c., swarm at all hours with *saunterers*. According to my ideas a Frenchman's life must be wretched, for he does not seem at all to enter into the charms of home—their houses are not calculated for it; they huddle together in nooks and corners, and the male part (judging from the multitudes I daily see) leave the women and children to get through the day as they can.

Their coffee-houses are some of them quite extraordinary; most of them are ornamented with Mirrors in abundance, but some shine with more splendour. In the Palais Royal there is one called "*Le Café de mille Colonnes*," which merits some description. It consists of three or four rooms—the largest is almost one mass of plate-glass mirrors, beautiful clocks at each end, and magnificent chandeliers; behind a raised table of most superb structure, composed of slabs of marble and plate-glass, sat a lady dressed in the richest manner, diamonds on head and hand, lace, muslin, &c. This is the landlady; by her a little boy, about four years old, stood in charge of a drawer from whence the

41. Eldest son of Edward Stanley, b. 1811

PARISIAN AMUSEMENTS

small change was issued; this, if it happened to be copper, was delicately touched by the fair hand, which was immediately washed in a glass of water as if contaminated by the vulgar metal. She never spoke to the waiters, but rung a golden bell; her inkstands, flower jars—in short, every article on the table was of the same metal or of silver gilt. The tables for the company were fine marble slabs; the room was from the reflection of all the mirrors, as you may suppose, a perfect blaze of light, and yet altogether the place looked dirty, from the undress and shabby coats of the company. The French never dress for the evening unless going out to parties, and they always look dirty and unlike gentlemen; the former is not the case, in fact for they are constantly washing and bathing.

An hour or two before I was in this extraordinary coffee-house I had traversed a spot as opposite to it as could well be—the catacombs!—a range of vaults nearly half a mile long, about eighty feet underground, in which are deposited all the bones from all the cemeteries in Paris. I suppose we were in company with some millions of skeletons, whose skulls are so arranged as to form regular patterns, and here and there was an altar made of bones fancifully piled up, on the sides an inscription in Latin, French, &c. Behind one wall the bodies of all who perished in the massacres in Paris were immured. They were brought in carts at night and thrown in, and there they rest, festering not in their shrouds but in clothes. Such a mass of corrupt flesh would soon have infested all the vaults, so they were bricked up.

I wish to recommend our hotel to any people you may hear of coming to Paris—Hôtel des Estrangers, Rue du Hazard, kept by Mr. Meriel. Its situation is both quiet and convenient; it is really not five minutes' walk from the leading objects of Paris, and the people have been civil to us beyond measure.

The Catacombs Paris

CHAPTER 4

On the Track of Napoleon's Army

On leaving Paris, Edward Stanley planned to follow the traces of the desperate campaign which Napoleon had fought in the early months of that year (1814) against the Allies, and in which he so nearly succeeded in saving his crown for a time.

As, however, the English travellers did not intend to return again to Paris, they reversed Napoleon's line of march and started to Fontainebleau by the road along which the Emperor rode back in hot haste on the night of March 30th, to take up the command of the force which should have been defending his capital, and where the sight of Mortier's flying troops convinced him that all hope was at an end.

When they had visited Fontainebleau, where the final abdication had taken place on April 11th, they turned north-east to Melun and posted on through towns which had been the scenes of some of the most desperate fighting in that wonderful campaign, when Napoleon had seemed to be everywhere at once, dealing blows right and left against the three armies which, in the beginning of January, had advanced to threaten his Empire—Bülow in the north, Blücher on the east, and Schwarzenberg on the south.

They passed through Guignes and Meaux, by which Napoleon's army had marched after his victory over Blücher at Vauchamps on February 14th, in the rapid movement to reinforce Marshal Victor, and to drive back Schwarzenberg from the Seine.

Through Château Thierry, where on the 12th of February the Emperor and Marshal Mortier had pursued Russians and Prussians from street to street till they were driven over the Marne, and whence the French leader dashed after Blücher to Vauchamps.

Through Soissons, which the Russians under Winzengerode had

100

bombarded on March 3rd, and forced to surrender, whereby Blücher and Bülow were enabled to join hands.

Through Laon, where Blücher retreated after Craonne, and where he finally shattered Marmont's forces in a night attack.

By Berry au Bac, where the Emperor crossed the Aisne on his way to fight Blücher at Craonne, the scene on March 7th of one of the bloodiest battles of the war.

On to Rheims where, after Marmont's disaster at Laon, Napoleon beat the Russians just before he was forced to rush southwards again to contend with Schwarzenberg and his Austrians.

Finally they reached Châlons, which had been Napoleon's starting-point for the whole campaign, and where he had arrived in the closing days of January after having taken his last farewell of Marie Louise and of the King of Rome.

After Châlons they turned eastwards, following the line of fortresses for which Napoleon had staked and lost his crown, and reached the Rhine by Verdun, Metz, and Mayence; thence to Aix-la-Chapelle, Lille, and Brussels, which had by the Treaty of Paris, in May, been ceded with the whole of Belgium to the Netherlands.

EDWARD STANLEY TO HIS WIFE.

Melun, July 14th.

We quitted our hotel yesterday morning at six for Fontainebleau.

There is nothing particularly interesting about the road, which is almost an incessant avenue. About half-way we passed a fine *château* of Marshal Jourdan's.

The forest of Fontainebleau commences about four miles from the town and extends some nine or ten miles in all directions. At first I was in hopes of being gratified with the sight of fine woods, but, with the exception of a few patches of good oaks, the remainder is little better than underwood and dwarflings.

We went into the heart of the forest to see an old *hermitage* now inhabited by a keeper and his family. They had been visited by *Cossacks*, but had received no injury whatever; on the contrary the poor woman related with all the eloquence of truth and the French animation that from their own soldiers they had suffered all that cruelty and rapacity could devise—indeed, the house and gardens bore evidence to the facts—window shutters pierced with bullets, broken doors, furniture gone, and above 800 *francs'* worth of honey destroyed out of pure wantonness—in short the poor people seemed quite ruined. I received a similar account in the town.

Fontainebleau is a dull, melancholy-looking place, with a very extensive ugly palace—interesting only from the late events. Scarcely a soul appeared about; we crossed the large court in which Buonaparte took his last farewell and embraced the Imperial Eagles, called by some loyal French "The vile cuckoos." Our hostess was, I presume, a staunch imperialist, who thought she could not shew her zeal for the Emperor in a stronger manner than by imposing on Englishmen. She began by asking 16s. for a plate of eight little wretched mutton chops; we resented the imposition, although the sudden appearance of four or five officers of the imperial guard almost rendered it doubtful whether we ought to act too warmly on the defensive, as they seemed to patronise our hostess; however, we refused to pay and retired unimposed upon.

The imperial guard here are supposed to be particularly attached to the Emperor, and of course averse to Englishmen, but I was agreeably surprised to find three out of the four really something like gentlemen in their manners; we entered into conversation, which I managed as dexterously as I could, manoeuvring between the evil of sacrificing my own opinions on one side, and of giving them offence on the other; it was a nice point, as I perceived a word beyond the line of demarcation would have inflamed them in a trice. One happened to differ with another on a political point, which produced a loud and rapid stamping with the feet, accompanied by a course of pirouettes on the heel with the velocity of a dervish, which fully proved what might be effected on their tempers had I been disposed to try the experiment. They called themselves the Ex-Imperial Guard. On retiring I shook hands with them, and with as low a bow as the little King of Rome, said "*Messieurs les Gardes d'Honneur, Je vous salue.*" ...

Letter 7

Monday, July 19th.

. . .The history of Buonaparte immediately preceding, and subsequent to the surrender of Paris, was never actually known—I will give it you.

The capitulation took place on the 30th (March). In the evening of that day he arrived at Fontainebleau without his army. Rumours of fighting near Paris had reached him. He almost immediately set off with Berthier in his carriage for Paris, and actually arrived at Villejuif, only six miles from the capital; when he heard the result he turned about and appeared again at Fontainebleau at 9 the next morning. When he alighted, the person who handed him out, a sort of head-porter of the palace, who was our guide, told me he looked "*triste, bien triste*"; he spoke to nobody, went upstairs as fast as he could, and then called for his plans and maps; his occupation during the whole time he staid consisted in writing and looking over papers, but to what this writing and these papers related the world may feel but will never know; his spirits were by no means broken down; in a day or two he was pretty much as usual, and it is said he signed the abdication without the least apparent emotion.

We heard he was mad, but I can assure you from undoubted authority that he was perfectly well in mind and body the whole time, and, notwithstanding his excessive fatigues, as corpulent as ever; indeed, said our guide, "War seems to agree with him better than with any man I ever knew." Buonaparte laid out immense sums in furnishing and beautifying the *palais* here. I got into his library, the snuggest room you ever saw, immediately below a little study in which he always sat and settled his affairs; his armchair was a very comfortable, honest, plain armchair, but I looked in vain for all the gashes and notches which it was said he was wont to inflict upon it.

I could not perceive a scratch, he was too busily employed in that said chair in forming plans for cutting up Europe; within three yards of his table was a little door, or rather trap door, by which you descended down the oddest spiral staircase you ever beheld into the library, which was low and small; the books were few of them new, almost all standard works upon history—at least I am sure four out of five were historical—all of his own selection, and each stamped, as in fact was everything else from high to low, far and wide, with his N., or his bees or his eagle—all of which Louis XVIII is as busily employed in effacing, which alone will give him ample employment: but to return to the books.

Amongst the rest I found—Shakespeare . . . and a whole range of Ecclesiastical History, which, if ever read, might account in some degree for his shutting up the Pope as the existing representative of the animals who have occasioned half the feuds and divisions therein recorded. There was a chapel, which he regularly attended on Sundays and Saints' days. His state bed was a sort of state business, very uncomfortable, consisting of five or six mattresses under a royal canopy with two satin pillows at each end.

During his residence he never stirred beyond the gates, though

I could not discover that he was at all under restraint, or in any way looked upon as a prisoner; we were told in England (what are we not told there?) that he feared the people, who would have torn him in pieces; this is an idle story. I rather suspect the people liked him too well, besides which his Guards were there, and by them he is idolised. He generally took exercise in a long and beautiful gallery, called the Gallery of Francis I., on both sides of which were busts of his great generals on panels ornamented with the N., and some name above alluding to a victory; thus above one N. was *Nazareth*, which puzzled me at first, but I afterwards heard he had cut up some Turks there; besides the gallery, he walked every day up and down a terrace; he dined every day in a miserable (I speak comparatively) little passage room without any shew of state; he was affable to his attendants and is liked by them.

His abdication room is not one of the state apartments—it is a shabby ante-room; I could almost fancy that in performing this humiliating deed he had retired as far as possible from the halls and *saloons* which were decorated by his hand, and had witnessed his Imperial magnificence. Most of the marshals were in the room, and it would have been a tour indeed to have glided through the hearts of each when such an extraordinary performance was transacting. It was in the great court before the palace that he took his leave, not above 1,500 troops were present. At such a moment to have heard such a speech, delivered with the dignity and stage effect Buonaparte well knew how to give, must have produced a strong effect—how great (how sad I had almost said) the contrast!

The stones were overgrown with grass; nobody appeared, no voice was heard except the clacking of half a dozen old women who were weeding on their knees, and all the windows were closed. The dreary, deserted present compared with the magnificent past excited nearly the same feelings as if I had been looking on Tadmor in the wilderness. After passing the Imperial prison we were ushered into the apartments of the Imperial prisoners, the poor Pope and his sixteen cardinals. I had quite forgotten the place of their confinement, and was a little surprised when the man said, "Here, Sir, dwelt for nineteen months the holy conclave of St. Peter." He must have led a miserable life, for though he was allowed two carriages, with six and eight horses to each, he neither stirred out himself nor allowed any of the cardinals to so do, saying he did not think it right for prisoners.

Buonaparte saw him in January, I think the man said, for the last time. So much for Fontainebleau. Few have followed their master to Elba. Roustan the Mameluke and Constant his valet were certainly very ungrateful; one of them—I forget which—to whom Buonaparte had given 25,000 *francs* (about £1,200) the day before he left Fontainebleau, applied to the Duc de Berri for admission into his service; in reply the *Duc* told him his gratitude ought to have carried him to Elba, but though it had not, if he (the Duke) ever heard that Buonaparte wished to have him there, he would bind him hand and foot and send him immediately.

None of the Royal allies have been to Fontainebleau at the time or since, except the King of Prussia, who came *incog.* a few days ago. This the guide said he had heard since; he had, indeed, seen three persons walking about, but he had not shewn them the palace nor spoken to them. That it was the King of Prussia was confirmed by a curious little memorandum I found wafered over a high glass on the top of the room in which we dined, and which caught my eye immediately; I shewed it to the people of the house, who said they had not observed it before, but remembered three gentlemen dining there on that day. "*Sa Majesté le Roi de Prusse accompagné du Prince Guillaume son fils a diné en cette appartement avec son premier Chambellan Mr. Baron D'Ambolle, le 8 Juillet, 1814.*" . . . This is the way the King of Prussia always went about in Paris, nobody knew him or saw him. . . .

From Fontainebleau we went to Melun and kept proceeding through Guignes to Meaux. At Guignes we began to hear of the effects of war: 15,000 Russians had been bivouacked above the town for a week. Buonaparte advanced with his troops, on which they retired, but troops do not walk up and down the earth like lambs, but rather like roaring lions, seeking whom they may devour; however, here let us insert once for all the account I have invariably received from sufferers throughout the whole theatre of war—that the conduct of the Russians and French was widely different; the former generally behaving as well as could possibly be expected, and pillaging only from necessity; the latter seem to have made havoc and devastation their delight. They might perhaps act on principle, conceiving that it was better for the treasure and good things of the land to fall into their hands than the enemy's.

At a little shabby inn at Guignes where we breakfasted Buonaparte had slept. The people described him dressed "*comme un perruquier*" in a grey great-coat; he clattered into the house, bustled about, went to his room early, and appeared again at 9 the next morning, but "*J'en reponds bien*" that he was not sleeping all that time. If from Guignes we traversed a country where we heard of war, at Meaux we began to see the effects—before a picturesque gateway we descended to cross the bridge over a stone arch which had been blown up. Shot-holes marked the wall, and within the houses were well bespattered with musket balls. It was the first visible field of battle we had crossed, and to heighten the interest, while we were looking about and asking particulars of the people, up came bands of Russian troops of all descriptions, *Cossacks* included, 1,500 having just entered the town invalided from Paris on their return home.

To be sure, a more filthy set I never beheld. The country is pretty well stocked with *Cossack* horses; they were purchased at a very cheap rate—from 25 shillings to 50 a piece. We have had several of them in our carriage, and find them far more active and rapid than the French, though smaller and more miserable in appearance. My conversation with the Russians (for I made it a point to speak to everybody) was rather laconic, and generally ran thus, " *Vous Russe, moi Inglis*"—the answer, "You *Inglis, moi Russe*, we brothers"—and then I generally got a tap on the shoulder and a broad grin of approbation which terminated the conference.

You know the chief event which occurred at Meaux was the explosion of the powder magazines by the French on their retreat, for which they were most severely, and, I think, unjustly, censured in our despatches—indeed, after seeing and hearing with my own eyes and ears, I feel less than ever inclined to put implicit faith in these public documents. The magazine was in a large house where wines had been stored in the cellar—about half a mile to the west of the town upon a hill. About 3 o'clock in the morning the explosion took place with an "*ébranlement*" which shook the town to its very foundation. In an instant every pane of glass was shattered to atoms, but the cathedral windows, which were composed of small squares in lead, escaped tolerably well, only here and there some patches being forced out. The tiles also partook of the general crash. Many, of course, were broken by the shower of shot, stones, &c., which fell, but the actual concussion destroyed the greater part.

Numbers of houses were remaining in their dilapidated state, and presented a curious scene. We went to see the spot where the house stood, for the house itself, like the temple of Loretto, disappeared altogether. Some others near it were on their last legs—top, beams, doors, all blown away. Even the trees in a garden were in part thrown down, and the larger ones much excoriated. Only one person was killed on the spot, supposed to have been a marauder who was pillaging near the place. Another person about half a mile off, driving away his furniture to a place of safety, was wounded, and died soon afterwards.

From Meaux, I may say almost all the way to Châlons, a distance of above 150 miles, the country bore lamentable marks of the scourge with which it has been afflicted. I will allow you—I would allow myself perhaps, when I look back to the circumstances connected with the war—to wish that all the country, Paris included, had been sacked and pillaged as a just punishment, or rather as the sole mode of convincing these infatuated people that they are the conquered and not the conqueror of the Allies.

Wherever I go, whatever field of battle I see—be it Craon, Laon, Soissons, or elsewhere—victory is never accorded to the Russians. "*Oh non, les Russes étaient toujours vaincus.*" One fellow who had been one of Buonaparte's guides at Craon had the impudence to assure me that the moment he appeared the Allies ran away. "Aye, but," said I, "how came the French to retreat and leave them alone?" "Oh, because just then the *trahison* which had been all arranged ninteen months before began to appear."

Again, at Laon I was assured that the French drove all before them, and gained the heights. "Then," said I, "why did not they stay there?"

"Oh, then reappeared '*la petite trahison*,'" and so they go on, and well do they deserve, and heartily do I wish, to have their pride and impudence lowered. But when I see what war is, when I see the devastation this comet bears in its sweeping tail, its dreadful impartiality involving alike the innocent and the guilty, I should be very sorry if it depended on me to pronounce sentence, or cry "havoc and let loose."

On the 14th we slept at Château Thierry—such an inn, and such insolent pigs of people! Spain was scarcely worse ... added to the filthiness of the place, a diligence happened at the same time to pour forth its contents in the shape of a crew of the most vulgar, dirty French officers I ever saw. It was well we had no communication with them, for by the conversation I overheard in the next room there would have been little mutual satisfaction: "*Oh! voici un regiment* (alluding to us five) *de ces Anglois dans la maison! où vont-ils les Coquins?*" "*Moi je ne sais pas, les vilains!*"

Luckily they all tumbled upstairs to bed very soon, each with a cigar smoking and puffing from beneath the penthouse of their huge *moustachios*, during their ascent, by the by, keeping the Landlady in hot water lest they should break into her best bedroom, of which she carefully kept the key, telling me at the same time she was afraid of their insisting upon having clean sheets. By their appearance, however, I did not conceive her to be in much danger of so unfair a demand. We had the clean sheets, damp enough, but no matter—she remembered them in the Bill most handsomely, and when I remonstrated against some of her charges, for I must observe that we dined in a wretched hole with our postillions, she checked me by saying, "*Comment, Monsieur, c'est trop! Cela ne se peut pas; comme tout ici est si charmant.*" . . .

There was no reply to be made to such an appeal, so I bowed, paid, and retired. Then the bridge was blown up, the streets speckled with bullets. Near the bridge, which had been smartly contested, the houses were actually riddled, yet here the Emperor stood exposed as quiet and unconcerned amidst the balls as if (to use their own expression) he had been "*chez lui.*"

As we advanced the marks of war became stronger and stronger, every village wore a rueful aspect, and every individual told a tale more and more harrowing to the feelings. The Postmasters seem to have been the greatest sufferers, as their situation demanded a large supply of corn, horses and forage, all of which, even to the chickens, were carried off. One poor woman, wife of a postmaster, a very well-behaved, gentlewoman-like sort of person, told me that when 80,000 Russians came to their town she escaped into the woods (you will remember the snow was then deep on the ground and the cold excessive) where for two days she and her family had nothing to eat. The *Cossacks* then found her, but did no harm, only asking for food. I mention her case not as singular, for it was the lot of thousands, but merely to shew what people must expect when Enemies approach.

Soissons was the next place, and compared with the scene of desolation there presented all that we had hitherto seen was trifling.

I little thought last February that in July I should witness such superlatively interesting scenes. With the exception of Elba alone, ours has been the very best tour that could have been taken, and exactly at the right time, for I apprehend that a month ago we could not have passed the country. . . .

Letter 8

Mayence, July 22nd.

Our speed outstrips my pen. I am to retrace our steps to Soissons, whereas here we are upon the banks of the Rhine, which is hurrying majestically by to terminate its course amongst the dykes of Holland.

The nearer we came to Soissons [1] the nearer we perceived we were to the field of some terrible contest, and the suburbs, where the thickest of the fight took place, presented a frightful picture of war, not a house entire. It seems they were unroofed for the convenience of the attacking party, or set on fire, an operation which took up a very short space of time, thanks to the energetic labours of about 50,000 or 60,000 men. Indeed, fire and sword had done their utmost—burnt beams, battered doors, not a vestige of furniture or window frames.

I cannot give you a better idea of the quantity of shot, and consequent number of beings who must have perished, than by assuring you that on one front of a house about the extent of our home, and which was not more favoured than its neighbours, I counted between 200 and 300 bullet marks. I was leaning against a bit of broken wall in a garden, which appeared to be the doorway to a sort of cellar, taking a sketch, when the gardener came up and gave me some particulars of the fight. He pointed to this cave or cellar as the place of shelter in which he and 44 others had been concealed, every moment dreading a discovery which, whether by friend or foe, they looked upon as equally fatal. Fortunately the foe were the discoverers.

Upon the termination of the battle, which had been favourable to the Allies, in came a parcel of Russians upon the trembling peasants. Conceiving it to be a hiding-place for French soldiers, they rushed upon them, but finding none, satisfied themselves with asking what business they had there, and turning them out to find their way through blood and slaughter to some more secure place of shelter. A small mill pool had been so completely choked with dead that they were obliged to let off the water and clean it out. With Sir Charles Stuart's dispatches cut out of the Macclesfield paper we ascended the cathedral, and from thence, as upon a map, traced out the operations of both armies.

Soissons is half surrounded by the Aisne, and stands on a fine plain, upon which the Russians displayed. Buonaparte, in one of his bulletins, abuses a governor who allowed the Allies to take possession of the town when he was in pursuit, thus giving them a passage over the river, adding that had that governor done his duty the Russians might have been cut off. In England this was all voted "leather and *prunello*" and a mere vapouring opinion of the Emperor's, but as far as I could observe he was perfectly right, and had the governor been acting under my orders I question much whether I should not have

1. Soissons had been taken in February by the Russians under Winzengerode.

Laon, July 16

30

30

30

LAON, HOUSES AND TOWER, 1814.

hanged him. In looking about we were shewn a sort of town hall, with windows ornamented with the most beautiful painted glass you ever saw—nice little figures, trophies, landscapes, &c.—but a party of Russians had unfortunately been lodged there, and the glass was almost all smashed. I procured a specimen, but alas! portmanteaus are not the best packing-cases for glass, and in my possession it fared little better than with the *Cossacks*. However, if it is pulverised, I will bring it home as a souvenir. . . .

From Soissons to Laon the country is uninteresting except from the late events. With the exception of the first view of the plain and town of Laon, we passed village after village in the same state of ruin and dilapidation. Chavignon, about four miles from Laon, seemed, however, to have been more particularly the object of vengeance; it was throughout nearly a repetition of the suburbs of Soissons. Laon rises like a sort of Gibraltar from a rich and beautiful plain covered with little woods, vineyards, villages, and cornfields; the summit is crowned with an old castle, the town with its cathedral towers and a parcel of windmills. Buonaparte had been extremely anxious to dislodge the allies; for two days made a furious and almost incessant attack, which was fortunately unsuccessful owing, to speak in French terms, to *la petite trahison*, in plain English, the bravery of the Russians, who not only withstood the repeated shocks, but pursued the enemy all the way to Soissons, every little copse and wood becoming a scene of contest, and the whole plain was strewed with dead.

Since quitting Rouen I do not recollect any town at all to be compared with Laon either in point of scenery without or picturesque beauty within; it is one of the most curious old places I ever saw—round towers, gateways, &c. We took up our quarters at an odd-looking inn, with the nicest people we had met with for some time. They spoke with horror of the miseries they had undergone in this inn, not much larger than Cutts' at Wilmslow; they had daily to feed and accommodate for upwards of two months 150 Russians of all descriptions, and this at a moment when provisions were, of course, extremely dear.

The landlord's daughter with two friends were imprisoned, actually afraid of putting their noses beyond the keyhole; luckily they could make artificial flowers, and two of them drew remarkably well; a favourite dog of the landlord's was their companion. A *cossack* had one day taken him by the tail with the firm intent to put him on the kitchen fire, the bare recollection of which kindled all our host's anger, and he declared that had his poor dog been roasted, though he well knew the consequence, he should have shot the *cossack*; fortunately the dog escaped, but as his Master assured me, never smelt or heard a *cossack's* name mentioned afterwards without popping his tail between his legs and making off with the utmost speed.

Both at this place and at Soissons we met with people with whom Davenport[2] had lodged, and in both places he has established a character which reflects the highest credit on his activity, humanity, and generosity. He was no idle spectator; he went about endeavouring by every means in his power to alleviate the miseries of war by protecting persons and property, and by administering to the wants of the sick and wounded of every description. . . .

On the 16th we quitted Laon for Berry au Bac, passing through Corbeny and close to the heights of Craon, upon which a battle was fought which might be considered as the *coup de grâce* to the French. The Emperor commanded in person; he talked nearly half an hour with the postmaster, whom he summoned before him; if the man spoke truth, his conversation appears to have been rather childish. After asking many questions about the roads and country, he vented a torrent of abuse against the Russians, upon whom he assured the postmaster it was his intention to inflict summary punishment, and, indeed, according to the French translation of the business, he actually did so, though I never could find out that any other of the Imperial troops remained to enjoy the victory on these said heights, saving and except the wounded and killed; one spot was pointed out where in one grave were deposited the remains of 3,000. . . .

In this village of Corbeny there had been sad devastation; but it was at Berry au Bac that we were to see the superlative degree of misery. This unfortunate little town had been captured seven times—four times by the Russians, three times by the French; their bridge, a beautiful work of three arches, only completed in December, was blown up March 19. The houses fared no better; whole streets were annihilated—chiefly for the sake of burning the beams for firewood by the Russians—but the walls were in great measure knocked over by the French, for what other purpose than wanton cruelty I could not learn. Pillage and violence of every description had been excessive. Some of the inhabitants died of pure fright; a gentleman-like-looking man assured me his own father was of the number.

Even here the *Cossacks* were complimented for their compara-

2. E. D. Davenport, Esq., of Capesthorne, Cheshire, 1778-1847.

BERRY AU BAC

tive good behaviour, while the French and the Emperor were justly execrated—"*Plait à Dieu*" said a poor man who stood moaning over the ruins of his cottage, "*Plait à Dieu, qu'il soit mort, et qu'on n'entendît plus de Napoléon*";—the old woman, his wife, told me they only feared the *Cossacks* when they were drunk. An old *cossack* had taken up his quarters with them—"*Ah c'était un bon Viellard; un bon Papa.*"

One day a party of twenty or thirty drunken *cossacks* broke into their yard, and insisted on entering the house; the old woman said she had nothing to fear and would have opened the door, but the *cossack* seized her, saying, "There is but one way to save you," and taking her by the arm, shewed her to his companions as his prize and threatened the man who should touch his property with instant death. They did not dispute the matter with him and retired quietly. When they were out of sight he told her to follow him, and led her three or four miles up the country amongst the woods and left her in a place of safety, taking a kind leave of her and saying, "I have done all I could for you, now farewell"—and she saw no more of him. . . .

We arrived at Rheims on the evening of the 16th, a large, fine, regular, dull-looking city in a dull-looking plain. The cathedral is grand enough, but I felt no wish to remain till the Coronation. Hitherto we had seen inanimate vestiges of war, at Rheims we were to see the living effects. By accident we passed the door of a large church or hall which had been converted into an hospital for 400 Russian prisoners, and on benches near the porch were seated some convalescent patients without arms or legs. We stopped to speak to them as well as we could, and upon saying we were Englanders, one of the Russians with evident rapture and unfeigned delight made signs that there was a British soldier amongst their number, and immediately four or five of them ran to bring him out; and such a poor object did appear dragged along, his legs withered away and emaciated to the last degree.

He had been wounded at St. Jean de Luz in the thigh, and subsequently afflicted with a fever which had thus deprived him of the use of his limbs. We gave something to those who were nearest, and on my asking if any Prussian was there to whom I could speak in French, as I wished to express our desire but inability to relieve all, I was conducted through the wards to a miserable being who was seated with his head suspended in a sling from the top of the bed, both legs dreadfully shattered, and unable to support himself upright through extreme weakness.

During the whole of supper-time the hospital and this Englishman hung heavy on my mind; I felt as if I had not done enough, and that I might be of use in writing to his friends. Accordingly about 10 o'clock I went again to the gate and begged admittance. On mentioning my wish to see the Englishman, I was immediately allowed to enter, and conducted up the wards. On each side were small beds, clean, and in admirable order; there was nothing to interrupt the silence but our own echoing footsteps and the groans of the poor patients all round. The nurses were in the costume of nuns, and from religious principles undertake the care of the sick—there was something very awful in marching up the aisles with these conductors at this time. My poor countryman was asleep when I came to his bedside. I took down memorandums of his case, and promised to write to his friends, and left him money to assist him on his road home, should he (of which I much doubt) ever recover.

I staid with him some time; in the course of the conversation some wounded Prussians came up on their crutches, and it was quite gratifying to see their kindness and goodwill to this poor fellow who, sole of his nation and kindred, was wasting away amongst strangers. They patted him on his head, called him their *cher* and *bon garçon*, lifted him up that he might see and hear better, and he assured me that by them and by all the attendants he was treated with the utmost kindness and attention. Amongst 400 wounded soldiers whose deep groans and ghastly countenances announced that many were almost passing the barrier which separates the mortal from the immortal, with their nurses by my side holding their glimmering tapers, each arrayed in the order of their religion and wearing the cross as the badge of their profession, was a situation in which I had never before been placed.

In offering ministerial advice, and, I trust, affording religious consolation under circumstances so solemn and peculiar, you may conceive that I did speak with all the earnestness and fervour in my power. I told the nurses who and what I was, and so far from entertaining any illiberal ideas as to the propriety of my interfering in what might be called their clerical department, they expressed the greatest pleasure and seemed to rejoice that their patient was visited by one of his own ministers. . . . Thus ended my visit to the hospital at Rheims, which I never can forget.

We travelled the next day to Verdun, bidding *adieu* to the Hibberts at Châlons.

You will ask if we have seen any vestiges of war on the soil such as bodies. We have met with a tolerable quantity of dead horses by the roadside and in ditches, but only one human being, half scratched up by a dog, has appeared; a few rags of uniform dangling upon the skeleton bones called our attention to it.

Verdun is a very comfortable town of considerable extent decently fortified; the number of English there was from 1,000 to 1,100; they were all sent off in a hurry. At 5 in the evening they received the order, at 7 the next morning the greater part were off, and 24 hours afterward the Allies hovered round the town. The French boast, and nobody can contradict the assertion, that the Allies were never able to take their fortresses; certainly not; for they never attempted. Instead of losing their time in besieging, they left a few to mark the place and went on. . . . The English prisoners seem to have enjoyed every comfort they could expect—in fact, their imprisonment was in great measure nominal; with little difficulty they were allowed to go as far as they wished; they were noticed by the inhabitants, and many have married and settled in France. I think the prisoners in England have not been so well off, and complain with reason.

We went to the English church and theatre, and saw as much as we could for half a day. For the honour of my country I lament to say that many here contracted heavy debts which are not likely to be paid. Some instances were mentioned, the truth of which were proved by letters I read from the parties themselves, little creditable to our national character, and by persons, too, who ought to have known better. On the 18th we left Verdun for Metz. I had always winked at and generally encouraged the addition of another passenger behind our cabriolet. The road was quite crowded with straggling soldiers going or returning to their several homes or regiments. We rarely passed in a day less than 200 or 300, and really sometimes in situations so very favourable to robbing that I am surprised we were never attacked, their appearance being generally stamped with a character perfectly congenial to the *banditti* trade—dark, whiskered, sunburnt visages, with ragged uniform and naked feet.

Sometimes we were more fortunate than at others; for instance, stragglers from the Hamburg garrison, whose wan faces bore testimony to the fact they related of having lived for the last 4 or five months on horseflesh; but our charitable assistance was to be this day most abundantly rewarded. We overtook a poor fellow, more wretched than most we had seen, toiling away with his bivouacking cloak tied round him. He, too, solicited, and misunderstanding my answer, said in the most pitiable but submissive tone, "*Alors, Monsieur ne permettra*

VERDUN BRIDGE

pas que je monte?"

"*Tout au contraire,*" said I, "*Montez tout de suite.*" After proceeding a little way I thought I might as well see who we had got behind us, and guess my astonishment when I received the answer. Who do you imagine, of all the people in the world, Buonaparte had raked forth to secure the Imperial Diadem upon his brow, to fight his battles, and deal in blood, but—A monk of La Trappe. For three years had he resided in Silence and solitude in this most severe society when Buonaparte suppressed it, and insisted that all the Noviciate Monks in No. 36 should sally forth and henceforth wield both their swords and their tongues; with lingering steps and slow our poor companion went.

In the Battle of Lutzen[3] he fought and conquered. In Leipsic[4] he fought and fell—the *wind* of a shot tore his eye out and struck him down, and the shot killed his next neighbour upon the spot; he was taken prisoner by the Swedes, and was now returning from Stockholm to his brethren near Fribourg. The simplicity with which he told his tale bore ample testimony to the truth, but in addition he shewed me his Rosary and credentials.

After having talked over the battle I changed the subject, and determined to see if he could wield the sword of controversy as well as of war; and accordingly telling him who I was, asked his opinion of the Protestant Faith and the chief points of difference between us. He hesitated a little at first: "*Attendez, Monsieur, il faut que je pense un peu.*" In about a minute he tapped at the carriage. "*Eh bien, Monsieur, j'ai pensé,*" and then entered upon the subject, which he discussed with much good sense and ability, sometimes in Latin, sometimes in French; and though he supported his argument well and manfully, he displayed a liberality of sentiment and a spirit of true Christianity which quite attached me to him. I asked him his opinion of the *salvability* of protestants and infallibility of Catholics.

"*Ecoutez moi,*" was his reply. "*Je pense que ceux qui savent que la Religion Catholique est la vraie Religion et ne la pratiquent pas, seront damnés, mais pour ceux qui ne pensent pas comme nous. Oh non, Señor, ne le croyez pas. Oh mon Dieu! non, non! jamais, jamais!*"

"Are you *quite sure* a minister ought not to marry? You will recollect St. Peter was a married man."

"*Oh que, oui, c'est vrai, mais le moment qu'il suivit notre Seigneur on n'entend plus de sa femme.*" From this we proceeded to various other

3. May, 1813.
4. October, 1813.

topics, amongst others to the propriety of renouncing a religion in which we conceived there were erroneous opinions.

"*Señor, écoutez,*" said he, "can that religion be good which springs from a bad principle? *Les Anglois étaient une fois des bons Catholiques; le Divorce d'un Roi capricieux fut la cause de leur changement. Ah, cela n'était pas bon.*" ...

When we were on the point of parting he turned to me: "*Señor, j'espère que je ne vous ai pas faché, si je me suis exprimé trop fortement devant vous qui m'avez tant rendu service, il faut me pardonner, je suis pauvre et malheureux, mais je pensois que c'était mon devoir.*"

It was as lucky a meeting for him as for me. I assisted him with money to expedite him homewards, and he entertained and interested me all the way to Metz, when, much against my will, we parted, for had he been going to Pekin I should have accommodated him with a seat. ...

Letter 9

Cologne, July 25th.

If you could see what I now see, or form any ideas adequate to the scenery around me, you would indeed prize a letter which, though commenced at 4 in the morning, cannot be valued at a less price than two or three old castles; but it is not yet the moment to sing the praises of the Rhine. I shall only say that we slept at Bacharach, and that I am now looking at four old castles whenever I raise my eyes from the paper, and that a fine old abbey is only eclipsed by the gable end of a church, equally curious, which is almost thrusting itself into the window as if to look at the strangers.

Little enlivened our day after parting with our monk, unless I should except a good scene from a picture which happened at one of the post houses. No postillions were at home, so the Landlord himself was to drive—an enormous man, rather infirm, with a nightcap on his head, from whence emerged a long pigtail. It was necessary he should be put into his jack boots. By jack boots you are to understand two large things as big as portmanteaus, always reminding me of boots fit for the leg which appears in the castle of Otranto. Accordingly no less than four or five persons actually lifted the landlord into his boots, an operation which, from the weight and infirmities of the one and the extreme clumsiness of the others, took up nearly a quarter of an hour; and, of course, when fairly deposited in them he was unable to move, and further help was necessary to place him on the saddle. ... The first view of Metz, after traversing an uninteresting country, is remarkably fine.

It stands in a fine rich plain, near though beyond the reach of an eminence—for it does not deserve the name of a mountain—the sides of which are covered with woods, villages, and vineyards. There is something very grand in entering a fortified town—the clattering of drawbridges, appearance of moats, guns, sentinels, and all the other *etceteras* of war. Our passports were demanded for the first time. At length we were allowed to pass, and found ourselves in a large, clean town, chiefly remarkable for its cathedral, the painted window of which was equal to any I ever saw. The first thing we invariably do in these towns is to ascend the highest spire, from whence the general plan and position are at once explained. You need not be alarmed. There is no fever at present at Metz, or on the Rhine; but there has been.

From the close of 1813 and until the last two months not less than 69,000 sick or wounded have been in the hospitals of Metz—a large church contained about 3,000 at a time, the remainder were scattered about wherever they could find room, and many breathed their last in the streets. Of course, such a concourse of dead and dying infested the air to a certain degree, and a fever was the result. However, not above 200 or 300 inhabitants suffered. Of the sick troops from 1,200 to 1,500 per day were buried without the town, and quicklime thrown in. We supped with three or four Frenchmen and a Genoese officer, one of Buonaparte's Imperial *Elites* of the Guard. His form and countenance were quite Vandyck—I never looked upon a face so well calculated for a picture; his dark whiskers and black curling hair composed an admirable frame for a couple of the most expressive eyes; his manners were extremely gentleman-like, and you may conceive I did not talk and look at him with any diminution of interest when I found he was on his way home from Moscow. He had gone through the whole of the retreat, had almost reached the boundaries of Poland, when at Calick he was wounded, taken prisoner, and marched back to Moscow.

His description of the miseries of that horrible retreat was petrifying—when a horse fell it was instantly surrounded by famished Frenchmen, who devoured the carcase; not merely those who slept were frozen, but even sentries upon their posts. Yet with all this he imputed no blame to Buonaparte. The Russians, he said, had reason to thank the severity of their climate, without which they must have been completely conquered. I will say this, indeed, that the Russians themselves seem to consider their own efforts as rather secondary to the weather. Besides this officer we had a citizen of Metz, a young officer of the Polytechnique School who had fought at Montmartre, and a youth who was silent; the other three, however, made ample amends, talking incessantly, and all equally vehement in praise of Buonaparte. The officer blessed his stars that he had enough to live upon, and that he was now quitting a service which, having lost its brightest ornament, was no longer interesting or supportable.

The young Polytechnique was equally violent, with less of the gentleman to soften it down. He, too, was disgusted, and had retired for the same reason (these Frenchmen are sad liars after all). Of course, as he had been engaged with his school companions I thought I could not have a better opportunity of ascertaining the number killed at Montmartre, as it was invariably circulated and believed at Paris that this defence was noble to a degree and that the greater part perished by their guns. You will recollect that the Polytechnique cadets I met on the heights of Montmartre said the same, and yet the youth asserted that they had not lost a single individual, that only thirty were wounded, whereas they knocked over the Russians in countless multitudes.[5]

The citizen took the best ground for his Panegyric. He referred us to the roads, the public buildings, the national improvements which France had gained under the dynasty of Napoleon; and when I hinted the intolerable weight of the taxes (being one fifth on all rents and property) he made light of them, assuring me that Frenchmen had quite enough left for the comforts of life. When they all filled their glasses to drink to the health of their hero I turned to the Genoese officer and begged first to drink to the restoration of Genoa to that independence of which Napoleon had in great measure deprived her, adding that her present degradation was a cruel contrast to the dignified station she once held in Europe. His national superseded his Imperial feelings, and he drank my toast with great good humour and satisfaction; nor did he think it necessary in return to press me to drink success to the Emperor, though the citizen on my refusal, half in joke, half in earnest, said he wished I might be ill off for the rest of my journey.

My good fortune has not quitted me, however. The next morning on getting into the diligence we found only one passenger—Major

5. Subsequent accounts which I heard proved that this second account was nearer the truth than the first (E. Stanley).

Kleist, nephew to the celebrated Prussian General and to General Tousein—a Russian equally famous here though not so well known in England. His appearance was much in his favour; he talked a great deal; had commanded a regiment of the Russian Imperial Elites of the Guard (in which he still was) at the Battle of Leipsic and throughout the campaign; been engaged in every action from the Borodino to the capture of Paris; wounded two or three times; fought a French Officer in the Bois de Boulogne, and got his finger cut abominably; visited London and Portsmouth with his Emperor, dined with the Regent, &c.

He told me many interesting anecdotes and particulars, although, from a certain random way of speaking and the loose, unconnected manner in which his words dropped from him, I could not place implicit confidence in what he said, nor vouch for the accuracy of his accounts. He said decidedly that Alexander had visited the Princess of Wales in London incog.; he mentioned an anecdote which I cannot quite believe, because had it occurred in Paris we must have heard of it. One day when Eugène Beauharnais was with Louis XVIII. Marmont came in. Eugène, on seeing him, turned to the King, said, "Sire, here is a Traitor; do not trust in him; he has betrayed one master, he may betray you."

Marmont, of course, challenged him; they fought the next day and Marmont was wounded in the arm. He spoke highly of the King of Prussia as a military, unassuming, amiable, sensible man, and that he *does* visit the tomb of his wife.[6] Alexander, he said, was fond of diplomacy, an amiable man, very brave, but not much of a general. I asked him what he thought of the Duchess of Oldenburg. When I said she had excellent sense and great information, he simply replied, "*Oui, et peut-être un pen trop.*" Of Constantine[7] he spoke with indignation, and his whiskers vibrated as he described his detestable character— debauched, depraved, cruel, dishonest, and a coward. Constantine was abusing a colonel in very gross tones, a short time ago, for misconduct and incompetency in battle. "Indeed!" said the officer; "you must have been misinformed; this cannot arise from your own observation, as I do not recollect having ever seen you near me upon these occasions."

No wonder the Russians were moderate towards the inhabitants during the campaign—their discipline was severe enough. Our friend

6. Queen Louise, *née* Princess of Mecklenburg Strelitz.
7. Grand Duke Constantine, brother of Czar Alexander, 1779-1831.

the major caught seven *cossacks* plundering a cottage; he had them all tied up and knouted them to death by the moderate infliction of 1,000 blows each. In truth he seemed to hold the lives of these gentlemen, including the Calmucs, rather cheap. *"Pour moi,"* said he, *"Je considere un Cossac, un Calmuc et un Moineau à peu près comme la même chose."*

At St. Avold we again fell in with a regiment of Russians, or rather detachments from many regiments. Whoever they were they did not appear to be in high favour with the Major. "Our army," said he, "is divided into three classes—the first we can trust for discipline and ability; the second consists of Cossacks and other irregulars, whose business is reconnoitring, plundering, and running away when they see the Enemy; the men before you compose the third—fellows who know nothing and do nothing, but can stand quietly in the place assigned them and get killed one after another without ever thinking of turning their backs"; and their appearance was very like their character—patient, heavy, slumbering, hard-featured countenance; sitting or standing without any appearance of animation.

At St. Avold we began to lose the French language, and from this my fluency was reduced to signs, or at most to a very laconic speech— *"Ich Englander, Ich woll haben Brod mitt Café,"* &c. At Dendrich, a little village near Forbach, we crossed the new line of demarcation between France and Austria, and found the towns chiefly occupied by Bavarians. Unless I am much mistaken, this country will soon be a bone of contention; the people (as far as I can judge in three days) are dissatisfied, and the leaders of France look with a jealous eye on the encroachment, and an imaginary line of separation will not easily be respected.

Here I saw what is meant by a German forest—as far as the eye could reach all was wood. Austria may, if she pleases, by her new accession of territory become charcoal vendor to the whole world. The road is excellent, carried on in a fine, broad, straight line. Till Buonaparte spoke the word, there was no regular communication between Metz and Mayence, now there is not a more noble road for travelling. We were now in the hock country; in the villages we bought what I should have called wine of the same sort for 6d. a bottle. . . .

On Thursday, the 21st, we entered Mayence, over and through similar drawbridges, bastions, hornworks, counterscarps as at Metz; here we met a curious assemblage. By the first gate were stationed a guard of Prussians with the British lions on their caps, John Bull having supplied some Prussian regiments with uniforms. At the next gate a band of white Austrians, with their caps shaded with boughs of acacia (you will remember that their custom of wearing green boughs in their Hats was interpreted by the French into a premeditated insult). These, with Saxons in red, Bavarians in light blue, and Russians in green, made out the remainder of the motley crew. We found an excellent inn, and dined at a *table d'hôte* with about thirty people.

The striking contrast we already perceived between the French and Austrians was very amusing, the former all bustle and loquacity with dark hair, the latter grave and sedate with light hair; the Inns, accommodation, eating, &c., much cleaner; a band played to us during dinner, and I was pleased to see the Austrian *moustachios* recede with a smile of satisfaction as they listened to the "*Chasse de Henri Quatre.*"

There is little to be seen in the town. I found a most intelligent bookseller, and was tantalised with the number of fine engravings, &c., I might have purchased for a trifle. . . .

I have heard a curious political report repeated here, which is current all over the Continent—that Austria has sold the Netherlands and Brabant to England; the report gains credit probably because the towns in that part of the country are still garrisoned with British troops. Poor England is certainly not much beloved; we are admired, feared, respected, and courted; but these people will have, and perhaps with some reason, that upon all occasions our own Interest is the sole object of consideration; that our Treaties have the good of ourselves and not the peace of Europe at heart; and so far they carry this opinion, that I was very near getting into a quarrel with a fat man in the diligence who spoke it as a common idea that we fought with our money and not with our blood, for that we were too rich to risk our lives, and had there been a bridge that Napoleon would have been in London long ago. I told him he knew nothing at all about the matter (to which, by the bye, he afterwards virtually assented), and as a Frenchman's *choler* does not last long, we were good friends the rest of the journey, and he apologised for his behaviour, saying, it was a failing of his—"*de s'échauffer bientôt.*" Upon one point we agreed, too, in politics, *viz.*, being anti-Napoleonites.

Now for the Rhine. At 10 o'clock on Friday, July 22nd, in a little rotten, picturesque-looking boat and two men (preferring a private conveyance to the public passage boats for the convenience of stopping at pleasure) we left Mayence; the river here is about half a mile across, traversable by a bridge of boats. The Maine falls into it just above the town, and there appears nothing on the Frankfort or Strasburgh side to interest a traveller's eye, the country being flat vine or corn land. The Stream runs with a steady rapidity of about three and a half or four miles an hour, so that in a boat, with the addition of oars, you may proceed at the rate of about six miles an hour. The distance to Cologne is about 120 miles.

On the bank of the river we saw some of those immense floats preparing which are composed of timbers for the Holland markets. We glided with an imperceptible motion down the stream, expecting as we proceeded to behold the magnificent ruins of which we had heard so much. But, alas! village succeeded village, town followed town, and yet not a single turret made its appearance. We sat with our sketch books in battle array, but our pencils were asleep; we began to regret the uninteresting, even country we had passed from Metz to Mayence, and the time which might be called lost in coming so far for so useless a purpose, and to make vow after vow that we would never in future believe the account given by others respecting people and places.

By this time our appetites began to grow keen, luckily, just at the time when our spirits began to flag, and, accordingly, we went on shore at Rudesheim, famous for its excellent hock, and having dispatched a dinner and bottle of hock we ventured forth to explore, and, luckily, fell in with a little Gothic round tower, which, with the dinner, rather raised our spirits and enabled us to proceed four or five miles further to Bingen when we turned a corner...

I verily believe such another corner does not exist in the world. From the corner of Bingen must be dated the beauties of the Rhine, and from the corner of Bingen I commence my next letter; suffice it now to say that the moment we turned the corner we both, with one impulse, called out, "Oh!" and sat in the boat with our hands uplifted in speechless astonishment. ....

Letter 10

Aix la Chapelle, July 27, 1814.

I left you turning the corner of Bingen, now let me describe what there presented itself. On the left a beautiful picturesque town, with tower and picturesque-looking steeples placed each exactly on the spot an artist would have selected, with hills and woods on each side and a bridge running over a small river which emptied itself in the Rhine. Immediately before us, on a small islet, stood the tower of Mausthurm, or the Mouse turret, so called from a tradition that a baron once locked up a number of his *vassals* in a tower and then set fire to it and consumed it and its inhabitants, in consequence of which certain mice haunted him by day and by night to such a degree that he fled his country and built this solitary tower on its island. But all this would not do. The mice pursued him to his island, and the tale ends in his being devoured by them there.

On both sides the river hills covered with vines and woods rose abruptly, and on the right, tottering on a pinnacle that frowns over the flood, stood the castle of Ehrenfels. . . .

It would be quite impossible, and indeed unnecessary (as my sketch-book can best unfold the tale), to describe all we saw. For above 100 miles, with little interruption, the same scenery presented itself, attaining its superlative point of grandeur in the neighbourhood of Lorich and Bacharach. It might be called a perfect Louvre of old castles, each being a *chef d'œuvre* of its species. I could almost doubt the interference of a human hand in their creation. Placed upon elevated and apparently impossible crags, they look more like the fortresses of the giants when they warred against the gods than anything else. But the castles were not the only points of attraction. Every mile presented a village as interesting as the battlements which threatened to crush them to death from above. Each vied with its neighbour in picturesque beauty, and the people as well as the buildings in these remote nooks and corners partook of the wild character of the scenery.

A shower of rain and close of the day induced us to make Bacharach our sleeping-place. The landlord, with his nightcap on his head and pipe in his mouth, expressed no surprise at our appearance. The coffee and the milk and the hock came in due season when he had nodded acquiescence to my demand, and he puffed away with as much indifference as if two strange Englishmen had not been in his house. We found good clean beds, and should have slept very well but for the deep-toned bell of the church within a few yards of us, which tolled the time of night every half-hour, and for a watchman who, by way of murdering the little sleep which had survived the sound of the bell, sounded with all his might a cow-horn, and then, as if perfectly satisfied that he had awaked every soul in the village, bawled out the hour and retired, leaving them just time to fall asleep again before the half-hour called for a repetition of his exertions.

Every evening about dusk, in our course down the river, a curious Phenomenon presented itself which to me, as an entomologist, had peculiar charms. We were surrounded as far as the eye could reach with what appeared to be a fall of snow, but which, in fact, was a cloud of beautiful white *ephemera* just emerged from their chrysalis state to flutter away in their perfection for one or two hours before their death. I mention this circumstance now, whilst it is fresh in my memory, for I really should hesitate in relating it before company for fear of being accused of traveller's stories. I had heard of them before, and was therefore not so much surprised, though the infinite number was truly astonishing.

On Saturday, 23rd, we dined and spent an hour or two in Coblentz, which, situated at the junction of the Moselle with the Rhine, is strongly fortified towards the land. There is little worth notice in the town except a stone fountain erected by Napoleon, from the pipes of which run the united streams of the two rivers. Upon these are carved in large letters the two following inscriptions, the one immediately below the other in characters precisely similar:—

A.N. MDCCCXII.
Mémorable par la Campagne
Contre les Russes
Sous la Préfecture de Jules Dragon.

Vu et approuvé par nous
Commandant Russe de la ville de Coblentz
Le Ier. Janvier 1814.

At Coblentz as well as at Cologne the Rhine is passed by a flying bridge—*i.e.*, a large boat moored to several other smaller ones, whose only use is to keep the large one steady. It swings from bank to bank, according as the mooring line is placed on one side or the other, merely by the action of the current producing a sort of compound motion. Coblentz is completely commanded by the heights of Ehrenbreitstein, a rock as high as Dover, the summit and side covered with the ruins of the fortress which the French blew up. The people in this country are pretty well satisfied with the change of affairs. They led a life of unsupportable tyranny under the rod of Napoleon. The river was crowded with custom house officers.

Not a man could pass without being personally searched for coffee and sugar in every part of his dress. All they lament now is the uncertainty of their fate. Many expressed a hope that the report of their being sold to England might be true. All they want is certainty, and then their commerce will revive. As it is, nothing can be more uninteresting in a commercial point of view than this noble river. We did not see above a dozen merchants' *barks* in the course of 120 miles, and yet they say trade is tenfold greater than when Napoleon governed. Below Coblentz we passed some of the *châteaux* of the German Princes, which are generally large, uncomfortable-looking houses, fitted up, as far as external examination allowed us to judge, without taste. The river became rather dull, but at Andernach, where we slept, it began to improve and to promise better for the next morning, and for some miles we were not disappointed.

We were under the necessity of travelling on the Sunday, which in our situation I certainly held to be no crime. What I could do I did in inducing our Boatmen to attend their Mass. Religion, which appears to be nearly extinct in France, is by no means so in Germany. We find the churches all well attended and plentifully scattered over the whole country. In the course of the morning we passed a large chapel dedicated to St. Apollonius, and noted for its miracles, all of which were recorded by our boatmen with the air of implicit reverence and belief. It happened to be the festival of the Saint, and from a distance of ten or twenty miles even the road was crowded with persons going or coming to their favourite shrine.

You will recollect what Mme. de Staël says of the Germans' taste for religious music. Of this we had a specimen today. As we passed the height upon which the chapel stood a boat containing forty or fifty people put off from the shore and preceded us for several miles chaunting almost the whole way hymns and psalms. In the evening, soon after leaving Bonn, we came up with another containing about 120, who every quarter of an hour delighted us with the same strains. They glided with the stream, and gave us time to row alongside, and we continued in their company the remainder of the day.

Could I have heard and not have seen all would have been perfect, but the charm was almost broken by the heterogeneous mixture of piety and indifference, outward practice and inward negligence. Some were telling their beads and chattering *Pater Nosters*, some were at one moment on their knees, in the next quarrelling with their neighbour; but, after all, the general effect was so solemn and imposing that I was willing to spare my criticisms, and give them credit for perhaps more than they deserved. Conceive such a concourse of persons, on one of the finest evenings imaginable, floating silently with the stream, and then at a signal given bursting forth into songs of praise to God—all perfect in their respective parts, now loud, now low, the softer tones of the women at one time singing alone.

If the value of a Sabbath depends on the religious feelings excited,

I may safely say I have passed few so valuable. They had no priest amongst them, the hymns were the spontaneous flow of the moment. Whenever one began the rest were sure to follow.

When upon the subject of music I must be the advocate of Mme. de Staël. She has been accused of falsehood in stating that in the cottages in Germany a *piano forte* was a necessary piece of furniture. I cannot from my own knowledge go quite so far, but from my short experience of German manners I may safely say there is no nation in which music is so popular. We have heard the notes of pianos and harpsichords issuing from holes and corners where they might least be expected, and as for flutes and other instruments, there is scarcely a village in which, in the course of an hour, you will not hear a dozen.

At Cologne we were lodged at a French inn kept by the landlord and his wife alone—no waiters, no other attendance—and yet the house was spacious, clean, and excellent. I never met with more attention and wish to accommodate, and not only in the house; the exertions of our host were exerted still further in our behalf. He introduced us to a club chiefly composed of French Germans, who were as hospitably inclined as himself.

One gentleman invited us to his house, would give us some excellent hock, introduced us to his family, amongst the rest a little fellow with a sabre by his side, with curling locks and countenance and manner interesting as Owen's. Hearing I was fond of pictures and painted glass, he carried me to a fine old connoisseur, his father-in-law, whose fears and temper were a good deal roused by the "*peste*," as he termed it, of still having half a dozen *cossacks* in his house. However, they were officers, and by his own account did him no harm whatever; but for fear of accidents he had unpanelled his great dining-room. Our friend had a large and excellent house, in a style very unlike and far more magnificent than is usually met with in England. In return for his civility I was delighted to have it in my power to give him a few ounces of our Pecco tea which remained of our original stock.

Travelling in Germany is certainly neither luxurious nor rapid; the custom of hiring a carriage for a certain distance and taking post horses does not extend here, and you are therefore reduced to the following dilemma, either taking a carriage and the same horses for your journey or the "post waggon," or diligence, which is of the two rather more rapid. Of two evils we preferred the last, and at half-past 8 this morning were landed at Aix la Chapelle, having performed the journey of forty-five miles in 12 and a half hours shaken to death, choked with dust, and poisoned with tobacco, for here a great hooked pipe is as necessary an appendage to the mouth as the tongue itself.

Under the circumstances above mentioned, with the thermometer at about 98 into the bargain, you may conceive we were heartily glad to run from the coach office to the baths as instinctively as young ducks. On looking over the list of persons visiting the place, we were delighted to find the names of Lord and Lady Glenbervie[8] and Mr. North.[9] Accordingly, having first ascended the highest steeple in the town, and been more disgusted than in any place I have seen since Spain, with virgins and dolls in beads and muslins, and *pomatum* and relics of saints' beards, and napkins from our Saviour's tomb, and mummeries quite disgraceful, we went to call upon them. . . .

We find this, like every other town and village, swarming with Prussian troops. General Kleist commands, and has no less an army than 170,000. This seems very like a determination of the King of Prussia not to give up the slice he has gained in the grand continental scramble. Every uniform we saw was of British manufacture. An officer told me we had furnished sufficient for 70,000 infantry and 20,000 cavalry.

There is little to be seen in this place. The country about reminded me most of England; for the first time on the continent we saw hedges and trees of tolerable size growing amongst them. We were directed above all other things to pay our respects to the great gambling table. It is, indeed, one of the lions of the town; the room is splendid in size, and everybody goes to see it. It is open three times a day for about two or three hours each time. About fifty or sixty people were winning or losing round a large table at a game apparently something like *vingt un*; not a word was said, but money was shovelled to the right and left very plentifully. . . . I forgot to mention that near Linz on the Rhine we passed a headland fronted and inlaid with as fine a range of Basaltic columns as the Giant's Causeway, some bent, some leaning, some upright. They are plentiful throughout that part of the country, and are remarkably regular; all the stone posts are formed of them, and even here I still see them. . . .

Letter 11

Bruxelles, 29th.

After a night and greater part of two days passed in a species of oven

8. Lady Catherine North, sister of Lady Sheffield, married 1786, Sylvester Douglas, Lord Glenbervie.
9. Hon. F. North, fifth Earl of Guilford.

French Diligence.

called a French *diligence*, with Réaumur thermometer at 23—hotter, you will observe, than is necessary to hatch silkworms, and very nearly sufficient to annihilate your unfortunate brother and husband—did we arrive at Bruxelles. . . . I must give you a few details that you may fully understand the extent of our misery. We arrived at Liège all well, with only two other passengers; conceive our sorrow when on re-entering the diligence after dinner we found besides ourselves and a lady the places occupied by a Dutch officer, who sat gasping without his coat, and so far exhausted by the heat, though he had been ten years in Batavia, that his pipe hung dangling as if he had not breath sufficient to keep its vestal fire alive, and a lady with two children besides living intruders.

A net from the top was filled with bags, baskets, and band-boxes. Our night was sad indeed, and the groans of our fellow-travellers and the ineffectual fluttering of a fan which the officer used proved how little they were satisfied with the order of things. The children were crammed with a succession of French Plums, almonds, garlicked mutton, liqueurs, and hock, all of which ingredients the kind mother endeavoured to cement on their stomachs by basons of milk at sunrise, but no sooner had a few additional jolts brought these *bons-bons* into close contact than the windows were occupied the rest of the journey by the stretched-out heads of the poor children.

The heat has been more excessive for the last four or five days than has been experienced for many years in this country; and, in short, when *I* think it worthwhile to mention heat as the cause of real inconvenience, you may consider it such as would have thrown you into a fever. Enough of our personal sufferings, which you may easily conceive have been few indeed if the above is worth recording. . . .

I left Aix la Chapelle with no great regret. The country round it is pretty, much resembling Kent, but as a town or watering-place it has nothing to recommend but its gambling-table. I expected to have found a museum of human nature and national character.—*tables d'hôtes* crowded with the best bred of all countries, but just the reverse. There were *tables d'hôte's* at the minor inns tolerably frequented, but none at the most fashionable; there the guests lived by themselves. There is no point of rendezvous, no promenade, no assembly room, where the concentrated world may be seen. Like Swedenborgh's theory of living in the midst of invisible spirits, so at Aix la Chapelle (unless time and opportunity may have thrown him into private circles) a traveller may be surrounded by princes and potentates without knowing or benefiting by their illustrious presence; the Glenbervies made the same complaint.

From Aix to Liège we had the company of a very pleasant, well-informed citizen of Liège (indeed, all the military classes in Germany seem well informed), who in pathetic terms lamented his lot. In the cutting up of this grand continental dish Prussia has had Benjamin's mess in this part of the country. We have his troops, with few exceptions, forming a cordon within the Rhine from Saarbruck to Liège, and they are by no means popular. We have clothed them, and all the people feed them, besides having been called upon for contributions. It is flattering to see the high respect shown to the British character, which increases as opportunities occur of observing its effects. If we were like the people of Bruxelles (said our Liègeois) all would be well; we should rejoice in having a garrison. British troops, so far from exacting contributions or demanding free quarters, pay for everything, are beloved by the people, and money circulates, whereas under the Prussian government we pay all, are put to all manner of inconvenience, and receive neither thanks nor satisfaction.

They appear to have been peculiarly unfortunate in all wars. Poor Liège has received a thump from one, a kick from another, and been robbed by a third. The Austrians have burnt their suburbs, the Republicans sold their national and ecclesiastical Estates, and lately they have had the pleasure of being pillaged by French marshals and satisfying the voracious appetite of the Crown Prince, who put them to an expense of 150,000 *francs* in providing his table for seven weeks, and when they hinted that they thought it but fair their Royal visitor should pay for his own dinners, he departed, leaving his bills unpaid. He seems to have been secreting himself here like a cat in a barn watching the motions of the mice, acting solely from interested motives, and ready to pounce upon whatever might be safely turned to his own advantage.

When the French retreated out of Holland the Duke of Tarentum[10] did the poor people at Liège the honour of making their town a point in the line of his march. He stopped one night, and because the inhabitants did not illuminate and express great joy at his illustrious presence he demanded an immediate contribution of 300,000 *francs*, 150,000 of which were paid the next morning. Luckily the Allies appeared towards noon, and I hope his Grace will not get the remainder.

10. Marshal Macdonald, 1765-1840.

In the character of almost all these French military leaders there are such blots and stains that one sickens at the thought of being of the same species. It would be endless to recount the acts of rapacity committed by all these engines of Imperial France; conscious that their throne might one day fall, they lost no time in amassing wealth, and pillage was the watchword from the cathedral to the cottage. Lisle is in the hands of the French, and by their own account the people have suffered every species of misery, yet they are strong for Napoleon, garrison and citizen, and I cannot find that they ever vented their feelings in any other way than in nicknaming their General Maison [11] (a cruel tyrant who destroyed all their suburbs under pretence they might be in the way in case of a siege, which might have been done in a day had the Allies ever thought of such a thing); he is in consequence called General Brise Maison, and then the foolish people laugh and cry, "*Que c'est bon cela,*" think they have done a great feat and submit like lambs.

The country from Liège to Brussels wears the same Anglicised face—hedgerows and trees without any leading features. Bruxelles is a nice town—and really it was a gratification in passing the gate to see a fat John Bull keeping guard with his red coat. The garrison consists of about 3,000, amongst the rest a regiment of Highlanders whose dress is the marvel of the people. A French lady who came with us from Liège had seen some and expressed her utter surprise, and as if she was speaking to one who doubted the fact, she repeated, "*C'est vrai! actuellement rien qu'un petit Jupon—mais comment!*" and then she lifted her eyes and hands and reiterated, "*petit jupon—et comment,*" concluding, as if she almost doubted the evidence of her own senses, "*Je les ai vus moi-même.*"

At Bruxelles at least we expected to see a numerous and genteel *table d'hôte*, and in this hope took up our quarters at a magnificent hotel in the Place Royale—very fine indeed, and very full of English, much too full, for though we saw a few in the passages, or eyed them as they peeped out of their doors, and sat down with about fifteen or twenty at table, "They spoke not, they moved not, they looked not around." By dint of asking for salt and mustard, and giving my next neighbour as much trouble as I could to show I had a tongue which I should be happy to use, we towards the 3rd act of the entertainment began to talk, and ascended gradually from the meats to the wines (here, it is true, there was some prolixity), and then to other subjects pretty well,

---

11. General Maison, 1771-1840, one of the most faithful of Napoleon's generals.

though the burthen of my companion's song was that "the French were all d——d rascals and ought to be well licked." We tried the play; there we found a few English officers and one English lady, few of any other nation, not fifty altogether, in a house dismal and dirty. There is a delightful sort of wood and promenade called the park. . . .

DUTCH SHIPS.

CHAPTER 5

The Low Countries

After Brussels the travellers proceeded to Holland, and saw Antwerp on their way. They had now gone beyond the country which Napoleon's victories had made famous, and the chief military interest of the country through which they passed, just eleven months before Waterloo, was derived from two very melancholy events for an Englishman to record—the Walcheren Expedition and the storming of Bergen op Zoom.

Letter 12

Bergen op Zoom, July 31st.

. . .On leaving Bruxelles the country immediately loses its character, and becomes entirely Dutch, by which we exchange for the better, leaving dirty floors, houses, and coaches for as much cleanliness as soap and water can produce; I only regret from my experience of last night that they should be so much occupied in washing as to forget that drying is also a luxury, but there is no such novelty in this country, and so much to be seen that I have no time to catch cold. Our diligence from Bruxelles held ten people inside and three in front, and we had all ample elbow room; it was large, as you may suppose, as everything else in Holland is from top to bottom. Hats, coats, breeches, pipes, horns, cows—are all gigantic, and so are the dogs, and because the poor things happen to be so, they harness a parcel of them together and breed them up to draw fish-carts.

I yesterday met a man driving four-in-hand; in turning a corner and meeting three of these open-mouthed mastiffs panting and pulling, you might almost fancy it was Cerberus drawing the chariot of Proserpine—but I am wandering from the diligence, which deserves some description. It resembled a little theatre more than a coach, with front boxes, pit, &c., lined with common velvet. We had a curious collection of passengers. Opposite to me sat a prize thoroughbred Dutch woman as clean and tidy as she was ugly and phlegmatic, with a close-plaited cap, unruffled white shawl, and golden cross suspended from her neck. I took a sketch while she stared me in the face unconscious of the honour conferred. By her side sat a French woman crowned with the lofty towers of an Oldenburg bonnet. By my side a spruce, pretty, English woman, whom I somehow or other suspected had been serving with His Britannic Majesty's troops now occupying Belgium. She had on her right hand a huge Brabanter who spoke English, and had acquired, I have no doubt, a few additional pounds of fat by living in London.

Edward sat behind me in a line with the Brabanter's wife and a Dutch peasant. These, with two or three minor characters, completed our cargo, and away we went on the finest road in the world towards Antwerp between a triple row of Abeles and poplars, and skirting the bank of a fine canal upon which floated a fleet of Kuyp's *barks*, and by which grazed Paul Potter's oxen—the whole road was, in truth, a gallery of the Flemish school. By the door of every ale-house a living group from Teniers and Ostade, with here and there bits from Berghem and Hobbema, &c.

Halfway between Bruxelles and Antwerp is Malines. I had began to fear that I had lost my powers of observation, and was, therefore, no longer struck with the external appearance of the towns—in fact, that the novelty was gone, and that my eyes were too much familiarised with such objects to notice them. Happily Malines undeceived me, and convinced me I was still fully alive to whatever had any real peculiarity of character to entitle it to notice. With the exception of the villages on the Rhine, all the towns and houses I had seen lately had little to recommend them, and were like half the people in the world, possessed of no character of their own, their doors and windows like all other doors and windows, but Malines had doors and windows of its own, and seemed to take a pride in exhibiting its own little queer originalities; in every house was a different idea.

The people were of a piece with their dwellings; I could almost fancy I was permitted to inspect the toys of some Brobdignag baby who washed, cleaned, and combed the beings before me every morning and locked them up in their separate boxes every evening. When the nice green doors of the nice painted houses opened, I bethought me of the Dutch *ark* you bought for Owen, and was prepared to make my best bow to Noah and his wife, who I expected to step forth with Ham and Japhet, and all the birds and beasts behind them.

We approached Antwerp as the sun was setting behind its beautiful cathedral and shining upon the pennants of the fleet which Bonaparte has kindly built for the accommodation of the allied powers. The Antwerpers had a well-arranged promenade and tea garden, &c., about a mile from the house, well wooded. These, with all the houses in the suburbs, the French entirely destroyed, leaving not a wreck behind. I must acquit them of wanton cruelty here, however, as in sieges these devastations are necessary. We passed through a complete course of fortifications, and then entered what, from all I can perceive, is the best town I have seen on the continent.

It is a mass of fine streets, fine houses, and fine churches; the tower of the cathedral is quite a *bijou* 620 steps in height! but the ascent was well rewarded; from thence a very respectable tour of about thirty miles in every direction may be accomplished. Walcheren and Lillo (the celebrated fort which prevented our ascending the Scheld) were visible without any difficulty, with Cadsand and all the well-known names of that silly expedition,[1] rendered apparently more silly by seeing how impossible it would have been to have taken Antwerp unless by a regular siege, which might have been of endless duration; we might have bombarded the *basons* in which the men-of-war were deposited, and with about as much success as Sir Thos. Graham,[2] who, after expending a mint of money in bombs and powders, in the course of two days contrived to send about half a dozen shells on board the line of battleships.

I was on board the *Albania*, which had suffered the most. The extent of her damage was two shells which passed through the decks, exploding without much mischief, and a round-shot which shivered a quarter gallery and then fell on the ice—indeed, bombarding vessels, which are objects so comparatively small, is something like attempting to shoot wild ducks on Radnor Mere by firing over their heads with ball in hopes that in its descent it may come in contact with the bird's head.

About a dozen gun brigs were sunk, all of which we saw with their masts above the water; a few houses near the *bason* were shattered, and

---

1. This disastrous expedition to attack Antwerp sailed under the Earl of Chatham, July 20, 1809, and ended in total failure. The troops were withdrawn in December, 1809.
2. Sir Thomas Graham, 1748-1843, afterwards Lord Lynedoch.

about twenty townsmen killed. The country round Antwerp is quite flat, and appears, with the exception of two or three miles round the town, a perfect wood; fancy such a wood with the Scheldt winding through it, several roads radiating in lines straight as arrows, with here and there a steeple breaking the horizontal line, and you may suppose yourself at the top of the cathedral.

The town is large, with the river washing the whole of one side; on the south are the dockyards, with rope walks and everything in fine style; the destruction of these might have been practicable, as they are rather beyond the line of immediate fortifications, but probably they have works for their express protection, and the advantage gained must have been in proportion to the stores and vessels building. I counted sixteen or seventeen ships of the line on the stocks, two or three of 120 guns. In the Scheldt floated thirteen in a state of apparent equipment; in the *basons* nine—all of the line—thus completing a fleet of 39 fine ships, besides a few frigates and gun brigs innumerable—of these only two were Dutch.

It was curious to see such a fleet, and some of them were actually worn out, the utmost extent of whose naval career had been an expedition to Flushing. On descending the spire, we examined the carillons, which are a gamut of chiming bells of all sizes—the total number for them and the church is 82; by a clock work they play every seven minutes, so that the neighbourhood of the cathedral is a scene of perpetual harmony; they can also be played by hand. Most of the churches in this country have them. Our Guards in marching into Alkmaar were surprised and gratified in hearing the church bells strike up "God Save the King."

There are several good churches in the town, and once all were decorated with the works of Rubens, which Napoleon carried off. I should, however, be perfectly satisfied with a selection from the remainder. I saw a Vandyck on the subject of our Saviour recommending the Virgin Mary to St. John, which was incomparable; it quite haunts me at this moment, and, however horrible the effect of the bleeding figure on the cross, I do not wish to lose the impression. The Dutch have carried the art of carving in wood to a most extraordinary pitch of perfection. I am surprised it has not been more spoken of; some of their pulpits are really quite marvellous. Religion increases and, I think, improves.

There is less mummery here than at Aix and some other places I have lately seen, with the exception of a few little saviours in powdered wigs and gilt satin and muslin frocks, and a very singular figure as large as life, supposed to represent the deposition in the holy sepulchre, which was covered by a shroud of worsted gauze, studded over with enormous artificial flowers and tinsel like a lady's court dress.

Wherever we went, at whatever hour, Mass was performing to good congregations. The women here all dress in long black shawls, or, rather, hooded wrappers, which, as they knelt before their confessional boxes, were extremely appropriate and solemn. The English have a church here for the garrison; it is simplicity itself. They have even removed several fine pictures, the rooms having been a sort of museum—the Vandyck I alluded to among the rest. . . .

In our morning's tour we, of course, visited the celebrated *basons* for the men-of-war. "Still harping upon these ships," I can fancy you exclaiming; "when will he have done with them?" You must bear it patiently. It was on account of these said basons, in a great measure, that I came to Antwerp, so you must endure their birth, parentage, and education.

There are two *basons*, one calculated for sixteen, the other for thirty sail of the line; they are simple excavations. Nature never thought of such a thing, and gave no helping hand. It was Napoleon's work from first to last; the labour and expense must have been enormous. They open by dock gates immediately into the Scheldt, from whence each ship can proceed armed and fitted *cap à pie* (if she dares) to fight the English. They were begun and finished in two years, but improvements were suggested, and there is no knowing what more the Emperor intended to do. Precautions had been taken during the bombardment to preserve the ships. For instance, all the decks were propped up by a number of spars, by which means if a bomb fell it did no other mischief than forcing its way through and carrying all before its immediate course, whereas without the props it might have shaken the timbers and weakened the access considerably. In every ship also were two cartloads of earth, to throw over any inflammable substance which might have fallen on board.

From this mole hill of a truth was engendered a mountainous falsehood for home consumption. I read in the English Papers of the time that the French had scuttled their ships to the level of the water, and then covered them over with earth, which was carefully sodded!! Sir Thos. Graham's batteries were very near the *basons*, half-way between the village of Muxham, about two miles from the town and the nearest French battery. From one of the latter we had a perfect conception of the whole business. Without saying a word about my extreme partiality and fears for the safety of No. 1, and probable inconvenience which might ensue from loss of said No. 1 to Nos. 2, 3 and 4, I wonder much whether my curiosity would have allowed me to sleep quite in the back ground. The sight must from this point have been superb, as it was the intention to throw the bombs over this battery so as to make them fall in the *bason* amongst the ducks. The top of the Cathedral would have been perfection, but the Governor most vexatiously kept the keys. . . .

We found abundance of British troops here, remnants of all the regiments who had survived the storming of Bergen op Zoom, about 3,000 or 4,000. . . . They have no reason to complain of their quarters, though it is possible many of them may be of the same opinion with a soldier of the Guards, who, in reply to my question of "How do you like Antwerp?" said with great earnestness, "I like St. James's Park a great deal better." I observed several ladies with their "*petits chapeaux*," and I must do them the justice to say they are much handsomer than the French, German, or Dutch. . . . English curricles, coaches, and chariots are to be seen, and some few English horses, which are certainly better calculated for speed and pleasant driving than the heavy breed of this country. Flanders mares—as Henry VIII. tells us by comparing his queen to one—have never been remarkable for elegance and activity, and I was much entertained in seeing an Englishman break in a couple of these for a tandem.

. . . At our *table d'hôte*, where we met nothing but English merchants, I heard the report of the day that Belgium was to be a sort of independent state, under the Prince of Orange's government, according to its old laws and customs, and that he was to hold a court at Bruxelles. . . . The Prince of Orange is now in fact gone to make his public entrance into Bruxelles. . . .

There is a custom that the key of the town should be presented to the possessor or Governor of the town on a magnificent silver-gilt plate. When the *Cossack* chief came, as usual, the key was offered, which the good, simple man quietly took, put into his pocket, and forgot to return. When I saw the dish, the man told me this anecdote, and lamented woefully the loss of his key, which may possibly in future turn the lock of some dirty cupboard or other on the banks of the Don. It seems these *Cossacks* were immensely rich. Latterly I have been assured they could not fight had they been inclined, from the excessive height of their saddles and weight of their clothes; on the one they could scarcely sit, and with the others they could scarcely walk. They had always three or four coats or coverings, and in the folds of these were unkennelled 1,330 *napoleons* on one of them who happened to die at Bruxelles.

We quitted Antwerp after dinner yesterday for Bergen op Zoom by a new sort of conveyance; by way of variety we *"voitured"* it, *viz.*, hired a carriage, driver, and horses for Breda on our way to Amsterdam. It was a nice sort of gig phaeton, with comfortable seats for four, the driver on the front bench. I fear I must retract what I said in the beginning of this letter, as to the decided change in houses and people here. It was most conspicuous about Malines, but on this road there was nothing remarkable one way or the other.

Our road was, however, Dutch throughout. Upon a sort of raised dyke, between a monotonous avenue of stunted willows, did we jog gently on, with nothing to relieve the eye but here and there a windmill or a farm. On our left we saw, as far as eye could reach, the swamp (or I scarcely know what to call it), which fills up the spaces between the Main and South Beveland, and it almost gave me the Walcheren fever to look at it. The evening gun of Flushing saluted the sun as he sank to rest behind these muddy isles, and we begun to fear, as night drew on, that we should have to take up our night's lodging in the gig, for though he knew that the gates of the fortress were closed at 9, our sturdy Dutchman moved not a peg the faster. However, we escaped the evil, and 10 minutes before 9 we passed the drawbridge of the ditch leading to the Antwerp gate, which had been the grave of the 1st Column of Guards, led by General Cooke, on the 8th March. . . .

Note.

Storming of Bergen op Zoom, March 8, 1814.—Sir Thomas Graham had landed 6,000 men on October 7, 1813, in S. Beveland, in order to combine with the Prussians to drive the French from Holland.

On March 8, 1814, he led 4,000 British troops against Bergen op Zoom. They were formed into four columns, of which two were to attack the fortifications at different points; the third to make a false attack; the fourth to attack the entrance of the harbour, which is fordable at low water.

The first, led by Major-General Cooke, incurred some delay in passing the ditch on the ice, but at length established itself on the rampart.

The right column, under Major-General Skerret and Brigadier-

General Gore, had forced their way into the body of the place, but the fall of General Gore and the dangerous wounds of Skerret caused the column to fall into disorder and suffer great loss in killed, wounded, and prisoners. The centre column was driven back by the heavy fire of the place, but re-formed and marched round to join General Cooke. At daybreak the enemy turned the guns of the place on the unprotected rampart and much loss and confusion ensued. General Cooke, despairing of success, directed the retreat of the Guards, and, finding it impossible to withdraw his weak battalions, he saved the lives of his remaining men by surrender.

The Governor of Bergen op Zoom agreed to a suspension of hostilities for an exchange of prisoners. The killed were computed at 300, prisoners, 1,800.—Ed.

Letter 13

Hague, August 4, 1814.

Sterne pities the man who could go from Dan to Beersheba and say that all was barren, and I must pity the man who travels from Bergen op Zoom to Amsterdam and says that Holland, with all its flatness, is not worth visiting.

Oh Willow, Willow, Willow, here
Each stands bowing to another,
And every Alley finds its brother.

Nature never abhorred a vacuum more than she herself is abhorred by these Dutchmen; here rivers run above their levels and cattle feed where fishes were by nature intended to swim. Hogarth's line of beauty is unknown in Holland. No line can be either beautiful or palatable except that which (defined mathematically) is the shortest that can be drawn between two given points. But I have yet a great deal to say before I come to these roads. I left you at Bergen op Zoom, just arrived. On Sunday morning, after a little enquiry, we were glad to find there was a Protestant French church in the town, and thither we went. I cannot say much for the sermon; it was on 1 Cor. 7. 20, in which a great deal of French display of vehemence and action made up in some degree for a feeble prolixity of words; in one part, however, he made an appeal, which has at least had the effect of eloquence and certainly came home to the heart. He described the miseries the country had so long endured and the happy change which had now taken place.

But while he blest the change he lamented the tears which must be shed from the fatal effects of the war which produced it; and then turning to us, whom he perceived to be Englishmen, he proceeded: "It is for us to lament the sad disaster which this town was doomed to witness in the loss of our friends (our compatriots, I may say), who shed their blood for the restoration of our liberties." After church I went into the vestry to tell him who and what I was. As an English-man he shook me by the hand, and when he understood I was a Prot-estant minister he shook it again. Had he asked me to dine I should have accepted his invitation, but unluckily he lost my company by paying what he conceived to be a greater compliment.

Like an Indian warrior, he offered the calumet of peace and begged I would go home and *smoke* with him. Now, I would have gone through a good deal to have had some conversation with him, but re-ally on one of the hottest days of July, when I was anxious, moreover, to inspect the fortification, smoking would not do, and taking our leave he sent his schoolmaster, an intelligent man who had a brother a captain in one of our assaulting regiments, to be our guide and tell the melancholy tale.... And now let me see if I can make that clear to you which has never been made clear to anybody yet.

"At 10 o'clock," said our guide, "I was at supper with a little party, some French officers being present; about half after 10 some musket shots were heard; this was no uncommon sound and we took no notice; however, it rather increased, and the French sent a sergeant to know the cause, and remained chatting quietly. In about ten minutes in burst the sergeant, '*Vite, vite, à vos portes! Les Anglais sont dans la ville.*'"

I need not add the party broke up in a hurry; our guide sallied forth with the rest, and went on the ramparts for *curiosity*, but whilst he was gratifying this passion, on a pitch dark night, down drops a man who stood near him, and whiz flew some bullets, upon which he took to his heels, got home, and saw no more; indeed, had he been inclined it would have been impossible, for patrols paraded the streets and shot everyone who was not a French soldier. Thus far our schoolmaster was an eyewitness; for the remainder you must trust to my account from as minute an enquiry as I could make upon the spot with Sir T. Graham's dispatches in my hand, which threw very little light upon the subject.

Under the guidance of some inhabitants who had fled to the Eng-lish, soon after 10 o'clock, March 8th, the ground covered with snow and ice, our troops marched in silence to their respective posts. The

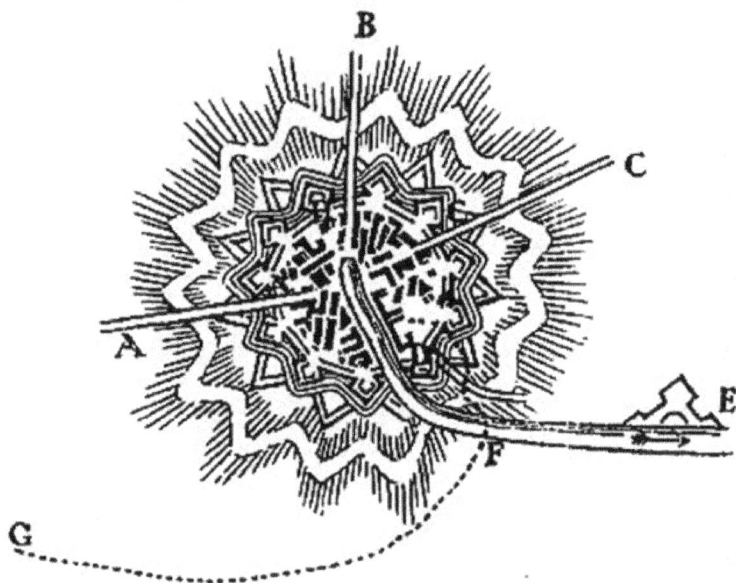

BERGEN OP ZOOM .

A. The Steenbergen Gate.
B. Breda Gate.
C. Antwerp Gate.
D. Water Gate.
E. Picket of veteran French Soldiers.
F. River or creek running into the town.
G. Side from whence the English approach.
H. Bastion near Breda Gate.

Guards, led by General Cooke, were to go round towards B and C, at A a false attack was to be made; another column was to force open the gates at B, and the 4th column, led by Generals Skerret and Gore, proceeded by the dotted line, crossed the river up to their middle, and skirting round between the works were the first to enter the town behind some houses which fronted the quay. Hitherto all went on well, and the object of all the columns was to concentrate at G, but no sooner had the 4th Column gained its point (from what cause nobody knows, for I cannot conceive that the immediate loss of its two generals was the sole cause) than all subordination seems to have been at an end, and the men, instead of going on, occupied themselves with revelling and drinking and getting warm in the houses by the quay, and though many prisoners were taken, they were imprudently left unguarded with arms in their hands, which they very soon turned against their captors with fatal success.

The doors and windows in this part of the town bore evidence of the business which for a short time was carried on. The Guards gained their point, and so did the column at B in part, for the French were killed in great numbers on Bastion H, in fact, eleven bastions were taken, and all before midnight; but from this period till 7 in the morning, when the affair closed, I can give you no clear account. Nobody seemed to know what was doing, all appears to have been con-fusion—not a gun was spiked, none were turned towards the town. In the meantime the French were no inactive observers of what was passing; they came forward most manfully, fighting hand to hand, and though I could not find out that there was the slightest reason for suspecting they were at all prepared beyond what was usual, or aware of the attack, they contrived to be instantly at the right point, and though with barely 3,000 men to defend works, the inner circle of which is at least two miles in circumference, and with 3,900 men at-tacking, they remained master of the field, killing near 400 and taking 1,500 prisoners.

The French general was an elderly man who left all to his *aide de camp*. He was, in fact, the head, and has been rewarded most deservedly in the ribbon of the Legion of Honour. The French, it is supposed, lost 500 or 600 men. The number was certainly great, and they were aware of it, for they buried their dead directly, to prevent the possibility of counting. The Bergen op Zoom people say it is utterly impossible to account for the failure of the assault but on the supposition that the English were led to conclude that the French would make no resistance or that they were badly officered. I should be sorry to believe the latter, and yet I heard from good authority that many of these, instead of encouraging their men at the water post gate, were actually busied in collecting braziers and fires to warm themselves and rest upon their arms.

It may be supposed that wading on such a night upwards of fifty yards in mud and water must have been dreadfully cold, but I can scarcely conceive that upon a service so important cold could have any influence; however, never having led an assault under such circumstances I can be no judge. Were I to give my own opinion, it would be this: That the affair was entrusted to certain general officers who were unfortunately killed in the beginning of the action; that no precautions appear to have been provided against such accidents, and no remedy applied to the confusion thereby created—the columns knew not what to do, each on gaining its point possibly waiting for orders to proceed; that the darkness increased the confusion—in short, that "*the right hand knew not what the left hand did*," and that the French acted with incomparable bravery and skill.

It should be added that most of their troops were conscripts. It is an ugly story altogether, and I shall say no more. A sketch of the works in and near the Antwerp gate will give you some idea of the spot which has proved the grave of so many fine officers and men. At 4 o'clock we quitted the town for Breda—the greatest part of the road inexorably flat and uninteresting; but what is lost in the country is gained in the Towns, villages, and people—they are *sui generis*. For three hours did we toil through a deep sand between parallel lines of willows of the same size, shape, and dimensions; then for three hours more did we proceed at a foot pace over a common; this brought us to Breda just in time for the gates, through which we trotted to the usual rattle of drawbridges, chains, &c.

By the bright light of the moon at night and earliest dawn of the following morning we rambled through the streets. Breda was one of the last towns which got rid of its French garrison without a siege; it departed one night without beat of drum, and the *Cossacks* came in to breakfast, leaving the trembling inhabitants to doubt whether in escaping Scylla they were not approaching Charybdis. However, they behaved tolerably well. "Did they pillage?" said I to a Breda lady who travelled with us in the diligence.

"*Oh non,*" she replied; "*seulement quelque fois ils prenaient des choses sans payer.*"

Thus a *cossack* comes into a shop, makes signs he wants some cloth. The Dutchman, delighted with the idea of accommodating a new purchaser, takes down his best pieces. The *cossack* looks them over, fixes on one, takes it up, pops it under his arm, and walks off, leaving the astonished vendor gaping behind his counter to meditate on the profits of this new verbal ceremony.

After the *Cossacks* came the Prussians, who remained a long time and were little better than the French—they lodged in free quarters, domineered without mercy, and paid for nothing. All the Prussian officers I have seen appeared gentleman-like men, but they are nowhere popular. The English succeeded the Prussians, they were all "*charmants*"; then came the Dutch who were "*comme ça*," but then "*n'importe*" they were their own countrymen. I rather begin to like the Dutch women. The next day in the diligence we had my present informant, a lively, talkative damsel of Breda, a very pretty girl of the same town who talked nothing but Dutch, and an old lady who would have been perfect if everything had been as charming as her dress.

The ladies are elegant and apparently well-behaved, with all the liveliness of the French. We met with no adventures till we came to a river; here a regiment of Dutch cavalry impeded our progress and luckily gave us time to get our breakfast; the next river brought us in contact with a detachment of artillery waggons. Our diligence consisted of a machine with six seats inside, a cabriolet in which sat Edward and myself, on a little seat before us the driver with his legs dangling for want of a footboard. His patience had been rather put to the test by the cavalry, but the artillery quite upset him, and on getting entangled amongst their train, uttering two of the French words he had learnt from his servitude under the Emperor, *viz.*, "*sacré bleu*," he popped his pipe into his pocket, threw the reins into my hands, and jumped down to request the officer's permission to pass.

Under existing circumstances I confess I did not much like the responsibility of the charge committed to me, but fortunately our conductor soon returned with permission to pass. We got out while he drove his four in hand quietly into the boat, every cranny of which was filled up by soldiers and artillery horses, which, as if to shew off the pomp of war, capered and reared before our sedate steeds, who only wanted pipes in their mouths to rival the impenetrable gravity of their driver. It is necessary to cross the Waal before you get to Gorum. When we got to the bank not a boat was to be had. With some difficulty at last our coachman procured a miserable punt with a boy.

Dutch diligence on board a boat.

What with our trunks and passengers we were quite enough for it; indeed, the female part of our crew hesitated for some time; and well they might, for no sooner had we shoved from the shore than a leak was discovered which threatened serious consequences. It gained rapidly; the old lady above mentioned was in despair, and sat with her thumb crammed over the spouting orifice the whole time, while a young man baled with his shoes as fast as possible. This was not all. The stream carried us down, and our driver—no great sailor—caught crabs at every other pull; then we got upon a bank. Really I begun to think it would be quite as well to be safe now, but as for *fear*, it was out of the question, the lamentations of the women, and terrors of the old lady in particular, kept us quite in spirits. The last event was the total overthrow of the driver by a sudden bump against the bank.

Poor fellow! he was not only well drenched, but his head cut by falling against the seat of the boat in his overturn. Though every nerve vibrated with compassion, it was quite impossible to avoid laughing. Luckily a glass of vinegar well rubbed upon the wound soon set him to rights and good humour. Gorum and Naard were the last two towns which the French retained, and poor Gorum suffered sadly. The suburbs, tea gardens, avenues, walks, &c., were all destroyed by the French to prevent the Prussians coming in, and their houses and heads knocked about with shot and shells to drive the French out. Luckily the French listened to the entreaties of the people and capitulated.

I wish they would bombard Knutsford or Macclesfield or some of our towns for an hour or two, just to shew them what war is. Bang, whiz, down comes a shell and away goes a house. War and slavery have quite reconciled the Dutch to the abdication of Napoleon. In answer to the question, "*Êtes vous content de ces changements?*" you meet with no doubtful shrug of the shoulders, no ambiguous "*mais que, oui*"; an instantaneous extra whiff of satisfaction is puffed forth, accompanied with the synonymous terms, "*Napoleon et Diable.*"

On leaving Gorum we acquired an accession of passengers—a protestant clergyman and a fat man, who looked much like a conjurer or alchemist. A protestant clergyman in Holland may be known by his dress—a cocked hat of a peculiar model covers a lank head of unpowdered hair. Nothing white appears throughout but the pipe in his mouth and cravat round his neck, a long black coat down to his ankles, with black worsted stockings and gold-headed cane. I must say they do not look over and above agreeable, and as they hate all innovations few have learnt French, so that I have been foiled in most of my attempts at conversation.

From Gorum to Utrecht the country improves; we had hitherto travelled sometimes on dyke tops, sometimes in dyke bottoms which only required the efforts of a few able-bodied rats to let the water in upon us. It is quite surprising to see on what a precarious tenure Holland is held. Take but a dyke away, overturn one dam, and see what discord follows—and this does sometimes happen. In 1809 the ice broke through near Gorum and carried away countless houses, men, cattle, &c. I have said the country improved, *i.e.*, we got into a land of villas and Trees, some of them beautifully laid out, and all, stable included, bright and clean as possible. Each, too, has its summer house perched by the canal side and (the evening being fine) well filled with parties of ladies and gentlemen. The road for many miles was ornamented with wooden triumphal arches and hung with festoons of flowers, &c., as a compliment to the Emperor Alexander, who passed about a month ago. . . .

. . . We arrived at Amsterdam on Monday night; here, again, all was new. Hitherto we had rode in carriages of various descriptions *with* wheels, but in Amsterdam you have them without wheels, drawn by a fine horse and driven by a man who walks by the side with his long reins. . . .

But what delighted me more than anything else was the prospect of suiting Owen and Mary exactly. What think you of a goat curricle? Goats are regularly trained for draught, and are the prettiest things in the world, trotting in neat harness with two or three children. I shall, if I have time at Rotterdam, see if I can get a pair. Buonaparte was so delighted with them that he ordered four for the King of Rome. Amsterdam is a very large, gloomy town, intersected in all directions by water, monotonous in the extreme. Had I not been convinced by the evidence of my senses in looking down from a house top on several objects I had visited in different parts of the town, I should have suspected that our *Laquais de place* had amused himself by walking up and down the same street where canals with trees on each side do not keep the houses asunder; high buildings and narrow streets of dark, small brown brick constitute the character of the town, and, having seen one, you have seen the whole.

In the course of my walk I heard that two or three Englishmen were settled in the town. I called on one, the Reverend Mr. Lowe, with little of the Englishman left but the language. He had been there thirty years and held a Presbyterian church. I asked him if Napoleon

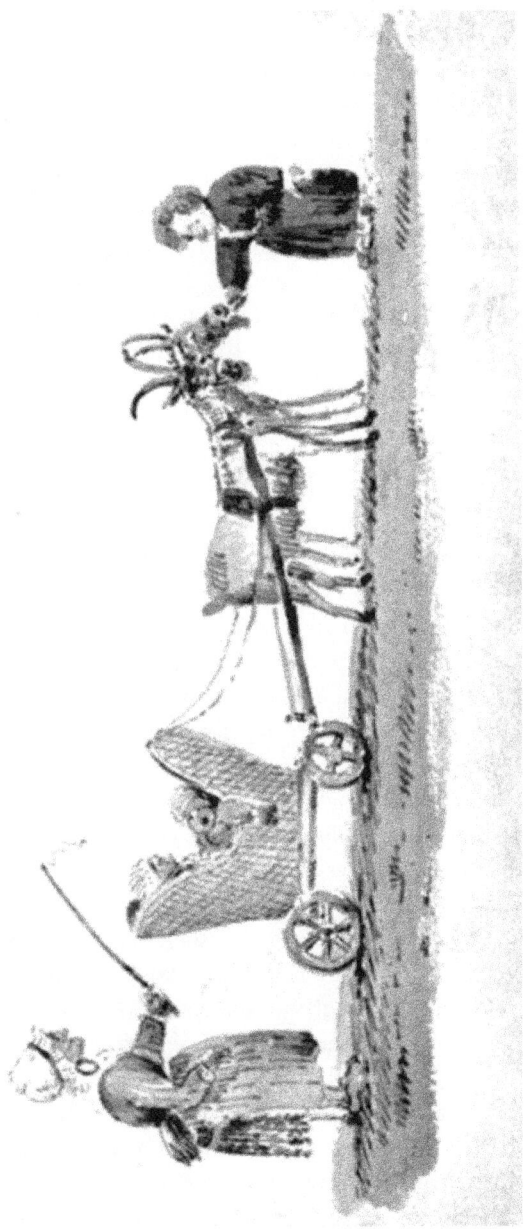

GOAT CARRIAGE FOR THE LITTLE KING OF ROME.

troubled the English settlers during the war. He said that, provided they conformed quickly to the laws and regulations, they experienced no persecution. Upon my asking if it was at all necessary to conceal his extraction, he exclaimed, "What, conceal my extraction, deny my country? Not for all the Emperors in the world. No, I have too much conscience and independence. To be sure, I was obliged by law to pray for the health and prosperity of Buonaparte every Sunday. But what signified that? God Almighty understood very well what I meant, and that I heartily wished his death all the time."

By long residence in Holland, he had adopted a good portion of Dutch impenetrability and slowness. He assured us nothing short of a week could give us the least chance of seeing the curiosities of Amsterdam, and when I told him that we were (according to our common custom of early rising) to be in North Holland by 6 o'clock in the morning, and had seen all by 11 o'clock which occupies a Dutchman's whole day, and gave him a few instances of our mode of operation, he threw himself back, raised his cocked hat to examine us more thoroughly, put his arms *akimbo* and exclaimed, "How do you support human nature. It must expire under such fatigue," and I found it quite impossible to convince him that my health for the last month had been infinitely better than usual.

But, after all, I fear you will find me growing old. I had a compliment paid to my grey hairs, in coming from Utrecht, which must be mentioned. The fat alchemist, above mentioned, squeezed himself into Edward's place in the diligence; on remonstrating to a young Dutch gentleman who spoke French, he replied, "*Que c'était vraiment impoli mais que c'était un viellard à qui on devait céder quelque chose, et je vous assure, Monsieur, comme vous êtes aussi un peu agé si vous aviez pris ma place je vous l'aurais cédé.*"

In Amsterdam there is little to be seen but the Palais, in which there is a splendid collection of Flemish pictures—two or three of the finest of Rembrandt—and without exception the most splendid room I have seen in Europe. It is the great hall of audience; King Louis [3] has fitted up everything in grand style. We went over what the Dutchmen cry up as an object which it would be unpardonable not to see—the Felix *meritus*, a sort of Lecture room with some wretched museums attached. I found nothing to interest me but a capital figure of a Dutchman, who came also to see the wonders. Nothing could exceed his at-

3. Louis Buonaparte, third brother of Napoleon, 1778-1846; King of Holland, 1806-1813.

titudes as he looked with an eye of incredulity whilst they explained a planetarium, examined with an air of conscious safety a snake corked up in a bottle, and ogled with terror a skeleton which grinned at him out of his case. I walked round and tried his perspective in all directions, and rather blushed when, with treacherous condescension, I requested him to use my glass that I might see how he looked peeping through a telescope. This is such a museum as will furnish me with samples of oddities for the rest of my life.

Letter 14

August 6, 1814.

Luckily we have a commodious cabin in the *Trechschuyt*, and no smoke or other intruders, so where I finished my last I will begin another.

As to the country, a peep once an hour will be sufficient; I will look out of the window and give you the result—five plover, a few fat cows, a good many rushes, and a canal bridge. At Amsterdam we dined at a regular Dutch *table d'hôte*; about twenty people, all of them eaters, few talkers; the quantity of vegetables consumed was quite surprising. With the last dish a boy came round with pipes and hot coals, which were soon followed by a tremendous explosion of tobacco from a double line of smokers, and as if the simple operation of puffing in and puffing out was too much for these drowsy operators, many of them leaned back in their chairs, put their hands in their breeches pockets, shut their eyes, and carried on the war with one end of the pipe in their mouths and the other leaning on their plates.

On Wednesday, Aug. 3rd, we crossed the Gulf by sunrise on a little tour into North Holland, to see the Village of Brock and Saardam, where the house in which the Czar Peter worked still exists. We landed at Buiksloot, from whence carriages are hired to different parts of the country. From Breda to Amsterdam they varied the diligences according to the number of travellers; sometimes we had a coach and four, and then a machine and three, and as our number diminished we were forwarded the last stage or two in a vehicle perfectly nondescript with two horses; it was a sort of cart painted white, hung upon springs, with an awning, but it was reserved for this morning to see us in a carriage far beyond anything before seen or heard of.

I am inclined to think it must have been the identical equipage (for it was a little the worse for wear) which the fairy produced from the gourd for the service of Cinderella—a sort of phaeton lined with

TABLE D'HOTE, AMSTERDAM.

red flowered velvet, the whole moulding beautifully carved and gilt, the panels well painted with flowers, birds, urns, &c., the wheels red and gold. It contained two seats for four persons, and a coach box painted, carved, and gilt like the body of the carriage; the whole was in a Lilliput style drawn by two gigantic black horses, whose tails reached above the level of our heads. It was exactly suited to the place where we were going, the village of Brock, which, like our vehicle, was unlike anything I had seen before. I have, in former letters, talked of Dutch cleanliness and neatness, but what is all I have said compared with Brock? Even the people have their jokes upon its superiority in this particular, and assert that the inhabitants actually wash and scrub their wood before they put it on the fire.

Lady Penrhyn's cottages must yield the palm, they are only internally washed and painted, but in Brock, tops and bottoms, Outside and in, bricks and all, are constantly under the discipline of the paint brush, and as if Nature was not sufficiently clean in her operations, the stems of several of their trees were white washed too! In fact, nothing seemed to escape—the milk pails were either burnished brass or painted buckets, and the little straw baskets the women carried in their hands came in for their share of blue, red, or green. They have such a dread of dirt, that entrance is limited to the back door only, the opening of the front door being reserved for grand occasions, such as weddings, funerals, &c. It is not accessible by carriages and horses, on account of several canals which intersect it; these sometimes widen, and in one part the houses stand round a pretty little lake. I can give you no better idea of the scene than a Chinese paper, whose neat summer houses and painted boats are all mixed together. Most houses have each a separate garden, kept in style equally clean. I really believe my own dusty shoes were the most impure things in the whole village.

We returned to Buiksloot and then proceeded to Saardam, on the top of a dyke, which keeps the sea from inundating the vast levels of North Holland. Saardam might be held up as the pattern of neatness had I not visited Brock first; as it is, I can only say that, though four times as large, it seems to be its rival in cleanliness and paint. The number of windmills is quite astonishing; it would require an army of Don Quixotes. I counted myself upwards of 130 in and close to the town; they say there are 1,200. Windmills seem great favourites with the Dutch. In the diligence near Utrecht my neighbour roused me by a sudden exclamation, "*Oh la vue superbe!*"

I looked, and beheld fourteen of them in a dyke! and yesterday,

SAARDAM.

on asking the *Laquais de place* if we should see anything curious at Saardam besides the *Czar's* house, he replied, "*Oh que, oui—beaucoup de Moulins!*" Peter the Great's house is a small wooden cottage close to the town, remarkable for nothing but having been his.

Alexander had put up two little marble tablets over the fireplace, commemorating his visit to the Imperial residence, on which something good and pointed might have been inscribed; as they are, it is merely stated that Alexander placed them on, and that Mrs. Von Tets Von Groudam stood by, delighted to see him so employed. We returned to Amsterdam by 3 o'clock and left it at four for Haarlem. In Protestant countries cathedrals are not always open; we found that at Haarlem open and a numerous congregation listening to a very respectable, venerable-looking preacher, whose voice and manner, style and action approached perfection. His eloquence, however, seemed to be in vain, for I observed many sleepers; and what had an odd effect, though customary in their country, the men with their hats on; they take them off, I believe, during prayers, but put them down during the sermon; we ascended the tower and enjoyed as extensive a view as heart could wish.

The sea of Haarlem is an immense lake separated from the Gulf by a flood gate and narrow dam. The French had a block house and batteries here. In truth, Holland does not require above twenty guns to keep out all the enemies in the world. Different, indeed, are the Dutch from the French in the facility and liberality of access to their curiosities. It required some eloquence and more money to induce the key-keeper to let us go up; and on asking whether the organ was to play, he assured us it was not, but that if we wished it, the performer would sound the notes for sixteen *shillings*; this was a gross imposition to which we were little inclined to submit; but luckily, as we were coming down, we heard it opening its great bellows and re-echoing through the body of the church.

We almost broke our necks in running downstairs, and leaving the Dutch guide to take care of himself, we found our way into the organ loft, to the visible annoyance of the performer, who, seeing we were strangers, thought himself sure of his eight florins, but his duty and the church service compelled him to go on, and he shook his head and growled in vain at our guide, who at this time appeared, intimating that he should take us away, as having no business there, but in vain. I heard the organ, counted the 68 stops, examined at my leisure the stupendous instrument, while he was under the necessity of continuing

PETER THE GREAT'S HOUSE, SAARDAM.

his involuntary voluntary, till my curiosity was satisfied. We took up our residence at an Hotel *in the Wood*, so-called from being the place of promenade and site of the new palace, but *ci-devant* residence of Mrs. Hope, and, in fact, from being also a respectable wood of tolerably sized trees.

By the best chance in the world here, too, we fell in with a *fête* on the river. Some great *burgomaster* had married himself, and all the world of Haarlem came forth in boats, decorated with colours, and bands of music in procession up the river to pass in review before the Princess of Orange, an elderly-looking woman. She sat in the window of a summer house overlooking the river, and the festive procession assembled before her. It was a lovely evening, and nothing could be more gay and animating than the scene.

We this morning at 6 quitted Haarlem in the boat in which I am now writing as comfortably as in my own room, the motion scarcely perceptible, about five miles an hour; by good luck few passengers, and those above looking at a man who is at this incessant Dutch employment of painting. The boat is as clean as a china dish, but possibly it may not have been painted since last week. Edward has just daubed his hand by looking out of the window. I am rather puzzled in getting on here. Very little French is spoken; among the common people none, and we converse by signs.

. . . Their money, too, is puzzling beyond measure. My stock consists of 5 *franc* pieces (French), upon which, exclusive of their not always understanding what they are, there is a discount; this, of course, adds to the confusion, and now I despair of understanding the infinite variety of square, hexagon, round coins of copper and silver and base metal which pass through my hands.

We passed two hours at Leyden as actively employed as a foxhunter. We found a man who spoke French, told him our wishes, gave him a list of what was to be seen in the town, and then desired him to start, following him on the full trot up and down churches, colleges, townhalls, &c. These towns are so much alike, that having seen one the interest is considerably lessened. Leyden, however, has the honour of possessing one of the finest streets in Holland; though capable of accommodating 65,000 souls, there are not more than 20,000, which gives it a melancholy appearance. In one part there is an area of about three or four Cheshire acres planted with trees and divided with walls, which in 1807 was covered, like the rest of the town, with good houses, but it happened that a barge full of gunpowder passing

DUTCH FISHERMEN.

through the canal, blew up, killed 200 people, including a very clever Professor Lugai, and destroyed all the houses. It was a sad catastrophe, to be sure; but now, as it is all over, and all the good people's mourning laid aside, I think the town may be congratulated as a gainer. I could fill up my letter with the anatomical preparations of the celebrated Albinus; but though I am very partial to these sights, I doubt whether you would be amused by a description of dried men, with their hearts, lungs, and brains suspended in different bottles. The town is full of booksellers' shops, in which capital Classics might be procured and divers others old books. The windows were also well filled with new works translated into Dutch; few, I think, original; amongst others, I saw *Ida of Athens!* [1] ...

It is not easy to trace the sieges of Philip 2nd in these towns, as the fortifications are most of them extinct, fortresses of more modern construction being now the keys of the country. Neat villas and gardens by the canal side marked our approach to the seat of government— and a very first-rate town the Hague is, though I cannot conceive how the people escape agues and colds in autumn. Stagnant canals and pools, with all circulation of air checked by rows of trees, cannot be healthy. Unfortunately for us, Lord Clancarty is at Bruxelles with the Prince of Orange. The Hague appears, from what I have seen, to be a better town for permanent residence than Bruxelles or Antwerp. The houses are all good, which implies a superior quality of inhabitants.

In the evening we took a drive to Scheveningen, a fishing village about two or three miles distant, through a delightful avenue. It is one of the fashionable resorts of the town, and is absolute perfection on a hot day, though pregnant with damp and dew in the evening. I told you of dog carts at Bruxelles, but here seems to be the region of despotic sway of the poor beasts. I believe that I am not wrong in stating that nearly all the fish is carried by them from Scheveningen to the Hague; and the weight they draw is surprising. We passed many canine equipages; in one sat a fisherman and his wife drawn by three dogs not much bigger than Pompey—he with his pipe in his mouth, she with an enormous umbrella hat, as grave as Pluto and Proserpine. I saw several nice goat gigs; moreover, I am determined to have one for Owen...

...It is quite extraordinary with what excessive silence and gravity these people carry on their affairs. On returning from Scheveningen at a good round trot, we came in contact with another carriage.

1. A novel by Lady Morgan.

DUTCH CARRIAGE.

Luckily no other accident happened than breaking their traces and grinding their wheels. But though disabled by our driver, not a syllable of complaint or commiseration was uttered by one party or the other. Our driver proceeded, leaving them to take care of themselves. I observed, too, that in manoeuvring the vessel in passing the Gulf yesterday, where some tacks were necessary, all was performed in perfect silence; no halloo-ing—a nod or a puff was alone sufficient. . . .

And so are we coming to the close of our tour—our next stage will be Rotterdam, from whence I shall bear my own dispatches. . . . In the course of my life this last month will bear a conspicuous place from the interesting and delightful scenes it has afforded me. I must confess I left England with some waverings and misgivings; the accounts of others led me to expect that disappointments, difficulties, and great expense would be the inevitable accompaniments of my course. But in no instance have I been disappointed, the difficulties too trifling to deserve the name, the expense nothing compared with the profits derived, and I have seen enough of men and manners, of things animate and inanimate, to make me quite at home in some of the great scenes which have just been performed. . . .

CHAPTER 6

The Waterloo Year

1814-1816.

The two years which intervened between Edward Stanley's second and third visits to France saw the Empire regained and lost by Napoleon, and the French Crown lost and regained by Louis XVIII.

In spite of the rose-coloured description of the comforts and pleasures of his journey with which the correspondence of 1814 closes, neither the rector nor his brother found it possible to travel on the Continent in 1815, which Lady Maria had foretold would be "a much more favourable time."

Such hopes must soon have been dashed by the proceedings of the Congress of Vienna, which, as was said, "*danse mais n'avance pas*," and gloomy forebodings are shewn in two letters from Lord Sheffield to his son-in-law, which were received at Alderley in the autumn of 1814 and the spring of 1815.

The first gives Lord Sheffield's view of the situation, and the second describes Napoleon's own remarks upon it to Lord Sheffield's nephew, Mr. Frederick Douglas.

LORD SHEFFIELD TO SIR JOHN STANLEY.

Sheffield Place, October 30, 1814.

It is time I should provoke some symptom of your existence. I have no letters from Frederick North, [1] but I can acquaint you that we had himself here, which is still better, and that he has been infinitely entertaining, after three or four months' tour on the Continent, from whence he arrived about three weeks ago, and where he proposes to return next week, to pass the winter at Nice with the Glenbervies and Lady Charlotte Lindsay, who are gone there, and, I might add,

1. F. North, afterwards 5th Earl of Guilford.

with many other English families. I begin to think I shall have more acquaintances on the Continent than in England; the migration there is beyond calculation.

The present is an anxious period. Perhaps there isn't in the history of the world a more complete instance of political imbecility than was exhibited in the late peace at Paris, especially in the Allies not availing themselves of the very extraordinary opportunity of securing the tranquillity of Europe for a long time.

I conceive that the most selfish ambition will not have been more hurtful than liberality run mad. And as I am not without apprehension of that fanaticism, which for some time has interfered even with Parliament, and to which there has been too much concession, I incline to the opinion that enthusiasm, as fanaticism, is generally more hurtful to society than scepticism. The fanatic measures are evidently systematic and combined.

Everybody now looks eagerly towards the Congress of Vienna. Talleyrand displays the cloven foot, by refusing to recognise the junction of all the Netherlands. However, the Bourbons, France, and all Europe may be thankful to Talleyrand.

You have often heard of Barthélemy.[2] His brother, a banker at Paris, first moved in the Senate the *déchéance* of the Buonaparte family. Alexander was treating respecting a Regency. The King of Prussia did not attempt to take a lead, but was well disposed to put down the dynasty. The Emperor of Austria had always declared that he would treat with Buonaparte for peace, under restrictions, still co-operating with the Allies.

While matters were in this state Talleyrand took the opportunity of sending a message to the Senate, saying that the family was deposed, and by this step decided the business.

Buonaparte never showed a disposition to treat and to agree to terms; but when he had seemingly agreed, he denied or broke off the next day. The failure or desertion of the marshals completed his overthrow.

It is surprising that he did not attempt to join Augereau's Army, [3] and retire into Italy, where he had forty thousand very good troops. At all events we must rest upon the pinnacle of glory and honour, although we have not secured a permanency of them. By premature concession we have yielded the means of securing the advantages we

2. A member of the Directory.
3. In the neighbourhood of Lyons.

had gained.

The affair at Lake Champlain[4] has been most unlucky, as it will encourage the Yankies, under the present inveterate and execrable Government, to persevere in a ruinous warfare—ruinous to the American States, and galling to this country, liable to be distracted by the efforts of an interested and mischievous faction, which, through lack of firmness in Government, often paralyses measures of the utmost consequence.

I have seen several letters from Madrid, and I have one from thence now before me of the 3rd inst.

A degree of infatuation prevails there which you could hardly conceive possible. The account comes from a very respectable and rational quarter. The most respectable characters are most violently persecuted, and the persons arraigned are confined in dungeons, no communication permitted; and persons convicted of the most atrocious acts are not even in disgrace.

While officers and soldiers invalided by wounds are starving, the King[5] is profuse to persons of no merit, and has given a pension of 1,000 dollars to a young lady who sang before him, &c., &c.

The Spanish funds, which on the King's arrival were at 85, are now at 50. The revenue is less than 20 millions of dollars, the expenditure nearly 50.

Spain is likely to be in as bad a state as ever, excepting the presence of a French army; consequently I conceive their Transatlantic Dominions will be lost to them.

Nothing, however, could be more favourable to our commerce than their emancipation. Such an event, and a proper boundary between us and the American States, would be the most favourable result of the war to this country.

There is an uncommonly good pamphlet published on this subject entitled *A completed View of the points to be discussed in treating with the American States*. I cannot do less than admire it, because it seems taken from my shop, or at least it adopts all the principles, with a considerable amelioration, by taking the Line of Mountains into the Lakes, and all the Lakes within our Boundary.

I am very much entertained with an anecdote in a letter of the 8th inst. now before me, from Switzerland, which states that the Princess of Wales dined a few days before with the Empress Maria Louisa and

---

4. The defeat of the British Flotilla by the Americans in September, 1814.

5. Ferdinand VII., b. 1784, d. 1833.

the Archduchess Constantine, [6] at Berne, and after dinner the Empress and Princess sang duets, and the Archduchess accompanied them. Two years ago nobody would have believed such an event possible.

All this vagabond Royalty is found extremely troublesome by travellers, filling up all the beds, and carrying away all the horses. The above dinner party reminds me of Candide meeting at the *table d'hôte* during the carnival at Venice, with two ex-emperors, and a few ex-kings. The Princess of Wales could not be prevailed on to remain more than ten days at Brunswick. She left Lady Charlotte Lindsay [7] and Serinyer behind her, and proceeded with Lady Elizabeth Forbes to Strasburg, where she found Talma, the renowned actor, and halted there ten days.

LORD SHEFFIELD TO SIR JOHN STANLEY.

Sheffield Place, February 1, 1815.

We are much entertained with Fred Douglas's[8] account of his visit of four days to the Isle of Elba.

On the third evening he had an interview with Buonaparte for an hour and a half—the conversation very curious. He says that Buonaparte is not at all like any of his prints; that he is a stout, thick-set figure, which makes him look short; his features rather coarse and his eyes very light, and particularly dull; but his mouth, when he smiles, is full of a very sweet, good-humoured expression; that at first he strikes you as being a very common-looking man, but upon observing him and conversing with him, you perceive that his countenance is full of deep thought and decision.

He says he received him with much good humour, and talked to him of the English constitution, with which he seemed well acquainted; said that France never could have the same, because it wanted one of the principal parts of it, "*Les Nobles de Campagne.*" He talked also much about our church laws, of which he appeared to be well informed, but said he heard there was much ill humour in Scotland on account of the *union*! Frederick thought he meant Ireland, but found he really did mean Scotland, and had no idea that the union had taken place above a hundred years ago.

He said he did not think the peace would last; that the French

6. Daughter of the Duke of Saxe Coburg; married in 1796 to the Grand Duke Constantine of Russia

7. Daughter of the second Earl of Guilford: married, 1800, John, son of Earl of Balcarres; d. 1849.

8. Son of Lord Glenbervie, and nephew of Lord Sheffield.

nation would never submit long to give up Belgium, and that he would have yielded all except that; that he would have given up the slave trade, as it was a brigandage of very little use to France. He had a most extraordinary idea of how it should be abolished, *viz.*, he said he would allow polygamy among the whites in the West Indies, that they might inter-marry with the blacks, and all become brothers and sisters. He said that he had consulted a bishop upon this, who had objected to it as contrary to the Christian religion.

He seemed very anxious to know concerning the quarrels of the Regent and his wife, upon which subject F., of course, evaded giving him any answers. He said, "*On dit qu'il aime la mère de ce Yarmouth— mais vous Anglais, vous aimez les vielles femmes,*" and he laughed very much. He avoided speaking of Maria Louisa, but spoke of Joséphine with affection, saying, "*Elle étoit une excellente femme.*" He said that the motive of his expedition into Russia was, first, that it was necessary to lead the French Army somewhere, and then that he wished to establish Poland as an independent kingdom; for that he had always loved the Poles, and had many obligations to them. He talked of all his battles as you would of a show, saying "*C'étoit un spectacle magnifique.*"

When Napoleon had fulfilled his own prophecies of the prompt disturbance of the peace of Europe by landing at Cannes, just six days from the date of this last letter, Lord Sheffield writes again, after war had been declared by the Allies.

LORD SHEFFIELD TO SIR JOHN STANLEY.

Sheffield Place, March 24, 1815.

I was greatly oppressed by the first intelligence of Napoleon's invasion. I was afterwards re-elevated, and now I am tumbled down again.

To be sure, there never was such an execrable nation as the French. The much more respectable Hindoos could not more meekly submit to any conqueror that chooses to run through their country at the head of a set of miscreant soldiers. The Pretorian band that in the time of Imperial Rome used to dispose of Empires is perfectly re-established. Immediate notice was sent me from Newhaven of the Duke of Feltre's[9] (minister of war) arrival there, and of poor Louis's

9. General Clarke, 1765-1818. He took part in the negotiations for the Treaty of Campo Formio in 1797. He was made Duc de Feltre for his services against the English at Walcheren. He accepted service under Louis XVIII., and was his Minister of War, 1815-1816.

flight from Paris.

I immediately set out, with the intention of rendering service to the variety of wretches that were pouring in upon our coast, English and French, but on my way called at Stanmer, where I found that this famous minister of war was gone forward to London, that the few shiploads that had got over to Newhaven were disposed of, and an embargo having been laid on the ports of France, of course there was nothing more to be done on our coast.

I returned home at night, and just as I was going out of Stanmer Park I met the Duke of Taranto [10] entering, for whom Lord Chichester had sent his carriage. The Duke of Feltre brought the intelligence that the King was at Abbeville.

I was considerably annoyed, because it seemed like inclining to England, and relinquishing all hopes of France. At Abbeville he certainly might turn off to Lisle, where I hope he is gone, and there, if there be any loyal Frenchmen, they may flock round his standard.

All accounts, and letters, that I have seen from France agree that the country is almost universally against Buonaparte, and it is very clear all the Army is for him, and that all the marshals adhere to Louis, except two. If so, and Napoleon has not the aid of his old generals, he may find it difficult to manage the many Armies that he must keep on foot to repel the attacks that will be made on him from all sides.

I cannot help thinking he is in a bad situation still. When all the Russians, *Cossacks*, Croats, Hungarians, Austrians, and all Germany clatter round him, and our very respectable army from the Netherlands advances, if he has nothing but the army in his favour, he will be considerably bothered, and I hope the sentimental, silly Alexander will never be suffered to interfere with his "*beaux sentimens*" in favour of the monster. If he should be taken and I had the command I should never trouble Alexander nor anybody else, but take him by the Drum head, giving something like the sort of trial the Duc d'Enghien had and immediately extinguish him by exactly the same process, ceremony, &c., as he practised on the Duc d'Enghien.

After all, and the worst of all, is that I apprehend we must pay the piper to enable the above-mentioned hordes to take possession of France, and when there I flatter myself they will live upon the country.

---

10. Marshal Macdonald (made Duc de Tarente after the Battle of Wagram, 1809), b. 1765, d. 1840. He did not join Napoleon during the Hundred Days, but refused employment under the King, and served only as a simple soldier in the National Guard.

If we do not make some effort of the kind, all the money we have shed may be in a great degree thrown away. One great difficulty occurs to me, how will it be possible to dispose of the present French army if it should be conquered, and how raise a French army to maintain Louis's dominion?

If Napoleon should be utterly extinguished, it may be possible to do something, but if he escapes (yet I know not where he can go) a large foreign army must remain a long time in France.

I must conclude by observing what a very extraordinary, strange creature a Frenchman is! Instead of attending the King, or suppressing Navy *depôts* where there are only fifty loyal men, the minister of war flies to England, and, as he represented, in order to join the King in Flanders. At Paris he was certainly nearer Flanders than he was at Dieppe. . . .

Yours ever,
Sheffield.

The Victory of Waterloo ended all fears of a fresh Imperial despotism, and also all the hopes of those who, like Lord Sheffield and the Stanley family, were no great admirers of the Bourbon Dynasty.

Edward Stanley's desire to revisit France was now coupled with a wish to realise the scene of the late campaign, and he planned his journey so as to arrive there on the first anniversary of the battle, June 18, 1816.

He was accompanied by Mrs. Stanley, by his brother-in-law, Edward Leycester Penrhyn,[11] who had travelled with him in 1814, and by their mutual friend, Donald Crawford.

Mrs. Stanley's bright and graphic letters contribute to the story of their adventures, and are added to make it complete.

---

11. Edward Leycester had inherited in December, 1815, the fortune of his cousin, Lady Penrhyn, who directed in her will that he should assume the name of Penrhyn. He married, in 1823, Lady Charlotte Stanley, daughter of the 14th Earl of Derby.

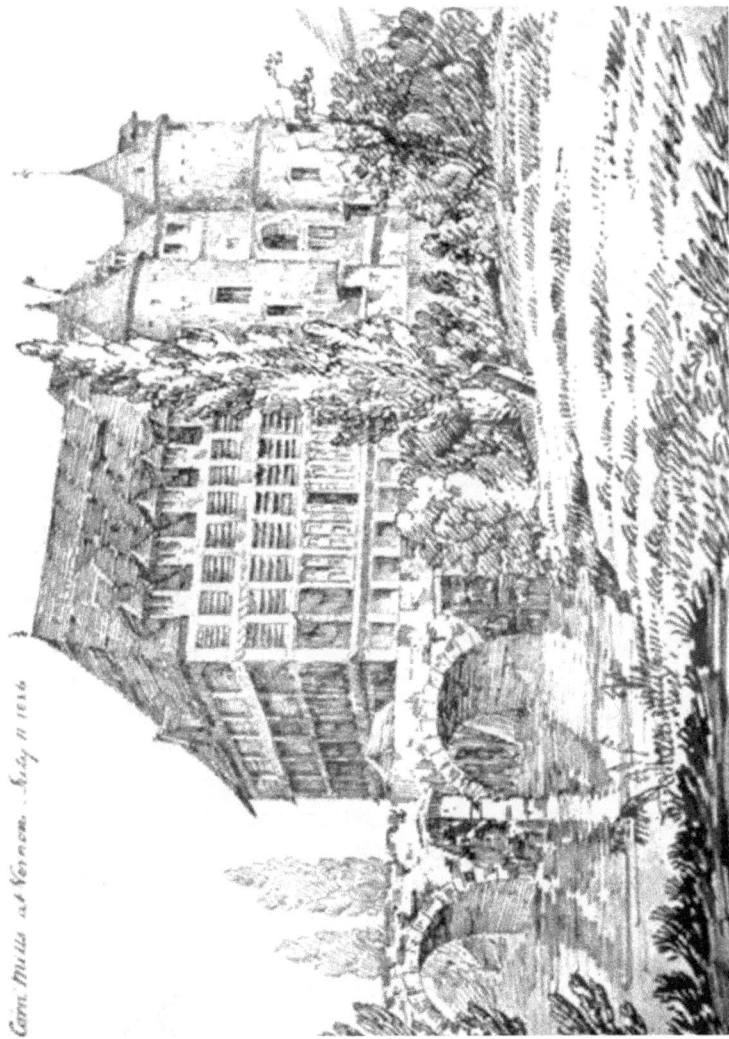

Corn Mills at Vernon. July 11 1816.

CORN MILLS AT VERNON, JULY 11 1816.

CHAPTER 7

After Waterloo

MRS. E. STANLEY TO LADY MARIA STANLEY.

Spring, 1816.

. . .Edward has long talked of a week at Waterloo, and all the rest of the plan came tumbling after one day in talking it over with Edward Leycester, as naturally as possible, and I expect almost as much pleasure in seeing Cambridge and being introduced to the looks and manners at least of E. L.'s friends, and in seeing him there as in anything else. We are to pay a visit to Sir George and Lady Scovell at Cambray, and perhaps to Sheffield Place, on our return. . . .

St. John's College, Cambridge,
June, 1816.

I am very glad to have this opportunity of seeing what a college life is, as well as seeing Cambridge itself and its contents animate and inanimate. I like both very much.

We had a very pleasant journey. The road is not only prettier by Ashbourne and Derby, but better, and, provided your nerves can stand cantering downhill sometimes, you get on faster than on the other road. We drank tea at Nottingham on Monday and went up to the castle.

We arrived at Cambridge by 6 o'clock on Tuesday evening, and found Edward deep in his studies. . . .

This morning we breakfasted with George,[1] and, after seeing libraries and people and buildings till I am tired, here I am, snug and comfortable, in Edward's room. . . .

We are off tomorrow for London.

---

1. Lord Pevensey, son of Earl of Sheffield.

Mrs. E. Stanley to Lady Maria Josepha Stanley.

Blenheim Hotel, London,
Saturday.

As we were coming yesterday Edward looked at the wind and decided that if Donald was not in the Thames then, he would have no chance of being here this week. We had not been here an hour when in he walked in high feather and gave me more reasons than I can remember for leaving his sisters and going with us . . . .

I have been to Waterloo[2] and in Buonaparte's carriage. He has given an alarm by writing to France in spite of all their precautions. . . . We have got our passports and arranged our going. Edward came back from the city with three plans—the steamboat, the packet, or a coach to ourselves to Ramsgate. We debated the three sometime, at last, on the strength of hearing that the steamboat had been out two nights on its passage once, we decided on the coach, and the places were just secured when Mr. Foljambe came in and told us he was going to Ramsgate on Tuesday with some other friends of Edward's, and that it was the nicest vessel ever seen and more punctual than any coach, which made us all very angry as you may guess. . . . We set out tomorrow morning and get into the packet at Ramsgate at 7 in the evening. Let me find a nice folio at Paris, care of Perrigaux, Banquier, and I shall not feel your handwriting the least interesting thing I have to see there.

Rev. E. Stanley to his niece, Louisa Dorothea Stanley.

Ramsgate, June 11th.

Rapidly went the coach from Canterbury, seventeen miles in an hour and a half. Fair blows the wind over the azure blue billow. "You will breakfast at Ostend," says the captain, "tomorrow."

"Oh, that Louisa were here!" says Donald.

"She would die of delight," says uncle, "and does not Uncle say true?"

Conceive the view from Nottingham Castle on the evening we left Alderley . . . a noble precipice, frowning over a magnificent plain, from the terraces of which we beheld immediately at our feet almost numberless—for I counted in a second 54—little pets of gardens, each adorned with a love of a summerhouse to suit; in the corners of the rocks many excavations and caverns fancifully cut out and carved, into which each of the proprietors of the above-mentioned gardens

2. Panorama by Barker, shown in London.

might at leisure retire and become his own hermit. Then how shall I touch upon the delights of Cambridge? How shall I speak of Edward's beauty in his cap, all covered with little bows, and a smart black gown? And how shall I speak of his dinner and his party? Such merriment! Such hospitality! Only think, Louisa, of dining, breakfasting and supping day after day with fourteen or fifteen most accomplished, beautiful, and entertaining young gentlemen! But no more, lest you expire at the thought! As for London, I cannot well tell you what I did or saw, such a confused multiplicity of sights and succession of business have seldom been experienced. At 6 this morning we started in the stage coach, the interior of which we took, excluding all intruders, and from hence at 3 o'clock on a lovely night, with an elegant moon, we embarked for Ostend.

(CONTINUED BY MRS. STANLEY.)

I have persuaded Uncle to carry his letter over the water that you may not have the anxiety of thinking for two days about the passage, which a gentleman who dined with us today informed us was the most precarious, dangerous, and uncertain known.

But I consoled myself with not believing the gentleman in the first place, and by thinking with Aunt Clinton that as Mrs. Carleton was drowned so lately at Ostend, it is not likely another accident should happen at present.

Here we are, waiting for the awful moment of embarkation, which I consider something like having a tooth out, but I live in hopes that, having been up early this morning and had 10 hours' jumbling, I may be sleepy enough to forget that I am on a shelf instead of a bed; so I have been just to admire the moon as we sail out of harbour, and then go to bed and find myself in sight of Ostend when I awake.

(E. STANLEY RESUMES NEXT DAY.)

A dead calm succeeded to a gentle breeze, and on the soft, sleepy billows we have reposed in the Downs, rolling ever since. To comfort us we have a beautiful packet and a limited number of passengers.

The discomfort consists in a rapid diminution of all our provisions and the consequent prospect of no tea, supper, or breakfast, or dinner tomorrow. One sailor said to another as he was skinning some miserable fish, "Aye, aye, they" (meaning the passengers) "will be glad enough of these in a day or two, and I was eleven days becalmed last year."

Kitty, to fill up an hour of vacuity, said she would draw, and to fill up my time this testifies that I have been thinking of you and wishing for your presence, for the novelty alone would keep you in full effervescence and banish all tediosity.

I have, moreover, been playing with a sweet little French dog brought by one of the sailors from Boulogne. The sailors have daily given him two glasses of gin to check his growth, and a marvellous dog of Lilliput he is! Pray, my dear Lou, drink no gin, for you see the consequences.

I had retired to bed, when Edward Leycester called me up to admire a beautiful display of Neptune's fireworks; wherever the surface of the waves was agitated, the circles of silver flashed and the drops were scattered far and wide.

The morning dawned upon us nearly in the same position, not a breath troubled the surface, smooth and still as Radnor Mere on the sweetest evening.

Famine began to stare us in the face; our provisions were nearly exhausted; two or more days might elapse before we reached Ostend.

We breakfasted on tea, fried skate and cheese. Breakfast at an end, it was proposed to board the nearest vessel and beg or borrow a dinner. In the tide course appeared a sail, about five miles distant.

The boat was lowered, volunteers stepped forward—Uncle, Edward, Donald, and a gentleman-like Belgian.

Away we went and by hard rowing we came alongside the strange sail in an hour. Three leaden figures, motionless as the unwieldly bark they manned, gazed curiously upon our approaching boat. Our Belgian friend hailed, but hailed in vain. They looked but spoke not. Again he spoke, and at length a monotonous "*yaw*" proclaimed that they were not dumb.

We went on board and found a perfect Dutch family on their way from Antwerp to Rouen. Out stepped from her cabin the captain's wife in appropriate costume, her close little cap, large gold necklace and ear-rings; and behind the captain's spouse stepped forth two genuine descendants of the nautical couple. Large round heads with large round (what shall I say?) Hottentots to match and keep up the due balance between head and tail.

Having explained our wants to the captain, he produced as the chief restorative an incomparable bottle of Schiedam, *i.e.*, gin. To each he offered a good large glass, and then in answer to our request for beef, four bottles of excellent claret, two square loaves. For this he asked a guinea, upon receiving which his features relaxed and he declared we should have two more bottles of claret. Upon hearing we had a lady in the packet he begged her acceptance of half a neat's tongue, some butter, and a bag of rusks. Loaded with them, we took a joyful leave of these sombre sailors and returned, with the orange cravat of our Belgian friend for a flag, in triumph to the packet.

But a truce to my pen. Ostend is in sight, and now we are all rubbing our hands and congratulating each other that wind and tide are in our favour and that we shall be in in a couple of hours.

Rev. E. Stanley to his niece, Isabella Stanley [3]

Bruges, June 14, 1816.

On our return from the Dutch vessel from which we recruited our exhausted store, we found our poor captain in sad tribulation, his patience exhausted, but his temper luckily preserved. Having paced his deck with a fidgeting velocity a due number of times, peeped through his glass at every distant sail or cloud to observe whether they were in any degree movable, and invoked Boreas in the most pitiable terms such as "Oh Borus! Now do, good Borus just give us a blow," we had the satisfaction at length, the supreme satisfaction, of perceiving a gentle curl upon the water which soon settled into a steady breeze, before which we glided away, delightfully enjoying our dinner upon the deck, during which our party manifested their respective characters in most charming style.

One Farmer Dinmont[4] and Dousterswivel, a Dutchman, were perfect specimens. A merry Belgian equerry to the Prince of Orange, laughed, joked, and amused us with sleight-of-hand tricks. Our Dutch beef, though doubtless salt far beyond due proportion, was relished by all, Dinmont excepted, who pronounced it, together with the dark-coloured bread, unfit for English hogs, and shook his head with a most significant expression of doubt at my assertion that I never enjoyed a better dinner in my life.

At five o'clock the low sand hills appeared to view in little nodules upon the horizon, and the Steeple of Ostend with its lighthouse were visible from deck. At 6 we were close in upon land, and in half an hour were boarded by a Dutch boat, but alas! there was nothing in its appearance to excite curiosity, and with the exception of large earrings you might have fancied yourself in Holyhead Harbour. Four stout, tall fellows, hard and resolute in feature and decided in action, proclaimed

---

3. Married Sir Edward Parry, K.C.B., the Arctic navigator, 1826.
4. Allusions to the characters in *Guy Mannering*.

their near alliance to British Jack Tars. They remained a little while and tried to cheat the passengers as much as possible, to take us on shore, but finding us determined to remain till the captain could get his own boat ready, they shrugged their shoulders, abused us in Dutch, and sailed away. We were too many for one boat, so taking Kitty and the best of our English passengers and honest Farmer Dinmont, with all the luggage, we pushed off from the vessel.

People of all descriptions, pilots, sailors, customs officers, soldiers, waiters soliciting customs for their respective turns. Porters regular and irregular, the latter consisting of a sort of light infantry corps of ragged boys. All these people, I say, were crowded together on a little peninsular jetty against which our boat was shoved, and no sooner had the oars ceased to play and our keel cleared the sand than all these people set up their pipes in every dialect of every tongue, French and English both bad of their sort, Dutch high and low, Flemish and German. All burst upon us at one and the same moment, and the *Cossack* corps of ragged porters all stept forward, arm, leg and foot, to claim the honour of carrying up (most probably of carrying off) our baggage.

By dint of words fair and foul, a shove here and a push there, I contrived to get Kitty under my arm and superintend, though with no small trouble and inconceivable watchfulness, the adjustment of our small portmanteaux, writing case, &c., in a wheelbarrow, which, from its formidable length of handle, bespoke its foreign manufacturer. On we jogged, but jogged not long; for before this accumulating procession could disperse we were arrested by a whiskered soldier, who in unintelligible terms announced himself a searcher of baggage. So to the custom house we went, when each trunk was opened and submitted to a slight inspection; the chief difficulty consisting in putting myself in two places at once—one close to the *depôt* of our goods in the barrow, the other before the officer with the keys.

Kitty was wedged in a corner with a writing case and, I think, Donald's sword. My English companion was equally on the alert, but Farmer Dinmont would have excited all your compassion, or rather admiration; for here amidst the din of tongues and arms, unable to move hand or foot, he stood with a smile of mingled resignation and wonder; at length, the search being concluded to the satisfaction of both parties, we recommenced our course, and in a few minutes Kitty found herself in a new world. Women and children unlike any women and children you ever saw; close caps with butterfly wings for the former, little black skull bonnets for the latter, in shape both alike, much resembling those toys which, if placed on their heads, by their superior specific gravity and extensive sacrifice of their lower projections instantly revolve and settle upon their tails.

"*Voici, Messieurs et Madame, entrons dans la Cour Impériale*," and another moment hoisted us within the covered gateway of this Hotel of Imperial appellation. Our arrangements for sleeping and eating being complete, we sat down on a bench before the door to gaze, but not to be gazed upon, for the good people never cast an eye upon us. On retiring to tea, good Farmer Dinmont's countenance relaxed as he flung himself into a chair; he put his hands upon the table and exclaimed, "Well, well, here I am sitting down for the first time out of Old England!" . . . A cup of tea, or rather a kettle full, for our salt beef had kindled an insatiable thirst, put him in good humour again, and, but for a sort of sigh or a look or a jerk which proved Old England to be uppermost in his thoughts, he appeared quite satisfied.

With some trouble Kitty secured the fly cap chambermaid and had taken possession of her room; having seen her safe, I descended to give orders for a warming-pan, leaving her (after having been two nights in her clothes) to the luxury of an entire change of linen and course of ablutions. On recrossing the court ten minutes afterwards I ran against a waiter running off with a warming-pan, glowing with red-hot embers.

"*Mais donc*" said I, "*Madame* wants a warming-pan. *Allons*, where is the chambermaid to carry it?"

"*Oh, n'importe*," replied this flying Mercury; "*c'est moi qui fera cela pour la dame!*"

Only guess Kitty's escape! Another moment and he would have been in her presence, warming-pan and all. By dint of remonstrating I checked his course and prevailed upon the maid to go herself with vast ill humour, innumerable shrugs, and some few "*Mon Dieu's*" and other suitable expressions. Kitty must herself be the interpreter of her own feelings in these lands of novelty. I am almost glad you were, none of you, here to witness what she will have such pleasure in describing. Our morning passed away in strolling over the town. Kitty and I dined at the *table d'hôte* with about twenty people.

Farmer Dinmont sent for a bottle of the best wine to try it and offered me a glass. I begged to propose a toast, "Prosperity to Old England." His features brightened up, he grasped the bottle, filled a bumper, and replied, "Aye, aye, with all my heart; that toast I would drink in ditch water." We left Ostend at 3 o'clock to take passage in the Bruges canal, and I do assure you we all felt quite sorry to leave our dear, good, honest John Bull.

At Saas we fell in with a specimen of Lord Wellington's operations. There is a formidable battery erected last year by way of guarding Ostend from a "*coup de main*"; it is singular that the English have placed a battery for the defence close to the celebrated sluice gates of this canal, which gates were blown up by Sir Evelyn Coote to prevent the French from inundating the country, when he invaded it some years before.

Behold us seated in a spacious room, for it does not deserve the diminutive name of "cabin," decorated with hangings of green cloth and gold border, on board a most commodious barge. Behold us on a lovely evening starting from the quay with full sail and three horses, a man mounted on one and cracking a great long whip to drive on the other two, which trotted away abreast at the rate of 4½ miles an hour. Behold us seated on this easy chair of Neptune! our ears deafened and our spirits enlivened by a band of music—trumpet, violin, and bass—admirably playing waltzes and other national tunes. When they had amused us on deck they went below to another class of auditors. Our fellow traveller, Mr. Trueman, followed them, and perceiving him to be English they struck up "God save the King."

A Frenchman called out "*Ba, ba*," a very expressive mode of communicating disapprobation, but seeing Trueman was of a different opinion, he ceased from his "*Ba, ba*," and stepping towards him made him a low bow. About 6 o'clock we arrived at Bruges, or rather to the wharf from whence passengers betake themselves and portmanteaux to barrows and sledges. As we approached our band resumed their musical exertions. A crowd assembled to welcome our arrival, Gigs, coaches (such coaches!!), Horsemen (such Horsemen!!), were parading. Such a light with such a rainbow shone upon such an avenue and such picturesque gate!!

Our baggage filled a car drawn by three stout men; and we all followed in the rear. . . . Bruges is a town affording five or six volumes of sketches; towers, roofs, gable ends, bridges—all in succession called for exclusive admiration. It was decided that we should rise at 4, breakfast at 6, and see all that was possible before 9, when we were to continue our route to Ghent. At 3 o'clock I was prepared, but a steady rain forced me reluctantly to bed again, but we did breakfast at 6, and did pick up two or three sketches.

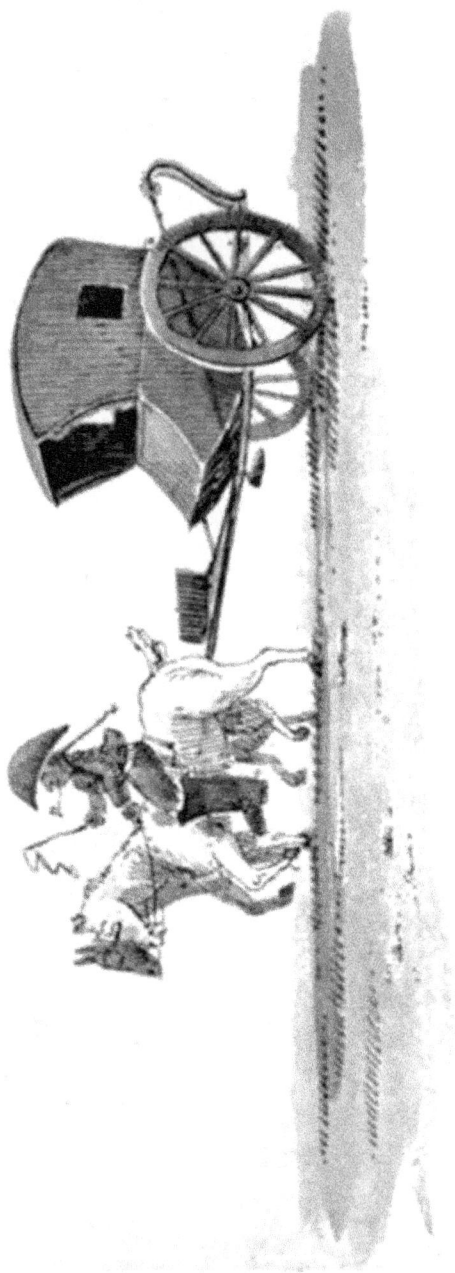

FRENCH CABRIOLET.

Brussels, June 18, 1816.

On the 18th of June, how can I begin with any other subject than Waterloo? . . At 8 this morning we mounted our *cabriolets* for Waterloo. Donald put on his Waterloo medal for the first time, and a French shirt he got in the spoils, and a cravat of an officer who was killed, and I wrapped myself in his Waterloo cloak, and we all felt the additional sensation which the anniversary of the day produced on everybody. It brought the comparison of the past and present day more perfectly home. Donald was ready with his recollections every minute of the day, what had been his occupation or his feeling. The Forest of Soignies is a fine approach to the field of battle—dark, damp, and melancholy. If you had heard nothing about it, you could hardly help feeling, in passing through it, that you would not like to cross it alone. There are no fine trees, but the extent and depth of wood gives it all the effect of a fine one, and an effect particularly suited to the associations connected with it.

The road—a narrow pavement in the middle with black mud on each side—looks as if it had never felt a ray of sun, and from its state today gave me a good idea of what it must have been. Sometimes the road is raised through a deep hollow, and it was not possible to look down without shuddering at the idea of the horses and carriages and men which had been overturned one upon another; in some parts the trees are *à la* Ralph Leycester, and you see the dark black of shade of the distant wood through them; but in other parts it is so choked with brushwood and inequalities of ground, that you could not see two yards before you, and no gorge was ever so good a cover for foxes as this for all evil-disposed persons.

At Waterloo we stopped to see the church, or rather the monuments in it, put up by the different regiments over their fallen officers. They are all badly designed and executed but one Latin one—not half so good as the epitaph on Lord Anglesey's leg which the man had buried with the utmost veneration in his garden and planted a tree over it; and he shows as a relic almost as precious as a Catholic bit of bone or blood, the blood upon a chair in the room when the leg was cut off, which he had promised my lord "*de ne jamais effacer*".

At Mont St. Jean Donald began to know where he was. Here he found the well where he had got some water for his horse; here the green pond he had fixed upon as the last resource for his troop; here the cottage where he had slept on the 17th; here the breach he had made in the hedge for his horses to get into the field to bivouac; here the spot where he had fired the first gun; here the hole in which he sat for the surgeon to dress his wound. He had never been on the field since the day of the battle, and his interest in seeing it again and discovering every spot under its altered circumstances was fully as great as ours.

After all that John Scott[5] or Walter Scott or anybody can describe or even draw, how much more clear and satisfactory is the conception which one single glance over the reality gives you in an instant, than any you can form from the best and most elaborate description that can be given! To see it in perfection would be to have an officer of every regiment to give you an account just of everything he saw and did on the particular spot where he was stationed.

Donald scarcely knew as much as Edward did or as the people about of what passed anywhere but just at his own station. But at every place it was sufficient to ask the inhabitants where they were and what they saw, to obtain interesting information.

Every plan I have seen makes it much too irregular, rough ground; it is all undulating, smooth ups and downs, so gradual that you must look some time before you discover all the irregularity there is. Hougoumont[6] is the only interesting point, and that by having an air of peace and retirement about it most opposite to what took place in it.

It is a respectable, picturesque farmhouse, with pretty trees and sweet fields all around it; the ravages are not repaired and many of the trees cut down. We left our carriages in the road and walked all over the British position, and henceforward I shall have a clearer idea, not only of Waterloo, but of what a military position and military plan is like.

At La Belle Alliance we sat upon a bench where Lord Wellington and Blücher perhaps met, and drank to their healths in Vin de Bordeaux. In spite of the corn, there are still bits of leather caps and bullets and bones scattered about in the fields, and you are pestered with children innumerable with relics of all sorts. We had heard magnificent accounts on our road here of all that was to be done on the field, balls, *fêtes*, sham fights, processions, and I do not know what, but they have all dwindled to a dinner given here to the Belgian soldiers and a Mass

---

5. John Scott, painter, 1774-1828.
6. Hougoumont was occupied by Byng's Brigade, and resisted the repeated attacks of the French throughout the battle.

HOUGOUMONT, JUNE 18TH

to be said for the souls of the dead tomorrow. However, we saw what we wished as we wished, and the impression is perhaps clearer than if it had been disturbed and mixed with other sights.

And now, being near 12, and I having walked about eight miles, and been up since 6, must go to bed, though I feel neither sleepy nor tired.

To Lucy Stanley.

June 24, 1816.

. . .Away with me to Waterloo!

We arrived at Brussels on the evening of the 17th, and at seven o'clock started for the scene of action. From Brussels a paved road, with a carriage track on each side, passes for nine miles to the village of Waterloo.

The forest (of Soignies) is, without exception, one of the most cut-throat-looking spots I ever beheld, . . . and for some days after the battle deserters and stragglers, chiefly Prussians, took up their abode in this appropriate place, and sallying forth, robbed, plundered, and often shot those who were unfortunate enough to travel alone or in small defenceless parties.

After traversing this gloomy avenue for about four miles, the first symptoms of war met our eyes in the shape of a dead horse, whose ribs glared like a *cheval-de-frise* from a tumulus of mud. If the ghosts of the dead haunt these sepulchral groves, we must have passed through an army of spirits, as our driver, who had visited the scene three days after the battle, described the last four miles as a continued pavement of men and horses dying and dead.

At length a dome appears at the termination of the avenue. It is the church of Waterloo. They were preparing for a mass and procession, and the houses were most of them adorned with festoons of flowers or branches of trees. . . .

. . .We turned to the right down the Nivelle road, for it was there Donald's gun was placed, and some labourers who were ploughing on the spot brought us some iron shot and fragments of shell which they had just turned up. The hedges were still tolerably sprinkled with bits of cartridge-paper, and remnants of hats, caps, straps, and shoes were discernible all over the plains. Hougoumont was a heap of ruins, for it had taken fire during the action, and presented a very perfect idea of the fracas which had taken place that day year. How different now! A large flock of sheep, with their shepherd, were browsing at the gate,

Interior of Hougomont June 18. 1816.

INTERIOR OF HOUGOMONT JUNE 18, 1816.

and the larks were singing over its ruins on one of the sweetest days we could have chosen for the visit. As I was taking a sketch in a quiet corner I heard a vociferation so loud, so vehement, and so varied, that I really thought two or three people were quarrelling close to me. In a moment the vociferator (for it was but one) appeared at my elbow with an explosion of French oaths and gesticulations equal to any discharge of grape-shot on the day of attack.

"*Comment, Monsieur,*" said I, "What is the matter?"

"*Oh, les coquins! les sacrés coquins*" and away he went, abusing the *coquins* in so ambiguous a style that I doubted whether his wrath was venting against Napoleon or against his opponents.

"*Oui,*" remarked I, "*ils sont coquins; et Buonaparte, que pensez-vous de lui?*" This was a sort of opening which I trusted would bring him to the point without a previous committal of myself.

It certainly did bring him to the point, for he gave a bounce and a jump and his tongue came out, and his mouth foamed, and his eyes rolled, as with a jerk he ejaculated, "*Napoleon! qu'est-ce que je pense de lui?*"

It was well for poor Napoleon that he was quiet and comfortable in St. Helena, for had he been at Hougoumont, I am perfectly convinced that my communicant would have sent him to moulder with his brethren in arms. Having vented his rage, I asked him if the French had ever got within the walls.

"Yes," he said, "three times; but they were always repulsed"; he assured me he had been there during the attack and that he saw them within; but added, "How they came in at that door" (pointing to the gate by which we were standing and which was drilled with bullets), "or when they came in, or how or where they got out I cannot tell you, for what with the noise, and the fire, and the smoke, I scarcely knew where I was myself."

One of the farm servants begged me to observe the chapel, which he hinted had been indebted to a miracle for its safety, and certainly as a good Catholic he had a fair foundation for his belief, as the flames had merely burnt about a yard of the floor, having been checked, as he conceived, by the presence of the crucifix suspended over the door, which had received no other injury than the loss of part of its feet. He had remained there till morning, when, seeing the French advance and guessing their drift, he contrived to make good his escape, but returned the following day. What he then saw you may guess when I tell you that at the very door I stood upon a mound composed of earth

La Belle Alliance.

and ashes upon which 800 bodies had been burnt. Every tree bore marks of death, and every ditch was one continued grave.

From Hougoumont we walked to La Belle Alliance,[7] crossing the neutral ground between the armies; a few days ago a couple of gold watches had been found, and I daresay many a similar treasure yet remains. At La Belle Alliance, a squalid farm house, we rested to take some refreshment. For a few biscuits and a bottle of common wine the woman asked us five *francs*, which being paid, I followed her into the house. Not perceiving me at the door, she met her husband, and bursting into a loud laugh, with a fly-up of arms and legs (for nothing in this country is done without gesticulation), she exclaimed, "Only think! *ces gens-là m'ont donné cinq francs.*" In this miserable pot-house did the possessor find 280 wounded wretches jammed together and weltering in blood when he returned on Monday morning. If I proceed to more particulars I foresee I should fill folios.

I must carry you at once to La Haye Sainte.[8] It was along a hedge that the severest work took place; it made me shudder to think that upon a space of fifty square yards 4,000 bodies were found dead. The ditches and the field formed one great grave. The earth told in very visible terms what occasioned its elasticity; upon forcing a stick down and turning up a clod, human bodies in an offensive state of decay immediately presented themselves. I found four Belgian peasants commenting upon one figure which was scarcely interred, and on walking under the outer wall of La Haye Sainte a hole was tenanted by myriads of maggots feasting upon a corpse.

Here stands the Wellington tree,[9] peppered with shot and stripped as high as a man can jump of its twigs and leaves, for every passenger jumps up for a relic. We stood upon the road where Buonaparte (defended by high banks) sent on, but *didn't* lead, 6,000 of his old Imperial Guard. They charged along the road up to La Haye Sainte, dwindling as they went by the incessant fire of 80 pieces of artillery, many of them within a few yards, till their number did not exceed 300. Then Napoleon turned round to Bertrand, lifted his hand, cried out, "*C'est tout perdu, c'est tout fini,*" and galloped off with La Corte and

---

7. Napoleon's army, on the day of Waterloo, occupied the plateau of La Belle Alliance.

8. A farm occupied by the King's German Legion under Major Baring; after a gallant resistance captured by the French at 4 o'clock on June 18th.

9. Wellington watched the battle from the shade of an elm-tree, which was afterwards sold to an Englishman, who made the wood into boxes and sold them as memorials.

Bertrand, [10] quitting most probably for ever a field of battle.

A continued sheet of corn or fallowed fields occupy the whole plain. The crops are indifferent and the reason assigned is curious. The whole being trampled down last year, became the food of mice, which in consequence repaired thither from all quarters and increased and multiplied to such a degree that the soil is quite infested by them.

Upon the heights where the British squares received the shock of the French cavalry, we found an English officer's cocked hat, much injured apparently by a cannon shot, with its oilskin rotting away, and showing by its texture, shape, and quality that it had been manufactured by a fashionable hatter, and most probably graced the wearer's head in Bond Street and St. James's. Wherever we went we were surrounded by boys and beggars offering eagles from Frenchmen's helmets, cockades, pistols, swords, cuirasses, and other fragments.

At Brussels they gave the Belgian troops a dinner in a long, shady avenue, which was more than they deserved, and in the evening the town was illuminated. In the newspaper I daresay there will be a splendid account of it, but it was a wretched display in the proportion of one tallow candle to fifty windows stuck up to glimmer and go out without the slightest taste or regularity.

From Brussels we started in a nice open *barouche* landau on Thursday, the 20th. We again crossed the Field of Waterloo and proceeded towards Genappes, a road along which we jogged merrily and peaceably, but which had last year on this same day been one continued scene of carnage and confusion: Prussians cutting off French heads, arms and legs by hundreds; Englishmen in the rear going in chase, cheering the Prussians and urging them in pursuit; the French, exhausted with fatigue and vexation, making off in all directions with the utmost speed.

At Genappes we changed horses in the very courtyard where Napoleon's carriage was taken . . . and were shown the spot where the Brunswick Hussars cut down the French general as a retaliation for the life of the Duke. The postmaster told us what he could, which was not much; the only curious part was that in his narrative he never called the Highland regiments "*Les Écossais*," but "*Les Sans Culottes*." The setting sun found us all covered with dust, rather tired and very hungry, and driving up, with some misgivings from what we had heard and

10. General Bertrand, 1773-1844; fought in Egypt and distinguished himself at Austerlitz and in the campaigns of Wagram and Moscow. He followed Napoleon to Elba and to St. Helena.

WATERLOO.

from what we saw, to our inn at Charleroi. "This is an abominable-looking house," said Donald. "Oh, jump out before we drive in and ask what we can get to eat."

"Well, Donald, what success?" we all cried like young birds upon the return of the old one to the gaping, craving mouths in their nest. "The landlady says she has nothing at all in the house, but if you will come in thinks something may be killed which will suffice for supper." This was a bad prospect. . . .

We three went on in quest of better accommodation, and drove first to enquire at the post house. The first question the postmaster asked was, What could induce us to come to a place from which there was no exit? We told him we wished to go to Maubeuge. Had you seen his shoulders elevate themselves above his ears. "To Maubeuge! Why, it is utterly impossible."

"Well, then," we said, "to Mons."

"*Le chemin est éxecrable.*"

"To Phillippeville."

"*Encore plus mauvais.*"

As a proof of which he told us that a government courier had two days before insisted upon being forwarded thither, that they had sent him off at 2 in the morning, to insure him time before daylight, that at 9 in the morning he was brought back, having proceeded with the utmost difficulty two *leagues*, and then being deposited in a rut by the fracture of his carriage. After a great deal of *pro* and *con* it was agreed that with more horses and great caution and stock of patience the road to Mons should be attempted, and we were directed to "*Le Grand Monarque*," a good name for these times, applicable to Buonaparte or Louis XVIII.

It was worthwhile to lose our way and encounter these unexpected difficulties for the amusement the landlady afforded us. We seemed almost at the end of the world. I am sure we felt so, for the people were so odd. Dinner she promised, and in half an hour proved by a procession of half a dozen capital dishes how wonderfully these people understand the art of cookery, in a place which in England would be considered upon a par with the "Eagle and Child."[11] We asked her about the road in hopes of hearing a more satisfactory account. With a nod and a shrug, and an enlargement of the mouth and projection of lip, she replied, "*Messieurs, je ne voudrais pas être un oiseau de mauvais augure, mais, pour les chemins il faut avouer qu'ils sont effroyables.*"

11. Inn at Alderley.

I will venture to say such a "*oiseau*" as our speaker has never before been seen or heard of by any naturalist or ornithologist. Her figure and cloak were both inimitable. She gave such a tragi-comic account of her sufferings last year, during the time of the retreat, and in 1814 when the Russians were there, that while she laughed with one eye and cried with the other, we were almost inclined to do the same. She had been pillaged by a French officer in a manner which surpassed any idea we could have formed of French oppression and barbarity. At one time the *Cossacks* caught her, and on some dispute about a horse, four of them took her each by an arm and leg and laying her upon her "*ventre*" flat as a pancake, a fifth cracked his knout (whip) most fearfully over her head, and prepared himself to apply the said whip upon our poor landlady.

By good fortune an officer rescued her from their clutches, but she shivered like a jelly when she described her feelings in her awkward position, like a boat upon the shore bottom upwards. Then she told us how her husband died of fright, or something very near it. Her account of him was capital, "*Il étoit*," said she, "*un bon papa du temps passé*," by which perhaps you may imagine she was young and handsome. She was very old and as ugly as Hecate.

Well, my sheet is at an end, and my hand quite knocked up. We did get to Mons, but the roads were "*effroyable*." At one moment (luckily we were not in it) the carriage stuck in the mud and paused. "Shall I go? or shall I not go?" Luckily it preferred the latter, and returned to its position on four wheels instead of two.

E. Stanley.

MRS. E. STANLEY TO LADY MARIA STANLEY.

And now to return to what pleased me first: Bruges—where I first felt myself completely out of England. The buildings were so entirely unlike any I have seen before that I could have fancied myself rather walking amongst pictures than houses. The winding streets are so interesting when you do not know what new sight a new turn will present; especially when, as in this case, the new sight was so satisfactory every time. Ghent is a much finer town but not near so picturesque; but we were fortunate in falling in here with a fine Catholic procession. We went to the top of the cathedral, and as we were coming down the great bell tolled and announced the procession had begun. We almost broke our necks in our hurry to get a peep, and we did arrive at a loop-hole in time to see the whole mass of priests and procession in slow motion down the great aisle and to hear their chant. It was very fine indeed, though to our heretical feelings the interest lies as much in the romantic associations connected with all the Roman Catholic ceremonies as in anything better. It is not in human nature not to feel more devotion in the imposing solemnity of such a church. The "descents from the cross" were just put up, and with the organ playing and mass going on, and the number of female figures with their black scarfs over their heads kneeling on chairs in different parts of the cathedral, we saw them to greater advantage than surrounded by French bonnets and other pictures in the Louvre. They are quite different to any Rubens I ever saw before; the colouring so much deeper and the figures so superior.

But no one should be allowed to enter that cathedral without the black scarf, which makes a young face look pretty and an old one picturesque; and there were several common people gazing at the picture with as much admiration and adoration painted on their faces as there probably was on ours.

At Brussels there were more pictures from the Louvre, but the brutes had packed up the Rubens without any covering or precaution whatever, and there they are with a hole through one, and the other covered with mildew and stains from rain and dirt. From Ghent we travelled in two cabriolets to Brussels, which were not quite so easy or pleasant as the canal boats; but the accommodations as far as Brussels have been really *superbe*. I have longed for the papers or the carpets or the marble tables in every room we have been in; and I have learned to consider dinner as a matter of great curiosity and importance, and I cannot wonder that Englishmen are not proof against the temptations of living well and so cheap.

Brussels is a nice place; there appear to be so many pleasant walks and rides in all directions. The country about is so pretty, and the town (with the exception of the steep hill which you must ascend to get to the best part of it) very cheerful and agreeable looking. . . . Every place swarms with English; we have met four times as many English carriages and travellers as we did on our road to London.

Our weather has been very favourable. We had a cool day for walking about at Waterloo, and the next day a delightful bright sunshine to show off the Palace of Laeken to advantage. It is the place where Bonaparte intended to sleep on the 18th, and he fitted it up. It is three miles from Brussels, commanding a view of the whole country and surrounded by trees and pleasure-grounds in the English style. After

Church of St Nicholas, Ghent. June 16, 1816

CHURCH OF ST. NICHOLAS, GHENT JUNE 16, 1816.

looking at buildings and towns so much, it was an agreeable relief to admire shady walks and fine trees. We went to the theatre, which was execrable, but at Ghent we were very much amused with some incomparable acting.

We left Brussels yesterday morning in a *barouche* and *three*, which is to take us to Paris. It holds us four in the inside and John on the box as nicely as we could wish and is perfectly easy. We suit each other as well in other respects as in the carriage. Donald is an excellent *compagnon de voyage*—full of liveliness, good humour, and curiosity, enjoying everything in the right way. He and Edward Leycester are my *beaux*, while E.S. does the business; which makes it much pleasanter to me than if I had only one gentleman with me. In short, we had not a difficulty till yesterday. We came by Waterloo again and picked up Lacoite to get what we could from him, and then to Charleroi, being told the road by Nivelles was impassable. The road to Charleroi was bad, and we did not arrive till 9, having had no eatable but biscuit and wine. Donald entered the hotel to enquire what we could have for dinner, and returned with the melancholy report that the woman had literally nothing, and did not know where any were to be procured, but that she would kill a hen and dress it if we liked!

We sent Donald and Edward, as a forlorn hope, to see if there was another inn, and after a long search they found one, whereupon the postillion found out that he had no drag-chain and could not properly descend the *montagne*. However, after some arguments, and my descent from the carriage, and Donald and John walking on each side the wheels with large stones ready to place before them in case they were disposed to run too fast, we arrived at the Inn at the foot of the Hill, from which issued an old woman who might have sat for Gil Blas' or Caleb Williams' old woman. When she heard where we were going, she shook her head and said she did not like to be *un oiseau de mauvais augure* but that the only road we could go was very nearly impassable. The people and the children in the street crowded round the carriage as if they had never seen one before, and, in short, we found that we had got into a *cul-de-sac*.

However, our adventures for the night finished by the old woman giving us so good a dinner and so many good stories of herself and the Cossacks, that we did not regret having been round, especially now when we are safely landed at Valenciennes without either carriage or bones broke—over certainly the very worst road I ever saw.

We shall be at Paris on Monday or Tuesday, I think. *Adieu.*

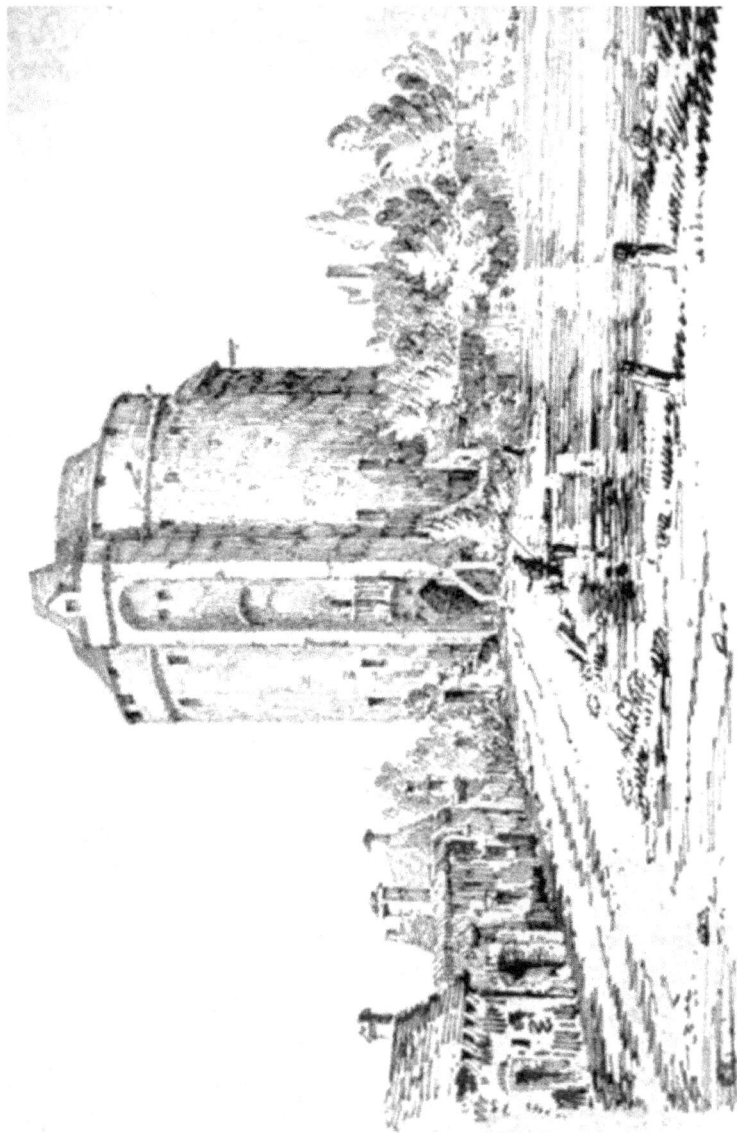

PORTE DE HALLE, BRUSSELS, LEADING TO WATERLOO.

Rev. E. Stanley to his niece, Rianette Stanley.

. . .Before leaving Brussels forever, it is impossible not to speak about the dogs. What would you say, what would you think, and how would you laugh at some of these wondrous equipages. You meet them in all directions carrying every species of load. They were only surpassed by one vehicle we met on the road drawn by nine, and as luck would have it, just as we passed, the five leaders fell to fighting and ran their carriage over some high stones. Then the women within began to scream and the driver without began to whip, which caused an inevitable scene of bustle and perplexity. . . .

At Quiverain we passed the line of separation between France and Belgium and were subjected to a close inspection by the Custom House officers, during which some bandana handkerchiefs of Edward's were for a time in great jeopardy, but they were finally returned and "*nous voilà*" in "*la belle France.*" The change was perceptible in more ways than one. Before we had travelled a mile we beheld a proof of this subjugated state in the person of a *cossack* "*en plein costume,*" with two narrow, horizontal eyes placed at the top of his forehead, bespeaking his Tartar origin. Upon a log of timber twenty more were sitting smoking. The Russian headquarters are at Maubeuge, but the *Cossacks* are scattered all over the frontier villages and are seen everywhere. We fell in with at least a hundred. They are very quiet and much liked by the people. The Duke of Wellington, when returning to Valenciennes a few days ago from Maubeuge, was escorted by a party of these gipsy guards.

On approaching Valenciennes other tokens of conquest appeared. A clean-looking inn, with a smart garden in Islington style, presented itself, bearing a sign with an English name containing the additional intelligence that London porter and rum, gin, and brandy were all there, and to be had.

Over many a window we saw a good John Bull board with "Spirituous Liquors Sold Here" inscribed thereon in broad British characters, unlike the "Spiritual Lickers" in the miserable letters upon the signboards at Ostend. As to Valenciennes, nothing was French but the houses and inns. The visible population were red-coated soldiers, and it was impossible not to fancy that our journey was a dream, and that we had in fact reopened our eyes in England.

Of hornworks, *demi-lunes*, and ravelines I shall speak to your Papa when I fight my battle once again in the armchair at the park or at Winnington; enough for you to know that we all breakfasted with Sir

Thomas Brisbane, a very superior man and a great astronomer, and though brave as a lion, seems to prefer looking at *la pleine lune* in the heavens than the host of *demi-lunes* with which he is surrounded in his present quarters. At Cambray Sir George Scovell[12] had most kindly secured us lodgings at Sir Lowry Cole's[13] house, which we had all to ourselves, as the general was in England. Where the French people live it is not easy to guess, for all the best houses are taken by British officers. They receive a billet which entitles them to certain rooms, and generally they induce the possessor to decamp altogether by giving him a small rent for the remainder.

We found Colonel Egerton, who married a Miss Tomkinson, in the garrison. We dined with them and the Scovell, and were received with the utmost kindness and attention by all. Colonel Prince and Colonel Abercromby (you know both, I believe) also dined there two days we remained.

On Sunday there was a procession. The most curious circumstance was that a troop of British cavalry attended to clear the way and do the honours, for the National Guard had been disarmed three days before in consequence of an order from the Duke of Wellington (nobody knows why). They gave up their arms without a murmur; some few, I believe, expressed by a "Bah!" and a shrug of the shoulders that it was not quite agreeable to their feelings, but "*voilà tout.*"

"I say, Jack," said a grenadier of the Guards to his companion, by whom I was standing as the procession came out of the church, "who is that fellow with a gold coat and gridiron?"

"Why, that's St. Lawrence," and so it was.

St. Lawrence led the way, followed by a brass St. Andrew as stiff as a poker and as much resembling St. Andrew as I conceive; but my companion the grenadier thought differently, for he pronounced him to be *a chef d'œuvre.* "Well now, Jack, that's quite natural." . . .

I must hurry you on to Compiègne, merely saying that we traversed a country fringed with immense forests in which wolves are born and live and die without much interruption, though we were told at one of the Inns that a peasant had, a day or two before, captured seven juvenile individuals of the species and carried them off uneaten

---

12. Sir George Scovell, 1774-1861, General. He fought in the Peninsula and at Waterloo.

13. Sir Lowry Cole, second son of first Earl of Enniskillen, General of 4th Division at the Battle of Salamanca. He received the thanks of both Houses of Parliament for his gallant services in the Peninsula. Commanded 6th Division at Waterloo.

by their disconsolate parents.

Our chief reason for visiting Compiègne was that we might see a Palace fitted up for Marie Louise by Bonaparte in a style of splendour surpassing, in my opinion, any palace I have seen in France.

MRS. E. STANLEY TO LADY MARIA J. STANLEY.

Paris, June 28, 1816.

And here I am—and what shall I tell you first? And how shall I find time to tell you anything in the wandering Arab kind of life we are leading? It is very new and very amusing and I enjoy it very much, but I enjoy still more the thoughts of how much I shall enjoy my own quiet home and children again when I get to them.

We arrived on Tuesday evening, and in half an hour I was in the Palais Royal in the Café de Mille Colonnes, and at night the brilliancy of the lamps and mirrors, glittering in every direction in every alley, displayed this new scene to me in the newest colours; and it was very like walking in a new world. . . .

The *fêtes* for the marriage of the Duc de Berri are unfortunately all over. Except the entertainments at the Court itself, a French party is a thing unheard of, and the only gaieties have been English parties to which some few French come when they are invited. The only gentlemen's carriages I have seen in the streets are English, and as to French gentlemen or ladies, according to the most diligent enquiries by eyes and tongue, the race has almost disappeared. . . .

If you admire Buonaparte and despise the Bourbons in Cheshire, what would you in Paris? where the regular answer to everything you admire is that it was done by Buonaparte—to everything that you object to, that it is by order of the Bourbons. In the library of the Hôpital des Invalides today, collected by order of Buonaparte for the use of the soldiers, there was a man pulling down all the books and stamping over the N's and eagles on the title-page with blue ink, which, if it did not make a plain L, at least blotted out the N; but I should apprehend that everyone who saw the blot would think more of the vain endeavour of Louis to take his place than if the N had been left.

. . . I have told you nothing about Valenciennes and how we break-fasted with two odd characters to come together in one, an astronomer and a soldier, *viz.*, Sir Thomas Brisbane, who enlivens his quarters wherever he goes by erecting an observatory immediately, and studying hard as any Cambridge mathematician every hour that he is not on military duty. His officers seem to have partaken in some degree of the spirit of their general, and to have made use of their position at Valenciennes to make themselves perfectly acquainted with all Marlborough's campaign, and they appeared to have as much interest in tracing all his sieges and breaches and batteries as their General in making his observations on the sun and the stars. . . . The Scovells were delighted to see us at Cambray; put us into Sir Lowry Cole's quarters, where we had a house and gardens all to ourselves. Lord Wellington had been at Cambray a fortnight before, and was all affability, good humour, and gaiety. . . . Sir Geo. Scovell gave many interesting details of his coolness, quickness, decision, and undaunted spirit.

EDWARD STANLEY TO BELLA STANLEY.

Paris, July 9, 1816.

It is absolutely necessary that a word or two should be said upon the palace at Compiègne, which was fitted up about seven years ago by Napoleon for Marie Louise. Having seen most of his Imperial abodes, I am inclined to give the preference, as far as internal decoration extends, to Compiègne. Gold, silver, mirrors, tapestry all hold their court here. The bath is a perfect specimen of French luxury and magnificence. It fills a recess in a moderately-sized room almost entirely panelled with the finest sheets of plate glass; and the ball room is so exquisitely beautiful that to see its golden walls and ceilings lighted up with splendid chandeliers, and its floors graced with dancers, plumed and jewelled, I would take the trouble of attending as your chaperon from Alderley whenever the Bourbons send you an invitation.

The gardens are like all other French pleasure grounds, formal and comfortless, but there is one part you would all enjoy. When Buonaparte first carried Marie Louise to Compiègne she expressed much satisfaction, but remarked that it was deficient in a Berceau; it could not stand in competition with her favourite palace of Schönbrunn. Now, a *berceau* is a wide walk covered with trellis work and flowers. She left Compiègne. In six weeks Napoleon begged her to pay another visit. She did so, and found a *berceau* wide enough for two carriages to go abreast and above two miles in length, extending from the gardens to the forest of Compiègne, completely finished. May you all be espoused to husbands who will execute all your whims and fancies with equal rapidity and good taste! In your *berceau* I will walk; but if you are destined to reside in golden palaces, you must expect little of Uncle's company.

Having travelled thus far, attend us to Paris and imagine yourself seated in a velvet chair in the Hotel de Bretagne, Rue de Richelieu, that is to say, when translated into London terms, conceive yourself seated in one of the hotels in or near Covent Gardens, close to theatre and shops and all that a stranger wishes to be near for a week when the sole purpose of his visit is seeing and hearing. We are within twenty yards (but if measured by the mud and filth to be traversed in the march I should call it a mile) of the Palais Royal, the fairy land of Paris, and Paradise of vice, and the centre of attraction to every stranger. Here we breakfast in coffee-houses, of which no idea can be formed by those who only associate the name of coffee-house with certain subdivided, gloomy apartments in England, where steaks and *Morning Chronicles* reign with divided sway, and where the silence is seldom interrupted but by queries as to the price of stocks or "Here, Waiter, another bottle of Port."

We dine at *restaurateurs*, choosing unknown dishes out of five closely-printed columns of *fricandeaus* and *à la financières*.

Before I proceed let me inform you of some simple matters of fact which I may forget if delayed. Such as that we found the Sothebys and Murrays, and Leghs of High Legh, and Wilbraham of Delamere Lodge. With the former we have made several joint excursions and contrived to meet at dinner. Mr. Sotheby is in his element, bustles everywhere, looks the vignette of happiness, exclaims "Good!" upon all occasions, from the arrangement of the skulls in the Catacombs to the dressing of a *vol au vent*. In short, they are all as delighted as myself, and that is saying a good deal.

Pardon this digression. Again to the point—to Paris. Where shall I begin? Let us take the theatres. We saw Talma last night, and the impression is strong, therefore he shall appear first on the list.

The play was *Manlius*, a tragedy in many respects like our *Venice Preserved*. The house was crowded to excess, especially the pit, which, as in England, is the focus of criticisms and vent for public opinion.

When a tragedy is acted no music whatever is allowed, not a fiddle prefaced the performance; but at seven o'clock the curtain slowly rose, and amidst the thunder of applause, succeeded by a breathless silence, Talma stepped forth in the Roman *toga* of Manlius. His figure is bad, short, and rather clumsy, his countenance deficient in dignity and natural expression, but with all these deductions he shines like a meteor when compared with Kemble. He is body and soul, finger and thumb, head and foot, involved in his character; and so, say you, is Miss O'Neil, but Talma and Miss O'Neil are different and distant as the poles. She is nature, he is art, but it is the perfection of art, and so splendid a specimen well deserves the approbation he so profusely receives.

The curtain is not let down between the acts, and the interval does not exceed two or three minutes, so that your attention is never interrupted. The scene closed as it commenced—with that peculiar *hurra* of the French, expressive of their highest excitement. It is the same with which they make their charge in battle, and proportioned to numbers it could not have been more vehement at the victories of Austerlitz and Jena than it was on the reappearance of Talma; and not satisfied with this, they insisted on his coming forth again. At length, amidst *hurras* and cries of "Talma! Talma!" the curtain was closed up, and my last impression rendered unfavourable by a vulgar, graceless figure in nankeen breeches and top-boots hurrying in from a side scene, dropping a swing bow in the centre of the stage, and then hurrying out again.

Theatres are to Frenchmen what flowers are to bees: they live *in* them and *upon* them, and the sacrifice of liberty appears to be a tribute most willingly paid for the gratification they receive; for, to be sure, never can there exist a more despotic, arbitrary government than that of a French theatre. A soldier stands by from the moment you quit your carriage till you get into it; you are allowed no will of your own; if you wish to give directions to your servant, "*Vite! Vite!*" cries a whiskered sentry. Are you looking through the windows of the lobbies into the boxes for your party, you are ordered off by a *gendarme*. I saw one gentleman-like-looking man remonstrating; in a trice he was in *durance vile*. A Frenchman at his play must sit, stand, move, think, and speak as if he were on drill, and yet he endures the intolerance for doubtful benefits derived from this rigid regularity.

In this play of *Manlius* were many passages highly applicable to Buonaparte, and Talma, who is supposed to be (*avec raison*) a secret partisan, gave them their full effect, but the listening vassals struck no octaves to his vibration. A few nights before we were at the Play in which were allusions to the Bourbons, and *couplets* without end of the most fulsome, disgusting compliments to the Duc de Berri, &c. These (shame upon the trifling, vacillating, mutable crew!) were received with loud applause by the majority of the pit. I did observe, however, that in that pit did sit a frowning, solemn, silent nucleus, but a nucleus of this description can never be large; a few *Messieurs* at three *francs par jour* would soon, when dispersed amongst them, like grains of pepper in tasteless soup, diffuse a tone of palatability over the whole and render it more agreeable to the taste of a Bourbon.

À propos, we have seen the Bourbons. The King is a round, fat man, so fat that in their pictures they dare not give him the proper *"contour"* lest the police should suspect them of wishing to ridicule; but his face is mild and benevolent, and I verily believe his face to be a just reflection of his heart. Then comes *Monsieur*, [14] a man with more expression, but I did not see enough to form any opinion of my own, and I never heard any very decisive account from anyone else. Then comes the Duchesse d'Angoulême. [15] There is no milk and water there. What she really is I may not be able to detect, but I will forfeit my little finger if there is not something passing strange within her. She is called a bigot and a devotee; she has seen and felt enough, and more than enough, to make a stronger mind than hers either the one or the other, and I will excuse her if she is both. She is thin and genteel, grave and dignified; she puts her fan to her underlip as Napoleon would put his finger to his forehead, or his hand into his bosom. She stood up, she sat down, she knelt, when others stood or sat or knelt, but I question whether if she had been alone she would have done all according to bell and candle, rule or regulation.

Then comes the Duchesse de Berri, [16] a young, pretty thing, a sort of royal kitten; and then comes her husband, the Duc de Berri, a short, vulgar-looking, anything but a kitten he is—but *arrête toi*. I am in the land of vigilance, and already my pen trembles, for there are gendarmes in abundance in the streets, and Messieurs Bruce and Co. in La Force, and I do not wish to join their party. In England I may abuse our Prince Regent and call him fat, dissipated, and extravagant, but in France I dare not say "Boo to a goose!" So, *Je vous salue, M. le Duc de Berri*.

À propos of the police. At the marriage of the above much honoured and respected *Duc* the illuminations were general. Murray's landlord was setting out his tallow candles, when Murray, guessing from certain innuendoes and shrugs (for before us English they are not much afraid of shrugging the shoulders or inventing an occasional "Bah!") that he would have been to the full as pleased if he had been lighting his candles upon the return of Napoleon, asked him, "*Mais pourquoi faites vous cela*? I suppose you may do as you like?"

---

14. Comte d'Artois, afterwards King Charles X.
15. Daughter of Louis XVI.
16. Caroline of Naples.

"*Comment donc!*" replied the astonished Frenchman; "do as I like! If I did not light my candles with all diligence, I should be called upon tomorrow by the police to pay a forfeit for not rejoicing."

With all this I think on the whole the Bourbons are popular; people are accustomed to being bullied out of their opinions and use of their tongues, and they are so sick of war, with all its inconveniences and privations, that they begin to prefer inglorious repose. English money is very much approved of here, but if it could be procured without the personal attendance of the owners, I feel quite confident the French would prefer it.

We are not popular. I suppose the sight of us must be grating to the feelings. We are like a blight on an apple-tree; we curl up their leaves, and they writhe under our pressure.

The constant song of our drunken soldiers on the *boulevards* commenced with—

Louis Dixhuite, Louis dixhuite,
We have licked all your armies and sunk all your fleet.

Luckily the words are not intelligible to the gaping Parisians, who generally, upon hearing the "*Louis Dixhuite*," took for granted the song was an ode in honour of the Bourbons, and grinned approbation. It is quite ridiculous, Paris cannot know itself. Where are the French? Nowhere. All is English; English carriages fill the streets, no other genteel Equipages are to be seen. At the play boxes are all English. At the hotels, restaurations—in short, everywhere—John Bull stalks incorporate. I see an Englishman with his little red book, the Paris guide, in one hand and map in the other, with a parcel of ragged boys at his heels pestering him for money. "*Monsieur, c'est moi,*" who am ready to hold your stick. "*Monsieur, c'est moi,*" who will call your coach.

About the Thuilleries, indeed, and here and there, a few "*bien poudréd*" little old men, "*des bons Papas du Temps passé,*" may be seen dry as Mummies and as shrivelled, with their ribbons and Croix St. Louis, tottering about. They are good, staunch Bourbons, ready, I daresay, to take the field "*en voiture*" for once, when taunted by the Imperial officers for being too old and decrepit to lead troops; an honest emigrant Marquis replied that he did not see why he should not command a regiment and lead it on "*dans son cabriolet.*"

We have been unfortunate in not arriving soon enough to be present at the Duke of Wellington's balls. At the last a curious circumstance took place. (You may rely upon it's being true.) Word was brought to him that the house was in danger from fire. He went down, and in a sort of subterranean room some cartridges were discovered close to a lamp containing a great quantity of oil, and it was evident they had been placed there with design. The first report was that barrels of gunpowder had been found, and strange associations were whispered as to Guy Fawkes and Louis XVIII. being one and the same; but the powder was not sufficient to do any great mischief, and the general idea is that had it exploded, confusion would have ensued, the company would have been alarmed, the ladies would have screamed and fled to the door and street, where parties were in full readiness and expectations of Diamonds, &c....

We stay over Monday, for there is a grand review on the *boulevards*. We have seen *cuirassiers* and lancers shining in the sun and fluttering their little banner in the air. The Bourbons, who are determined to root out every vestige of the past, are now stripping the troops of the uniform which remind the wearers of battles fought and cities won, and re-clothing them in the white dress of the "*ancien Régime,*" which is wretchedly ugly. They know best what they are about, and they certainly have a people to deal with unlike the rest of the world, but were I a Bourbon, I should be cautious how I proceeded in demolishing everything which reminded the people of their recent glory. Luckily the column on the Place Vendôme has as yet escaped the Goths, and its bronze *basso reliefs* are still the pride of Paris.

EDWARD STANLEY TO LOUISA STANLEY.

July 13, 1816.

Days in Paris are like lumps of barley sugar, sweet to the taste and melting rapidly away.... We have now seen theatres, shows, gardens, museums, palaces, and prisons. Aye, Louisa, we have been immured within the walls of La Force, and that from inclination! not necessity.

We procured an order to see Bruce,[17] and after some shuttlecock sort of work, sending and being sent from office to office and *préfet to préfet*, at length we received our order of admission.

In this order our persons are described; the man put me down "*sourcils gris.*"

"*Mais, Monsieur,*" said I, "they will never admit me with that ac-

---

17. Michael Bruce, one of the Englishmen who helped Lavalette to escape from prison. He was known as Lavalette's Bruce. He had previously tried to save Ney. Major-General Wilson and Captain Hutchinson were also concerned in Lavalette's escape.

count."

He looked at me again, "*Ah! vos cheveux sont gris, mais pour les sour-cils, non pas, vous avez raison,*" and altering them to "*noirs,*" he sent me about my business.

Bar and bolt were opened, and at length we found ourselves in the presence of these popular prisoners—Popular, at least, amongst the fe-male part of the world. I have reason to believe that a few of the Miss Stanleys had formed a romantic attachment for Michael Bruce, and there are few of our adventures which would, I think, have given you more pleasure than this visit. Your heart would have been torn from its little resting-place and been imprisoned for ever. Michael Bruce! such an eye! such a figure! such a countenance! such a voice! and so much sense and elegance of manner, and then so interesting! There he sat in a small, wretched room, dirty and felonious, with two little windows, one looking into a court where a parcel of ragged prisoners were playing at fives, the other into a sort of garden where others were loitering away their listless vacuity of time.

I will not tell you what he said, for it would but inflame a wound which I cannot heal, and because part of his conversation was secret, *i.e.*, of a very interesting and curious nature which I cannot write and must not speak of. "Oh! dear Uncle, why won't you tell? a secret from Michael Bruce in the prison of La Force!"

No, Louisa, I dare not speak of it to the winds. Captain Hutchin-son was his companion, Sir Robert Wilson is in another room. The captain has nothing very interesting in his manner or appearance. He is very plain, very positive, and very angry. Well he may be. So would you if, like him, you had been immured in a room about eight feet by twelve, in which you were forced to eat, sleep, and reside for three months. Their penance closes on the 24th, when Michael Bruce re-turns to London. I hope you are not going there this year.

From such a subject as Michael Bruce it will not do to descend to any of the trifling fopperies of Paris.

Let me, then, give you a short account of our visit to Fountain Elephant, which if ever finished, with its concomitant streets, &c., will be an 8th wonder of the world. Its history is this: On the site of the Bastille (of which not a vestige remains) Buonaparte thought he would erect a fountain, and looking at the plans of Paris, he conceived the splendid idea of knocking down all the houses between the Thu-illeries and this fountain and forming one wide, straight street, so that from the palace of the Thuilleries he might see whatever object he might be pleased to place at the extremity. This street is actually begun; when executed, which it never will be, there will be an avenue, partly houses, partly trees, from Barrière d'Étoile to the fountain, at least six miles. Having got this fountain in his head, he sent for De Non,[18] who superintended all his works, and said, "De Non, I must have a fountain, and the fountain shall be a beast."

So De Non set his wits to work, and talked of lions and tigers, &c., when Buonaparte fixed upon an elephant, with a castle upon his back, and an elephant there is. At present they have merely a model of *plaister* upon which the bronze coating is to be wrought, for the whole is to be in bronze with gilt trappings. He is to stand upon an elevated pedestal, which is already completed. The height will be about sixty feet, nearly as high as Alderley steeple. The castle will hold water; the inside is to be a room, and the staircase is to be in one of the legs. The porter who showed it was exceedingly proud of the performance, and when I expressed my astonishment at Buonaparte's numerous plans and the difficulty he must have been at to procure money, looking cautiously about him, he said, "*Oh, mais il avoit le don d'un Dieu,*" and then grasping my arm with one hand and tapping me on the shoulder with the other, and again looking round to see if then the coast was clear, he added, "*Mais il n'y est plus, ah, vous comprenez cela n'est-ce pas,*" and then casting a look at his elephant he concluded with a sigh and a mutter, "*Superbe, ah, pardi, que c'est superbe!*"

Kitty has been dressing herself *à la Française,* and we have been purchasing a large box of flowers, which we hope to show you in England, if the Custom House officers will allow us to pay the duties, but we hear most alarming accounts of their ferocity and rapacity. They will soon, it is said, seize the very clothes you have on, if of French manufacture; if so, *adieu* to three pairs of black silk stockings and as many pocket handkerchiefs, to say nothing of a perfect pet of an ivory dog which I intend to present to your mama, and to say nothing of five perfect pets for Maria and you four eldest girls of the family of Harlequin and Punch, to be worn on your necklaces during the happy weeks. They are of mother of pearl about an inch high, the most comical fellows I ever beheld.

It is necessary that I should tell you of the presents, because if they

18. Denon (1747-1825), a member of the Académie de Peinture. He made sketches in Egypt for Napoleon, quietly finishing them on the battlefield. He directed the Emperor what objects of art he should take from various countries to enrich the Louvre. Napoleon made him *Directeur-Général* of Museums.

are seized, you know I shall still be entitled to the merit of selecting them. We have bought a few books. A thick *octavo* is here worth about four or five shillings, and the duty is, we understand, about one shilling more. One is *A Life of the Duke of Marlborough*. Buonaparte said it was a reflection upon England not to have a life of her greatest Hero, and therefore he would be his biographer; accordingly he set his men to work and collected the materials. Report speaks favourably of it, but I have been so busied in looking and walking about that I shall not be surprised if I find that I have almost forgotten to read upon my return!

EDWARD STANLEY TO LOUISA STANLEY.

Tuesday morning, July 13th.

We are in Paris still, and do not depart till tomorrow, dedicating this day in company with the Murrays to St. Denis and Malmaison, and then I think we shall have seen everything worth seeing in or near this queer metropolis. One day last week we went to our old friend, L'abbé Sicard,[19] and attended a lecture in which about twenty of his young scholars exhibited their powers. The poor *abbé* was, as usual, dreadfully prolix, and occupied an hour in words which might have been condensed within the compass of a minute, and poor Massuer yawned and shut his eyes ever and *anon*. Clair was not there, and as we were under the necessity of going away before the lecture was closed, we could not renew our acquaintance. Since last year he has taught his pupils to speak, and two dumb boys talked to each other with great success. I will show you the mode when we meet, but as you are not dumb it will be a mere gratification of curiosity.

Our assignation which called us from the lecture was to meet the Sothebys and Murrays and many others at the Buvin d'Enfer, near which is the descent to the Catacombs, where upwards of three million of skulls are arranged in tasty grimaces through streets of bones, but my sketch book has long given an idea of these ossifatory exhibitions. Only think, a cousin of Donald's and a very great friend of mine, a Captain McDonald, whom you would all be in love with, he is so handsome and interesting, was shut up there a short time ago by accident, and if the keeper had not luckily recollected the number of persons who descended and discovered one was missing, he would very soon have joined the bone party.

---

19. Abbé Roch Ambroise Sicard, founder of deaf and dumb school at Paris, 1742-1822.

There is another *cimetière* called that of Père la Chaise, of a very different description, and infinitely more interesting. It is the grand burial-place of Paris; all who choose may purchase little plots of ground, from a square foot to an acre, for the deposition of themselves and their families. Its extent is about 84 French acres, and upon no spot in the world is the French character so perfectly portrayed. Each individual encloses his plot and ornaments it as he chooses, and the variety is quite astonishing. It appears like a large Shop full of toys, work-baskets, columns, little cottages, pyramids, mounts—in short, what is there in the form of a monument which may not there be found? A pert little column with a fanciful top, crowned by a smart wire basket filled with roses, marked the grave, I concluded, of some beautiful young girl of 15 or 16. Lo and behold! it was placed there to commemorate *"un ancien Magistrat de France,"* aged 62.

The most interesting are Ney's and Labédoyère's, [20] the former, a solid tomb of marble, simply tells that Marshal Ney, Prince of La Moskowa, is below. Both were rather profusely decorated with wreaths of flowers, it being the custom for the friends of the deceased to strew from time to time the graves with flowers, or decorate them with garlands. Soldiers have been often seen weeping over these graves, and it is by them these wreaths were placed. Ney's had just received its tribute of a beautiful garland of blue cornflowers: and the other a chaplet of honeysuckle.

By both graves were weeping willows. Mr. Sotheby's friend, the poet Delille,[21] sleeps beneath a cumbrous mass of marble, within which his wife immerses herself once a week, to manifest sorrow for one whose incessant tormentor I am told she was during his life. The inscriptions were for the most part commonplace. I copied out a few of the best. I was sorry to observe not one in twenty had the slightest allusion to religion. There was one offering which particularly attracted my attention and admiration. Over a simple mound, the resting-place of a little child, were scattered white flowers, and amongst them a bunch of cherries, evidently the tribute from some other little child who had thus offered up that which to him appeared most valuable. The exclusion of the selfish principle in this display of sentiment and feeling quite delighted me.

The day after we visited the Louvre it was closed, and none have been admitted since. I believe they are scratching out some N's or

---

20. Labédoyère, General (1786-1815). Shot at Grenelle, 1815.
21. French poet and Academician, 1738-1813.

PARISIAN RAT-CATCHER AND ITINERANT VENDORS.

eagles. I should conceive these to be the last of their species, for the activity and extent of this effacement of emblems related to Napoleon is past all belief. In a picture of Boulogne in the Luxembourg, amongst the figures in the foreground was a little Buonaparte, about two inches high, reviewing some troops. They have actually changed his features and figure, and, if I recollect rightly, altered his cockade and Uniform. ... In the Musée des Arts and Métiers are some models of ships; even these were obliged to strike their Lilliputian tri-colours and hoist the white Ensign. And now Paris, fare thee well. ... Thou art a mixture of strange ingredients.

"Oh," said the hairdresser who was cutting Kitty's hair yesterday, "had we your National spirit we should be a great people, *mais c'est l'Égoisme qui regne à Paris.*"

Their manner is quite fascinating, so civil, so polished. The people are like the town, and the town is like a Frenchman's *chemise*, a magnificent frill with fine lace and embroidery, but the rest ragged. The frill of the Thuilleries and Champs Elysées are perfect fairylands, the streets all that is execrable. No wonder the cleaners of boots and shoes are in a state of perpetual requisition. In one shop I saw elevated benches, on which sat many gentry with their feet upon a level with the cleaners' noses, where they sat like statues, and I was actually induced to go back to satisfy myself that they were real men. English notices are frequent in the streets, some not over correct in style; for example, over a hairdresser's in the Palais Royal—"The Cabinet for the cut of the hairs."

MRS. E. STANLEY TO LADY MARIA J. STANLEY.

St. Germain, July 16, 1816.

Surely you must have forgot what it is to be divided by land and sea from what you love, or when you were abroad you left nobody behind whom you cared about, or you would not fancy that I should not find time or inclination to read as many trifles as you can find to send, or that they should not give me almost as much pleasure, and be read with as much interest, as if I were shut up in the next dungeon to Mr. Bruce at La Force. ... While you were enjoying the view of Beeston Castle, we were eating strawberries and cream under the trees in the *Jardin des Plantes* on the only hot day we have had. ... I am in no danger of forgetting you, and if I have not written oftener, it has only been because Edward got the start of me in beginning to write in detail, and he is so inimitable in description that I could not go over the same ground with him. . ... I do wish I could give you one of our day's amusement, and jump you over here in mind and body to leave all your cares behind you. . . .

At last we have bid goodbye to Paris, but every day seemed to bring something fresh to see, and we stayed two or three days longer than we intended yesterday to see St. Denis. It is not so fine as most of the churches we saw in Holland, but the historical interest is so great and so curious that I would not have missed seeing it for the world. Over the door all the guillotined figures of the Revolution; in the church the repairs which were begun by Buonaparte, now finishing by Louis; every stone and step you go marked by some association of one or other of these periods.

As Buonaparte's own power increased, his respect for crowned heads and authorities increased, I suppose, and so he had put up *fleurs de Lys* himself for the Bourbons in one part of the church, and he had prepared a vault for himself, decorated above with bees and statues of the six Kings of France who had the title of Emperor. To this vault he had made two bronze doors with gold ornaments and gold lions' heads, one of which flew back with a spring, and discovered three keyholes, to which there were three golden keys. The Sacristy he filled with *chef d'œuvres* of the best French artists, representing those parts of the history of France connected with St. Denis and with his own views of Empire.

The beautiful white marble steps leading to the altar beneath which the seventh Emperor was to be laid were just finished when Louis XVIII. came to fill the tomb, which was just prepared, with the bones of Louis XVI., to depose the Emperor, to complete the marble pavement, and to extend the *fleurs de lys* over the whole church.

And upon the stone which now conceals the entrance to the vault the Duchesse d'Angoulême always kneels at the grave of her father, for the fine bronze doors are deposed also, only, I believe, because they were placed there by Buonaparte, and now they have to get into the Vault by taking up the stone. We got into the carriage full of Buonaparte, returned to Paris, and then got out again with the Murrays at Malmaison. It is the only enviable French house I have seen, and deserves everything Edward said about it, even without the statues and half the pictures which are taken away.

We spent three or four hours in the Thuilleries Gardens on Sunday. Buonaparte must have thought of gilding the dome of the Invalides when he was walking in the *Jardin des* Thuilleries, it suits the whole thing so exactly. A French crowd is so gay with the women's shawls and flowers that they assimilate well with the real flowers, and are almost as great an ornament to the garden. A shower came on just as we were standing near the palace, and at that moment the guards took their posts as a signal the King was going to Mass, so Edward and I followed the crowd to the *Salle des Maréchaux* (they would not admit Donald because he had gaiters, and Edward had luckily trowsers), and there we saw Louis XVIII. and the Duchesse d'Angoulême and *Monsieur* much better than we had done the Sunday before, with all the trouble of getting a ticket for admission into the chapel, and being squeezed to death into the bargain.

His Majesty is more like a turtle than anything else, and shows external evidence of his great affection for turtle soup. His walk is quite curious. One of his most intimate friends says that in spite of his devotion *Le Roi est un peu philosophe*. We staid on Monday to see a review. Donald introduced us to a Mr. and Mrs. Boyd, who have lived in France the last fourteen years, and have a terrace that overlooks the *boulevards*, so there we sat very commodiously and saw the King and the Duchesses de Berri and Angoulême, in an open *calèche*, pass through the double row of troops which lined the *boulevards* from one end to the other, and a beautiful sight it was. Mr. Boyd invited me to a party at his house in the country, and in the hopes of seeing that *rara avis*, a French lady or gentleman, I said yes. So I sent for a hairdresser, who came post haste, and amused me with his *politesse*, and Edward with his *politique*. I was quite sorry I could not have him again.

We dined with the Murrays, and then went on to Mr. Boyd, where I found myself the only lady there dressed amongst about forty. That is to say, their heads and tails were all in morning costume and mine in evening. . . .

I must go back one more day, and tell you how I went to be described for a passport to La Force on Saturday, and how I thought Mr. Bruce more of a hero young man than any I have ever seen. I recollect seeing him before, and thinking him a coxcomb, but a few years have mellowed all that into a very fine young man.

Making every allowance for seeing him in his dungeon in La Force, I think you would be delighted with his countenance. He spoke his sentiments with manly freedom, and yet with the liberality of one who thinks it possible a man may differ from him without being a fool, or a rascal. Lucy and Louisa would certainly have fallen in love with his fine Roman head, which his prison costume of a great coat

The Great Green Coach

and no neckcloth showed to great advantage.

And now, *adieu* Paris! At 2 o'clock on Wednesday a green coach, which none of you could see without ten minutes' laughing at least— three horses and a postillion! (what would I give just to drive up to Winnington with the whole equipage!)—carried us to Versailles, and there I longed for Louis XIV. as much as for Buonaparte at St. Cloud; for one cannot fancy anyone living in those rooms or walking in those gardens without hoops and *Henri quatre plumes*. If one could but people them properly for a couple of hours, what a delightful recollection it would be! Versailles ought to be seen last. It is so magnificent that every other thing of the sort is quite lost in the comparison.

I am glad I saw Paris and the Tuilleries and St. Cloud first. We saw the palace, and then we dined, and then we set out for the Trianon, and then we met with a guide who entertained us so much as to put Louis XIV. and all his court out of my head. Buonaparte never went to Versailles but once to look at it, but at the Trianon he and Joséphine lived, and it is impossible, in seeing those places, not to feel the principal interest to be in the inquiry—where he lived? where he sat? where he walked? where he slept?—so accordingly we asked our guide. "*Monsieur, je ne connais point ce coquin là*" soon told us what we were to expect from him, but his silence and his loyalty, and the combat between his hatred of the English and his hatred of Buonaparte was so amusing that we soon forgave him for not telling us anything about him.

He said "Bony" was only "fit to be hanged."

"Why did you not hang him, then?"

He could only shrug his shoulders.

"We should have hung him for you if he had come to England."

"*Ma foi! Monsieur, je crois que non.*" He told us the stories of the rooms and the pictures with all the vivacity and rapidity of a Frenchman, and with pretty little turns of wit. . . . Donald asked him if a cabinet in one of the rooms had not been given by the Empress of Russia to Buonaparte? He instantly seized him by the button with an air of triumph. "*Tenez, Monsieur, quand l'Empereur de Russie était ici, il a vu ce Cabinet et a dit; otez cette Volaille là*" (pointing to the compartment in which the Imperial eagles had been changed into angels). "*Je l'ai donné aux Français, et lui—il n'était pas Français.*"

In all the royal house the servants are equally impenetrable on the subject of Buonaparte. But sometimes it seems put on, sometimes they really do not know from having been only lately put there, but this man was a genuine Bourbonist and a genuine Frenchman.

We just got to St. Germain in time to walk on the terrace before evening closed in over the beautiful view. The palace and the town put me quite in mind of the deserted court in the *Arabian Nights*. . . .

EDWARD STANLEY TO HIS NIECES. TUESDAY MORNING.

I could fill another letter with the interesting things we saw yesterday at St. Denis and Malmaison, but we are off in an hour, and it is possible you may hear no more from these

Happy Travellers.

ALDERLEY RECTORY

www.ingramcontent.com/pod-product-compliance
Lightning Source LLC
Chambersburg PA
CBHW032054080426
42733CB00006B/268